WAVES AND WORDS

FINDING SERENITY IN AN AI WORLD

A Journey Through Sound, Poetry, and Digital Harmony

Redefining Peace in an Era of Intelligent Creativity

NATHAN NIFCO, Ph.D.

Copyright © 2025 by Nathan Nifco.

All rights reserved.

No part of this publication may be reproduced, stored, or transmitted in any form or by any means, electronic, mechanical, photocopying, recording, scanning, or otherwise without written permission from the publisher. This publication is designed to provide accurate and authoritative information in regard to the subject matter covered. It is sold with the understanding that neither the author nor the publisher is engaged in rendering legal, investment, accounting, or other professional services. While the publisher and author have used their best efforts in preparing this book, they make no representations or warranties with respect to the accuracy or completeness of the contents of this book and specifically disclaim any implied warranties of merchantability or fitness for a particular purpose. No warranty may be created or extended by sales representatives or written sales materials. The advice and strategies contained herein may not be suitable for your situation. You should consult with a professional when appropriate. Neither the publisher nor the author shall be liable for any loss of profit or any other commercial damages, including but not limited to special, incidental, consequential, personal, or other damages. It is illegal to copy this book, post it to a website, or distribute it by any other means without permission. Nathan Nifco asserts the moral right to be identified as the author of this work.

First edition

ISBN: 978-1-0694444-2-4 (paperback)

ISBN: 978-1-0694444-0-0 (ebook)

elchifbooks.com

Contents

WAVES AND WORDS: FINDING SERENITY IN AN AI WORLD		1
1.	Welcome	2
2.	Waves and Words: Finding Serenity in an AI World	3
3.	The Concept of a "Melodic Landscape" Defining the Immersive Union of Sound, Words, and Image	4
4.	Part I Awakening to the Need for Serenity	7
5.	Prelude to Part I Awakening to the Need for Serenity	8
6.	Navigating the Storm—Finding Calm in Chaos Strategies for Inner Peace Amid Turmoil	9
7.	The Modern Chaos – Why Serenity Matters Now A World in Overdrive	14
8.	Art and Sound – Gateways to Inner Peace Melodic Landscapes as Portals to Inner Calm	18
9.	Twelve Pillars of Wellness Twelve Pillars That Anchor Every Melodic Landscape	22
11.	Part II The Symphony of Serenity	37
12.	Prelude to Part II The Symphony of Serenity	38
13.	Learning to Listen Mindfully Cultivating Awareness through Sound	39

14.	Harnessing Sound for Body and Mind Curating Melodic Landscapes for Body, Mind, and Spirit	42
15.	Balancing Silence and Sound for Serenity How Piano, Poetry, and Visuals Begin in Stillness	47
16.	The Science of Serenity – Sound and Hormones The Neuroscience of Melodic Landscapes	51
17.	Applying Peace – Sounds' impact on Body and Mind Practical Ways to Use Sound for Well-Being	57
19.	Part III Poetry as Path to Peace	60
20.	Prelude to Part III Poetry as Path to Peace	61
21.	Poetry's Alchemy Turning Emotion into Healing Verse	62
22.	The Roots of Poetry's Calming Power Exploring Why Verse Heals	68
23.	Healing Through Poetry – A Reader's Guide How to Engage with Verse for Emotional Healing	71
24.	Verses of the Soul: A Journey Through Poetry's Heart Exploring the Depths of Human Experience in Poetry	77
26.	Part IV Weaving Words and Waves Together	84
27.	Prelude to Part IV Weaving Words and Waves Together	85
28.	The Synergy of Poetry and Melodic Landscape When Word and Melody Unite	86
29.	Rhythm and Resonance – Where Sound Meets Verse When Verse Begins to Sing	88
30.	The Power of Silence in Poetry and Sound The Pauses That Express and Heal	92

31.	Crafting Words and Waves Art in Action: Writing and Composing from Serenity	95
33.	Part V Living a Life of Serenity	101
34.	Prelude to Part V Living a Life of Serenity	102
35.	Staying on Course – Signs to Realign Recognizing When You've Strayed from Serenity	103
36.	The Cracks of Wellness Recognizing When Balance Fades	113
37.	Causes of Cracks in the Twelve Pillars of Wellness What Undermines Our Well-Being	115
38.	The Awake Heart – Cultivating Serenity Through Consciousness Mindfulness as a Path to Inner Peace	131
39.	Nurturing Serenity in Creative Life How Art Sustains the Soul	137
40.	Emotional Grounding in an AI-Driven World Staying Centered Amid Screens	141
41.	Waves of Serenity: Navigating Emotional Dependence on AI Maintaining Emotional Balance in a Tech-Dependent World	146
42.	Serenity as a Shield: Mitigating the Impact of Internet Loss and Outage Building Resilience Against Digital Disruptions	158
43.	Harmony Amidst the Machine – Serenity in an AI-Driven World Finding Peace in a Technology-Saturated Environment	162
44.	Emotions and Meaning of the Twelve Pillars of Wellness Understanding the Emotional Foundations of Well-Being	169
45.	Living the Twelve Pillars of Serenity Integrating Wellness Principles into Daily Life	177
47.	Part VI My Creative Serenity Journey	189

48.	Prelude to Part VI	190
	My Creative Serenity Journey	
49.	The Lifelong Journey of Creative Serenity	191
	A Personal Story of Art and Peace	
50.	Wellness in Verse – Poetry's Pillars	202
	Integrating Wellness Principles into Daily Life	
51.	Healing Words: Poetry's Strength	211
	Music as sanctuary provides a refuge	
52.	Threads of Serenity – Music and Poetry Intertwined	222
	The Restorative Strength of Poetry	
53.	Behind the Harmony: Crafting My Work	230
	The Creative Process Behind the Book	
54.	Twelve Pillars of Wellness	232
	Lessons Learned from My Practice	
55.	Charting Your Course to Serenity	240
	Creating Your Personal Map to Inner Peace	
56.	Uniting the Pillars of Wellness for Lasting Serenity	245
	Building Your Framework for Lasting Peace	
58.	Part VII	256
	The Symphony of Tomorrow – Weaving Art, Spirit, and Harmony	
59.	Prelude to Part VII	257
	The Symphony of Tomorrow – Weaving Art, Spirit, and Harmony	
60.	Reflecting on the Journey	258
	Lessons from Our Path to Serenity	
61.	The Irreplaceable Human Spirit	261
	What Makes Us Truly Human in a Digital Age	
62.	Envisioning a Harmonious Future	264
	How We Can Build It Together	
63.	Music, Poetry, and our Human Soul	267
	Personal Transformation Through Art	

65.	Conclusion	271
	A Call to Harmony	
66.	Epilogue: Harmony in Life	274
	A Vision for the Future	
67.	Additional Resources	276
	Major forms of poetry	
68.	Poetry Referencing Serenity	281
69.	Poetry Without Borders – Multicultural and Secular Traditions	285
70.	Resources for Ambient Sounds	288
	Sources for Free Ambient Sounds	
71.	Original Piano Compositions	291
72.	Serenity Collection	292
	Original Piano Compositions	
73.	Quest Collection	293
	Original Piano Composition	
74.	Enlightenment Collection	295
	Original Piano Compositions	
75.	Endearment Collection	296
	Original Piano Compositions	
76.	Nature Collection	297
	Original Piano Compositions	
77.	Guided Exercises with Poetry and Sound	298
78.	Biblical Passages on Serenity	299
	Old Testament Passages on Serenity	
79.	Your Serenity Compass: The Twelve Pillars	304
80.	Key Studies on Internet Disruptions	308
	Summary of Key Studies and Findings	
81.	Glossary	310
82.	References	322

WAVES AND WORDS

FINDING SERENITY IN AN AI WORLD

A Journey Through Sound, Poetry, and Digital Harmony

Redefining Peace in an Era of Intelligent Creativity

NATHAN NIFCO, Ph.D.

Welcome

Dear Reader,

Welcome to this journey of discovery. As you begin this book, let me introduce you to serenity—a profound state of calm and peace that touches your heart, mind, and spirit. Serenity is more than just a moment of quiet; it's a personal refuge of emotional balance and mental clarity, free from stress or chaos.

Serenity is a multifaceted concept that encompass a state of profound calm, peace, and tranquility both, internally and externally.

This dynamic peace is both a goal and a practice, nurtured through mindfulness, acceptance, and being fully present. In a noisy, fast-paced world, serenity offers you a gentle space to find clarity, build resilience, and reconnect with what makes us human.

"For it is in the gentle quiet, in the language of waves and words, that new awareness can rise."

May this vision of serenity inspire you, as a new reader, to embrace its transformative power for personal growth and deeper connection.

elchifbooks.com

Waves and Words: Finding Serenity in an AI World

A Journey Through Sound, Poetry, and Digital Harmony

Redefining Peace in an Era of Intelligent Creativity

This book takes you on a transformative journey through the interplay of music, poetry, and digital harmony. In an era where AI shapes our realities, we explore how melodic landscapes—curated Melodic Landscapes paired with verse—can restore balance. From ancient traditions to modern practices, discover how these elements converge to foster serenity, helping you navigate the digital world without losing your human essence. Each chapter builds on this foundation, offering tools to integrate art into your life for lasting peace.

This book is your guide to rediscovering peace amid the digital storm. Whether you're overwhelmed by AI notifications or seeking deeper human connections, join us in exploring how melodic landscapes—blends of poetry and sound—can restore balance. Let's begin this harmonious journey together

Embark on a transformative journey where music's rhythms meet poetry's verses in a digital harmony. In this AI-driven age, we navigate the tension between technology and tranquility, using melodic landscapes to bridge the gap. From thematic collections to practical exercises, discover how these elements foster serenity, turning chaos into calm through intentional, human-centered practices.

The Concept of a "Melodic Landscape"

Defining the Immersive Union of Sound, Words, and Image

The "Melodic Landscape" represents a revolutionary innovation in the realm of original piano compositions, designed to transcend the traditional boundaries of instrumental music. This term merges the idea of a "soundscape" (an immersive auditory environment) with "melodic" elements (fluid harmonic and rhythmic structures), aiming to create multisensory experiences where the piano is not merely an instrument but a portal to integrated narrative worlds. In essence, a Melodic Landscape is a piano composition that evokes vivid scenarios, as if the listener were wandering through a real landscape, enriched with melodies that guide emotions and imagination.

This innovation is supported by a unique conceptual structure: **twelve foundational pillars**, which serve as the philosophical and technical underpinnings of the creation, and **five thematic collections** (Enlightenment, Serenity, Endearment, Nature, and Quest), which organize the Melodic Landscapes into coherent sets, as will be fully elaborated in the following chapters. What makes this approach unique is the harmonious integration of poetry (as a narrative and lyrical element), music (centered on the piano as the primary axis), and multimedia (including visuals, projections, or digital elements). This triad intertwines to generate a holistic experience: poetry provides the written and narrated emotional script, music brings it to life, and multimedia visualizes it, creating a synesthesia that stimulates multiple senses simultaneously.

Below, I detail this structure comprehensively, illustrating how each component contributes to the innovation of the Melodic Landscape.

The Five Collections: Thematic Groupings

The five collections—**Enlightenment, Serenity,** Endearment**, Nature, and Quest**—organize the Melodic Landscapes into thematic sets, each exploring a distinct aspect of the Melodic Landscape. Each collection includes several melodic landscapes accompanied by original poems and multimedia elements (such as videos, digital art, or interactive installations). This structure facilitates presentations in concerts, albums, or immersive experiences, where the harmonious integration is evident: poetry is recited or projected, music is performed live, and multimedia is activated in sync.

Enlightenment: Focused on introspection and mental clarity. The Melodic Landscapes' feature contemplative melodies with minimalist harmonic progressions; poetry explores the search for inner truth; multimedia includes abstract visuals that evolve slowly, like light patterns symbolizing illumination.

Serenity: Centered on calm and inner peace. Fluid, gentle melodies evoke tranquility; poetry describes states of rest and harmony; multimedia incorporates videos of serene landscapes, like lakes at dawn, synchronized with the music.

Endearment: Explores warm, affective emotions such as love and compassion. Delicate melodies with warm chords; intimate, emotive poetry; multimedia with soft visuals, like family portraits or moving flowers, reinforcing emotional connection.

Nature: Inspired by terrestrial landscapes (forests, oceans, mountains). Melodic Landscapes with organic, undulating melodies; descriptive poetry celebrating biodiversity; multimedia with 360° videos of natural environments, designed for complete sensory immersion.

Quest: Visions of epic journeys, both physical and spiritual. Melodies with dynamic, contrasting elements blending acoustic and electronic touches; narrative poetry about   adventures and discoveries; multimedia with virtual reality or animations transporting listeners to imaginary worlds.

Each collection can expand indefinitely but remains anchored in the twelve pillars to maintain coherence.

Harmonious Integration of Poetry, Music, and Multimedia

The true innovation of the Melodic Landscape lies in how poetry, music, and multimedia integrate without overshadowing one another. **Poetry** serves as the narrative skeleton, providing texts recited during performance or printed in booklets, guiding the listener through the story. **Piano music** is the melodic soul, translating poetry into notes that evoke the described landscapes. **Multimedia** adds a visual and tactile dimension, such as videos projected in concerts or interactive apps allowing the audience to influence the experience.

For example, in a melodic landscape from the **Nature** collection, a poem about a forest is recited while the piano mimics the wind in the leaves, and a video of moving foliage is projected, creating a harmony where each element reinforces the others. In the Quest collection, a melodic landscape might include an epic poem about a stellar journey, accompanied by expansive melodies and AI-generated visuals of galaxies in motion. This integration is not additive but synergistic: poetry inspires the melody, music gives rhythm to the visuals, and multimedia completes the emotional cycle.

Conclusion

The Melodic Landscape is not just a label; it is an artistic philosophy that redefines Melodic Landscapes as an immersive, multidisciplinary experience. Supported by the twelve pillars and the five collections—**Enlightenment, Serenity, Endearment, Nature, and Quest**—this innovation invites creators and listeners to explore new horizons, where the harmony of poetry, music, and multimedia generates a lasting, transformative impact.

Part I
Awakening to the Need for Serenity

"The first and greatest victory is to conquer yourself."
– Plato

Prelude to Part I
Awakening to the Need for Serenity

Picture this: your phone buzzes relentlessly, the world outside hums with chaos, and inside, your thoughts race—sound familiar? In this storm, serenity feels like a distant shore. Here, we begin exactly where you are—breathing in the chaos, ready to step onto the path toward serenity.

In a world that often spins out of control, the demands of daily life can leave us overwhelmed and disconnected, stirring a quiet longing for peace—a sanctuary within ourselves. This prelude invites you to recognize the chaos within and around you and the need to cultivate serenity as a response to modern stressors. This journey aligns with an awakening theme, emphasizing that serenity is a vital state to reclaim by reconnecting with our inner selves.

Embark on a transformative journey where music's rhythms meet poetry's verses in a multisensory harmony. In this AI-driven age, we navigate the tension between technology and tranquility, using Melodic Landscapes—immersive piano compositions woven with poetry and synchronized visuals—to bridge the gap. From thematic collections to guided immersions, discover how these elements foster serenity, turning chaos into calm through intentional, human-centered practices.

From thematic collections to experiential engagements, discover how these elements foster serenity, turning chaos into calm through intentional, human-centered practices.

Through the following chapters, we'll explore the stressors of modern life, understand their impact on our well-being, and discover how the intertwined arts of poetry, piano, and visual storytelling can guide us toward serenity. Here, we begin exactly where you are—breathing in the chaos, ready to step onto the path ahead.

Navigating the Storm—Finding Calm in Chaos

Strategies for Inner Peace Amid Turmoil

Welcome, friend! Imagine starting your day already feeling the weight of the world—emails piling up, notifications buzzing, and a to-do list that stretches beyond the horizon. Does the constant ping of notifications leave you drained? This book offers a path to peace through poetry and sound.

If your heart races, your thoughts feel foggy, and a quiet unease creeps in, you're not alone—it sounds familiar, doesn't it? This is the chaos within, a storm many of us navigate daily. In this chapter, we'll walk together through the modern-day stressors stirring this turmoil, uncover their impact on our minds, bodies, and spirits, and discover why cultivating serenity isn't just a luxury—it's a lifeline. Through relatable stories, simple insights, and a touch of self-reflection, we'll begin to find calm amidst the storm. Let's take that first step together.

A Day in the Life of Stress

Meet Sarah, a marketing executive whose day begins at 6 a.m. with a phone already glowing with emails. By 8 a.m., she's juggling conference calls, looming deadlines, and family responsibilities. Lunch happens at her desk, and by evening, she's too drained to enjoy her kids. This relentless cycle leaves her drained—maybe you've lived a version of Sarah's story—caught in a loop where stress builds not just from big events but from constant daily pressures, like a backpack growing heavier with each step. The good news? There's a way through, and it starts with understanding what we're up against.

Modern-Day Stressors and Their Impact

Life today can feel like a high-wire act. Work pressures, family responsibilities, financial worries, and the endless scroll of social media keep us tethered to a constant hum of "go, go, go." Add the ping of notifications and the expectation to always be "on," and it's no wonder overwhelm has become a modern hallmark. This chaos doesn't just rattle our minds—it ripples through our bodies and spirits. Tension headaches, restless nights, or a nagging sense of disconnection might sound familiar. Over time, chronic stress can spiral into burnout or even physical ailments, like a weight pressing harder each day. But here's the spark of hope: recognizing this burden is the first step toward lightening it.

To guide you on this journey, we'll draw upon the Twelve Pillars of Wellness—timeless principles, each paired with a symbolic crystal. These pillars, which we'll explore in depth later in **Part VI: My Creative Serenity Journey**, form the foundation for building lasting serenity. Through sound and poetry, you'll discover how to embody each one.

The Signs of Stress Overload

Stress doesn't whisper—it shouts through our bodies and emotions. Physically, you might notice tight shoulders, fatigue that lingers despite sleep, or a racing pulse. Emotionally, it can show up as irritability—snapping at a loved one over spilled coffee—or anxiety that keeps your thoughts spinning. Maybe tasks that once felt doable now loom large, or you feel distant from what you love. These are your body and soul waving a flag, saying, "Hey, we need a breather." Spotting these signs isn't about blame—it's about awareness, the first seed of change.

Defining Serenity: Calm Amidst the Storm

So, what's the antidote to this chaos? Serenity. Picture a quiet harbor where boats rest while waves crash beyond, or a candle glowing steadily in a gusty room—images of calm holding firm amidst turmoil. Serenity isn't just the absence of stress—it's a deep, abiding peace you can carry within, even when life gets loud. Unlike relaxation—a fleeting sigh after a long day—serenity is a home you build inside yourself. It's the strength to face traffic jams or tough talks with a clear mind and steady heart. What does serenity feel like to you? Maybe it's a memory waiting to be reclaimed.

The Benefits of Serenity

Why chase this calm? Because serenity is a gift that keeps giving. For your mind, it's clarity—like wiping fog from a window to see clearly again—boosting focus and creativity. For your body, it's a balm, lowering cortisol, easing tension, and letting your system heal. For your spirit, it's connection—a quiet gratitude that lifts you up. Science shows that finding calm regularly can lower anxiety and improve health, such as reducing blood pressure—powerful, isn't it? Serenity isn't escape; it's your body exhaling after a long day.

Why Serenity Matters Now

In a world that glorifies busyness, stress can feel like the price of admission. But it doesn't have to be. According to a February 2023 report (American Institute of Stress, 2023), 83% of U.S. workers experience work-related stress, with 25% identifying their job as the primary source of stress in their lives, costing the economy billions annually. Globally, the World Health Organization flags anxiety and depression as top causes of disability. These aren't just numbers—they're a call to action. Serenity isn't optional in this chaos—it's essential. It's the solid ground that keeps us from sinking, a light we can share with others. You're not alone in this, and the journey to calm is worth every step.

Instant Calm: Five Stress Busters

Feeling the weight? Try these quick anchors to find calm now:

- **Breathe Deeply:** Inhale for four, hold for four, exhale for four. Repeat and feel the ground beneath you.

- **Tune into a Melodic Moment:** Step outside—hear the birds or rustling leaves. Let nature's rhythm seed a larger landscape.

- **Whisper Words:** Speak a favorite poem or quote. Let its cadence wash over you.

- **Imagine Peace:** Close your eyes, see a quiet beach or cozy nook. Let stress melt away.

- **Enter a Melodic Landscape:** Play a gentle piano piece and let its melody guide you into visualized calm.

These moments are doorways into the Melodic Landscapes ahead—piano compositions fused with poetry and synchronized visuals that turn fleeting calm into lasting serenity.

Your Stress, Your Journey: A Self-Check

Stress hits us all differently—some feel it as worry, others as frustration. How does it show up for you? Grab a notebook and take a moment:

- How often do you feel swamped by daily tasks?

- Any physical clues—headaches, tiredness, tension?

- How's your mood—anxious, snappy, or distant?

- Has creativity or focus taken a hit?

Jot down what stands out. No judgment—just noticing. This is your starting point, a brave step toward calm.

Looking Ahead

We've faced the chaos and glimpsed serenity's promise—a calm that lifts us up and holds us steady. Where do you feel that longing for peace in your life? As we turn the page, we'll explore how poetry and sound—words and waves—become your companions on this journey. Having explored the storm within, let's now step back to see how the chaos of our world amplifies it—and why serenity is our urgent antidote. Let's keep going, together.

Having explored the internal storms we face, let's now turn our attention to the external chaos that surrounds us in the modern world.

The Modern Chaos – Why Serenity Matters Now

A World in Overdrive

Imagine waking to a typical morning: your smartwatch buzzes with a stress alert, an AI-curated newsfeed scrolls urgent headlines on your phone, and a delivery drone hums outside your window. This is our reality—a relentless chorus of signals drowning out any hint of stillness. When did you last feel truly at peace, not just quiet, but centered in a way that lingers? Modern chaos isn't merely noise; it's a tidal wave of distraction, expectation, and pace, pulling us from ourselves. This book begins here, in the swirl of that storm, because serenity isn't a luxury—it's a need we can't ignore. The journey ahead offers a path through sound and poetry to reclaim what's slipping away. But first, let's face the why.

The Noise of an AI-Driven Age

We're living in a world where artificial intelligence doesn't just whisper in the background—it's the loud, unceasing soundtrack of our lives. Algorithms on platforms like X (formerly Twitter) are meticulously designed to crank up the volume on our emotions, churning out feeds that spark outrage or obsession. Just last week, I glanced at my phone before breakfast and was swept into a storm of conflicting takes on a news story, my heart pounding before I'd even poured my coffee. Beyond social media, voice assistants deliver instant replies to every question, while synthetic music streams from smart speakers, earbuds, and even elevators. A 2024 DataReportal study found global screen time has spiked by 30% in the past five years, and it's no surprise—AI has mastered the art of keeping us tethered to its relentless rhythm.

Compare that to the past, when life unfolded to the gentle beat of nature: the crackle of a fire, the steady rise and fall of ocean tides. Now, we're surrounded by the ping of notifications, the buzz of endless connectivity, and the hum of automation—a noise that never takes a breath.

The Double-Edged Sword of AI

AI is a double-edged sword: it enhances efficiency with smart assistants and personalized content but slices into serenity through addiction and privacy erosion. While it can curate calming playlists, overreliance fosters emotional detachment. Balancing its edges requires human-centric boundaries, like unplugging to engage with authentic poetry and natural sounds.

Reclaiming Serenity with Human-Centric Practices

That's where human-centric practices come in—not as a rejection of technology, but as a way to balance its noise with something softer, something real. Think of stepping outside to listen to the waves crash against the shore. Imagine the tension melting from your shoulders as their steady rhythm washes over you, unhurried and unchanging. Or picture yourself curling up with a poem, letting its words unfold slowly, grounding you in the present with their quiet power. These aren't escapes from the modern world; they're lifelines, anchoring us back to ourselves while AI buzzes in the background. Try them for five minutes daily—they remind you what it feels like to breathe deeply, to let your thoughts settle instead of racing to keep up with the next notification.

The Fragmented Mind – Attention in Crisis

This noise doesn't just surround us—it splinters us. Neuroscience suggests our average attention span for a single task is now around eight to twelve seconds in high-distraction environments, down from longer stretches a decade ago. Cortisol, the stress hormone, spikes as we juggle a work call, a text thread, and an AI-drafted email—all in the same breath. I tried meditating once, only to have my smart speaker chirping mid-breath with a weather update; my calm shattered faster than I could blink. Our brains, wired for deep focus—think of a hunter tracking prey or a poet crafting a line—now stumble through a fog of multitasking.

The cost is steep: burnout, anxiety, a vague sense of drift. We're scattered, not just by sound but by the sheer volume of input vying for our minds. Serenity offers a counterforce—a way to gather those fragments back into wholeness. In Part IV, we'll explore the neuroscience of how piano-based Melodic Landscapes rewire stress into calm. For now, know this: chaos breaks us apart, but we can choose to mend. It starts with seeing the crisis for what it is.

The Loss of Quiet Spaces

Step outside, and silence feels like a myth. Cities thrum with horns, sirens, and the buzz of drones; even rural paths carry the faint whine of wind turbines or distant highways. I felt this last month, hiking a forest trail to escape the clamor. I craved quiet, but my earbuds—synced to an AI playlist—kicked in unexpectedly with a podcast. Yanking them out, I stood still, and only then did the wind's rustle and a bird's call reach me. That moment hit hard: silence isn't just vanishing from our world—it's fading inside us. A friend's child recently asked me, "What's quiet like?" The question stopped me cold.

We've unlearned how to pause. Homes pulse with AI chatter, streets with traffic, even our thoughts with endless loops of worry or to-dos. This loss isn't trivial—it's where serenity takes root. Without those gaps, sound loses its depth, and words their weight. Later, we'll reclaim silence's power, weaving it with poetry and waves. For now, it's enough to see what's at stake: a world without quiet is a world without peace.

Why Now? The Urgency of Serenity

Why does this matter now? Look around: mental health apps report a 40% surge in anxiety logs since 2020, a silent epidemic of frayed nerves. X debates rage louder,

AI bots stoking division with uncanny precision—scroll any thread, and you'll feel the heat. Headlines whisper unease about AI autonomy, a future where machines outpace us. A colleague confessed she hasn't slept without AI-generated white noise in years—its hum has become her lullaby, not her choice. This isn't dystopia; it's today, and it's pressing.

Serenity isn't passive here—it's rebellion. It's a human act of reclaiming agency in a machine-led world, a stance that says, "I choose calm amidst the storm." This book's promise—nurturing peace in an AI world—starts with that intent. The tools ahead—sound's resonance, poetry's balm, mindfulness's clarity—aren't escapes but lifelines. We can't wait for a quieter era; serenity is our now, a radical choice to stand still when everything else races.

Turning Toward the Calm

This chaos—noise, fragmentation, lost silence—isn't our defeat; it's our wake-up call. We're awake to the storm, and that's where the journey begins. The pages ahead, starting with the symphony of serenity, offer the how: ways to weave sound and words into a shield, a haven, a life. The pages ahead deliver this promise through Melodic Landscapes—piano compositions fused with poetry and synchronized visuals that transform fleeting calm into embodied serenity. Amid the clamor, a wave crashes soft, a word lingers true—here, serenity whispers its promise. Turn the page, not to flee, but to find what's waiting: a peace that holds, no matter the tide.

Now that we've seen how modern chaos affects us, let's discover how Melodic Landscapes—piano, poetry, and visual synesthesia—become gateways to inner peace.

Art and Sound – Gateways to Inner Peace

Melodic Landscapes as Portals to Inner Calm

Throughout history, art and sound have been revered not just for their beauty, but for their power to heal and transform. From the rhythmic chants of ancient rituals to the soothing verses of poetry, these creative expressions have long been pathways to wellness. In this chapter, we will explore how poetry and soundscaping—the art of curating sounds—can be uniquely powerful tools for cultivating serenity. We'll delve into the science behind their impact on our brain and emotions, and discover how these practices have been used across cultures to foster healing and peace. As we journey through this chapter, you'll begin to see how these timeless tools can be woven into your own life, offering a gentle yet profound way to nurture your well-being.

A Legacy of Healing: How Poetry and Sound Have Soothed Souls Across Time

Let's step back in time to see how poetry and sound have been cherished as sources of healing. Picture ancient Greece, where poetry wasn't just art—it was medicine for the soul, its power echoed in tales of gods like Apollo. Epic recitations of Homer's tales calmed listeners with their rhythmic flow. Across the world, indigenous cultures have leaned on sound in similar ways. In Africa, the steady beat of drums during rituals doesn't just unite communities—it's believed to mend spirits. Meanwhile, Japanese haiku offers a quiet pause, its brief lines inviting mindfulness by capturing nature's calm. And in medieval Europe, monks filled stone halls with Gregorian chants, their harmonies lifting hearts toward peace. These practices show us that poetry and sound have always been more than beauty—they're bridges to serenity, no matter the era or place.

The Science of Calm: How Words and Sounds Rewire Us

Now that we've glimpsed their historical roots, let's explore why these tools work so well. Science offers fascinating clues. When you listen to a soothing Melodic Landscape—like waves or birdsong—your brain waves can shift, boosting alpha and theta waves that usher in relaxation. These are like a slow, dreamy rhythm in your brain, helping you unwind or get creative.

   A 2015 study in the *Journal of Neuroscience* found that slow-tempo sounds lowers heart rate and stress levels, giving your body a break from the grind. Poetry does something similar. Research by Dr. James Pennebaker shows that writing or reading expressive words—like a heartfelt poem—helps untangle emotions, easing anxiety by making sense of what's inside. The rhythm of a poem, much like a lullaby, can even sync with your breath, coaxing your mind into calm. It's no wonder these practices feel so good—they're tuning your brain for peace.

Why Poetry and Soundscaping Stand Out

So, what makes poetry and soundscaping special compared to, say, a yoga class or quiet meditation? It's their knack for wrapping your mind and senses in something immersive yet simple. Reading a poem aloud engages your voice, your ears, and your heart all at once—blending thought and feeling into a moment of presence. Soundscaping, with its layers of curated sounds, can whisk you away to a forest or shoreline without leaving your chair. Unlike exercise, which focuses on your body, or visual art, which leans on your eyes, these tools dive straight into your emotions through sound and words. Best of all, they're easy to try—no fancy gear, hours of free time, or prior skill needed. A few lines of poetry or a short

Melodic Landscape can fit into even the busiest day, making serenity feel within reach.

A Moment of Change: Natalie's Story

Need a little inspiration? Meet Natalie, a 35-year-old teacher who felt swamped by deadlines and city noise. One day, she decided to try something new. Each morning, she read a short poem—like Mary Oliver's "Wild Geese"—letting its gentle words remind her to breathe. On her commute, she swapped honking horns for the sound of ocean waves. After a few weeks, she noticed a shift: her shoulders unclenched, her mind felt lighter. It wasn't magic—just the quiet power of poetry and sound giving her a daily dose of calm. Natalie's story shows how small steps with these tools can ripple into real peace.

Consider Natalia's story as a testament to transformation. Overwhelmed by her tech-heavy job, she discovered serenity through daily Melodic Landscape and poetry reading. One evening, amid a binaural beat session paired with a calming verse, she felt a profound shift—stress melted away, replaced by clarity. This moment of change highlights how accessible practices can rewire our responses to chaos, proving that serenity is within reach for anyone.

Bringing It Home: Simple Ways to Start

Ready to give this a go? Here are some easy ways to weave poetry and Melodic Landscapes into your life:

- **Start with Words:** Pick a short poem that lifts you up. Read it aloud—maybe over coffee—letting the rhythm settle into your day.

- **Pause with Piano**: Find or make a 5- to 10-minute playlist of calming sounds—think rain or soft waves. Listen during a break, eyes closed, and just be.

- **Write Freely:** Once a week, scribble a few lines of your own poetry. Start with "Right now, I feel…" and see where it takes you—no rules, just you.

- **Wind Down with Waves:** Play a gentle Musical Landscape as you get ready for bed. Let it ease you into sleep like a soft lullaby.

- **Picture the Scene:** While listening to piano, imagine a slow visual: mist rising from a lake, a candle flame in a dark room, or leaves drifting downstream. Let the image sync with the music.

Try one—or all—of these for a few days. Notice how you feel. You might be surprised at how these little acts plant the seeds of a Melodic Landscape in your everyday world.

Reflections: Your First Step Toward Serenity

As we've seen, poetry, piano, and visual synesthesia are gifts from the human spirit—tools that heal through rhythm, resonance, and imagery. They meet you where you are, offering a way to hush the chaos and find a steady calm. Whether it's the echo of an ancient chant, the flow of a verse, or your own quiet mornings, these practices show us that serenity isn't far off—it's waiting in the notes, words, and images around us.

With this foundation, we are ready to delve deeper into one of the most expressive and transformative art forms: **poetry**. In the next chapter, we will discover how poetry acts as *emotional alchemy*, turning our innermost feelings into sources of strength and peace—especially when fused with piano and visual elements in a full Melodic Landscape.

With an understanding of how art and sound contribute to wellness, we are ready to delve deeper into one of the most expressive and transformative art forms: poetry. In the next chapter, we will discover how poetry can act as emotional alchemy, turning our innermost feelings into sources of strength and peace.

Twelve Pillars of Wellness
Twelve Pillars That Anchor Every Melodic Landscape

The *Twelve Pillars of Wellness* represent a comprehensive framework for achieving holistic health and well-being, addressing the multifaceted nature of human life. These pillars encompass physical, mental, emotional, social, and spiritual dimensions, including essential areas such as nutrition, physical activity, sleep, stress management, emotional regulation, mental stimulation, spiritual connection, social relationships, environmental awareness, occupational satisfaction, financial stability, and personal growth.

Each pillar plays a vital role in fostering overall wellness, and together they create a synergistic effect where nurturing one area positively influences the others. By understanding and integrating these twelve pillars into daily life, individuals can cultivate a balanced, resilient foundation for a vibrant and fulfilling existence.

To guide you on this journey toward inner peace, picture a **circle of twelve hexagons**, each representing a pillar and paired with a crystal-inspired icon. This visual map will appear throughout the book and serve as a meditative focal point.

Throughout the coming chapters, we'll explore how Melodic Landscapes—the fusion of piano, poetry, and synchronized visuals—activate and strengthen each pillar. Take a moment now to glance at the diagram and notice which pillar calls to you—perhaps one stirred by a melody you cherish or a verse that moves you.

We'll weave these pillars into every chapter, with a deeper compositional dive awaiting in *Part VI: My Creative Serenity Journey.* For now, let this diagram be a gentle companion, illuminating each step toward the peace you seek.

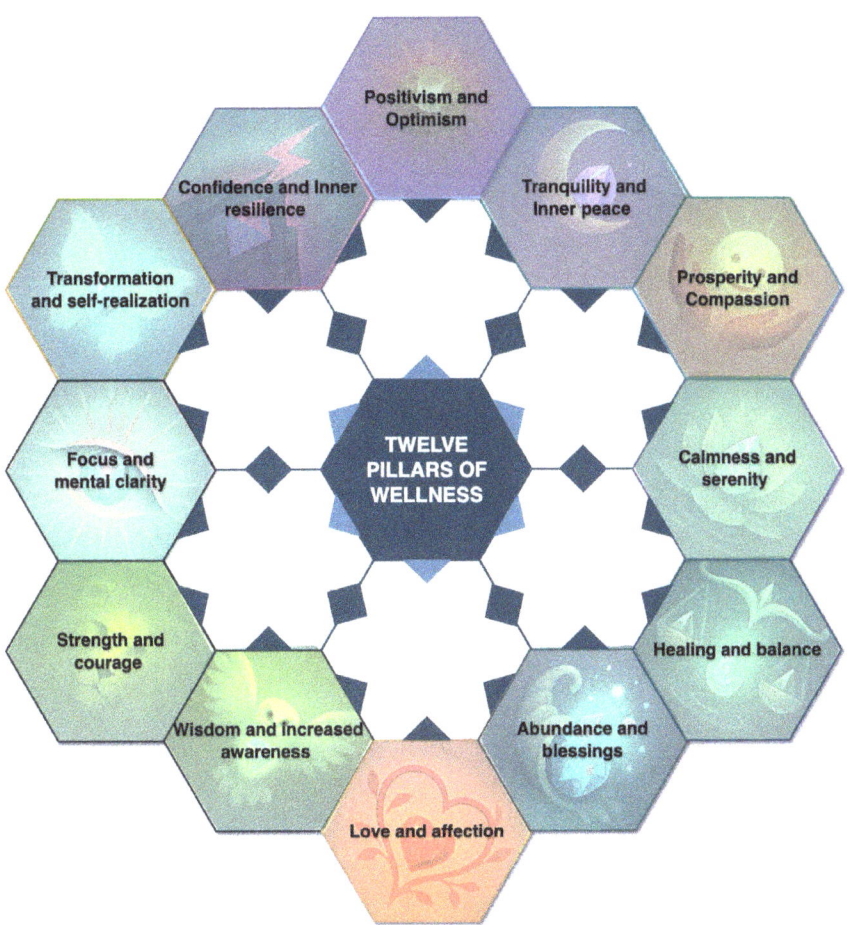

The Pillars in Action (Brief Overview)

Focus and Mental Clarity

Poetry sharpens attention to the present; piano quiets mental noise; visuals reduce visual clutter.

Calmness and Serenity

60-BPM melodies sync with resting heart rate; serene verse hushes turmoil; still-water visuals anchor peace.

Healing and Balance

Sustained tones promote parasympathetic rest; restorative verse mends emotional wounds; symmetrical visuals restore harmony.

Confidence and Inner Resilience

Resonant bass notes ground self-belief; resilient narrative arcs model recovery; bold color shifts reinforce strength.

Strength and Courage

Dynamic arpeggios build emotional muscle; narrative poetry models bravery; bold visuals inspire action.

Wisdom and Increased Awareness

Slow harmonic rhythm invites reflection; mindful verse deepens insight; evolving visuals mirror growth.

Tranquility and Inner Peace

Silence between notes creates refuge; tranquil verse steadies breath; moonlit visuals soothe the spirit.

Love and Affection

Warm chords evoke tenderness; intimate poetry nurtures bonds; soft visuals reinforce connection.

Abundance and Blessings

Gratitude-themed poems shift perspective; major-key resolutions uplift; golden-hour visuals cultivate contentment.

Prosperity and Compassion

Flowing left-hand patterns suggest flow; compassionate poetry builds empathy; community visuals foster belonging.

Positivism and Optimism

Ascending motifs spark hope; uplifting verse reframes challenges; sunrise visuals inspire forward motion.

Transformation and Self-Realization

Modulating keys mirror growth; revelatory verse unveils truth; metamorphic visuals reflect becoming.

These twelve pillars of wellness are the foundation upon which we can build a life of balance, harmony, and inner peace, guiding us toward a future where serenity is not just a fleeting moment but a way of being.

This vision inspires us to see these pillars as more than just principles—they are the stepping stones to a transformative journey. Imagine a life where well-being isn't a distant dream, but a vibrant reality you live every day. By embracing these pillars, you're not just chasing temporary calm; you're crafting a lasting sanctuary of peace and purpose.

The Pillars of Wellness and Their Icons

The Pillars of Wellness and their icons provide visual and symbolic guidance: Focus (clarity icon), Strength (courage symbol), etc. Each icon, often crystal-inspired, serves as a meditative tool, enhancing practices like soundscaping to build resilience against AI-induced distractions.

Icons in imagery hold a remarkable ability to influence personal transformation by serving as potent symbols that connect with our emotions, subconscious mind, and aspirations. Here's how icons impact personal transformation:

Emotional Triggers

Emotional triggers are stimuli that activate wellness pillars, such as a soothing melody evoking calmness or a verse sparking love. In AI contexts, these can counteract algorithmic stress—identify yours through mindful listening, using them as anchors to realign with serenity during digital overload.

These are the cues—sounds, words, or memories—that evoke specific feelings, helping activate the Twelve Pillars of Wellness. For instance, a gentle melody might trigger calmness, aligning with the Serenity pillar.

Icons tap into the subconscious, bypassing rational thought to evoke deep feelings. These emotional responses can shift your mindset, making icons catalysts for change.

Anchors for Goals and Values

Anchors for goals and values are symbolic reminders tied to the *Twelve Pillars of Wellness*, like a crystal icon for wisdom guiding daily intentions. In an AI era, these anchors ground us, helping set tech-free goals that align with core values, fostering sustained serenity through purposeful living.

Icons serve as visual and symbolic anchors, grounding your wellness journey. Each pillar's icon reminds you of core values like love or resilience, providing a focal point for meditation and goal-setting in an unpredictable AI era.

Connection to Something Bigger

Many icons carry collective meaning, linking you to a broader human experience. This connection can provide purpose or direction, fueling transformation by making you feel part of something larger than yourself.

Psychological Reinforcement

Your brain responds to visual cues. Icons you associate with strength, confidence, or peace can reinforce those qualities in your mind. In personal growth, surrounding yourself with meaningful imagery builds neural pathways that align with your desired change.

Icons in imagery are powerful because they distill complex ideas into simple, evocative forms. They trigger emotions, reinforce goals, and connect us to deeper meanings—all while working quietly in the background of our minds. For personal transformation, they're like tools in your pocket: subtle, yet capable of sparking profound change when they resonate with you. Choose your icons wisely—they might just shape who you become.

Below is a brief explanation of each pillar with their icon, detailing how they contribute to wellness, especially in times of chaos and an AI-driven world, and why they are essential for attaining serenity.

Focus and Mental Clarity

Concentrating on what matters and maintaining organized thoughts for effective decision-making. In chaotic times, they help you filter out distractions and reduce overwhelm. In an AI world, where information overload is common, they enable you to process data efficiently and avoid confusion. A clear, focused mind reduces anxiety and stress, creating a calm foundation for inner peace. Poetry sharpens focus by drawing attention to the present, while Melodic Landscapes quiet mental noise.

Calmness and Serenity

Calmness is the absence of agitation, and serenity is a profound peace. In chaotic times, calmness enables clear thinking amidst turmoil. In an AI world, it offers respite from fast-paced stimulation.

As both a pillar and goal, it directly builds and sustains a peaceful state.

Healing and Balance

Healing involves recovery from stress or trauma, while balance maintains equilibrium across life's aspects. In chaos, healing restores energy, and balance prevents burnout. In an AI world, they counteract the strain of constant connectivity. Feeling whole and steady promotes a calm, harmonious mind.

Confidence and Inner Resilience

Confidence is self-belief, and inner resilience is the ability to recover from setbacks. In chaos, they empower decisive action and perseverance. In an AI world, they support continuous learning amidst change. Trust in your capabilities fosters a steady, peaceful confidence.

Strength and Courage

Strength refers to physical and emotional resilience, while courage is the willingness to confront challenges directly. During chaos, they help you endure and tackle uncertainties. In an AI world, courage supports adapting to rapid technological changes, preventing feelings of inadequacy.

Knowing you can handle difficulties fosters a sense of security and peace.

Wisdom and Increased Awareness

Wisdom is gained from experience, guiding better choices, while increased awareness involves mindfulness of self and surroundings. In chaos, wisdom offers perspective to navigate challenges calmly. In an AI world, awareness of technology's impact ensures informed, ethical decisions.

Trust in your judgment and a mindful presence reduce inner turmoil, enhancing peace.

Tranquility and Inner Peace

Tranquility is a quiet state, and inner peace is internal harmony. In chaos, tranquility offers a mental refuge. In an AI world, it counters overstimulation from digital noise. Inner peace is the essence of serenity, providing a stable core amidst external storms.

Love and Affection

Love and affection represent emotional bonds and support from relationships. In chaotic times, they provide comfort and a sense of belonging. In an AI world, where digital interactions can feel cold, they maintain human connection. Feeling loved and supported counters isolation, fostering emotional tranquility.

Abundance and Blessings

This pillar reflects a gratitude-focused mindset, recognizing life's positives. During chaos, it shifts focus from scarcity to sufficiency, reducing despair. In an AI world, it counters the relentless pursuit of "more" by grounding you in the present. Contentment through gratitude nurtures a peaceful, satisfied state.

TWELVE PILLARS OF WELLNESS   33

Prosperity and Compassion

Prosperity ensures material and emotional security, while compassion fosters empathy for others.

In chaos, they build community and personal stability. In an AI world, compassion mitigates technology-driven disparities, enhancing social harmony. Security and connection to others create a serene, grounded life.

Positivism and Optimism

Positivism focuses on solutions and positivity, while optimism holds hope for the future.

In chaotic times, they prevent despair and inspire action. In an AI world, optimism fuels adaptability and innovation. A hopeful, positive outlook reduces fear, paving the way for calm.

Transformation and Self-Realization

Transformation is personal growth, and self-realization is understanding your authentic self.

In chaos, they enable adaptation to new realities. In an AI world, they anchor identity amid technological shifts. Aligning actions with purpose and values brings deep, lasting peace.

TWELVE PILLARS OF WELLNESS

End of Part I

Part II

The Symphony of Serenity

> "The music is not in the notes, but in the silence between.
> Melody is the essence of music."
> – Wolfgang Amadeus Mozart

Prelude to Part II
The Symphony of Serenity

In the whirl of daily life, we are surrounded by a cacophony of sounds—some jarring, others soothing. But what if we could curate the sounds around us to create a symphony of serenity? Soundscaping, the mindful practice of shaping our auditory environment, invites us to listen deeply and intentionally to the world around us. Through the chapters that follow, you will learn how to tune into everyday sounds, identify those that bring you calm, and create personalized Melodic Landscape that foster relaxation and emotional balance. Whether it's the rustling leaves or the soothing hum of background music, you'll discover how sound can be a powerful ally in your quest for inner peace.

Learning to Listen Mindfully

Cultivating Awareness through Sound

Close your eyes for a moment and listen—what do you hear? The hum of a refrigerator, the distant chirping of birds, perhaps the murmur of voices nearby. In this chapter, we cultivate the first step of every Melodic Landscape: mindful listening. By noticing everyday sounds, we identify which soothe and which stress. You'll create a Sound Map—a simple exercise that reveals how sound shapes your inner state and activates The Pillar of Focus and Mental Clarity. This is the foundation for curating personal Melodic Landscapes that turn chaos into calm.

The Art of Listening: Noticing Everyday Sounds

Welcome to *listen mindfully*—the seed of every Melodic Landscape. In busy lives, sounds fade into the background. This practice invites us to pause, tune in, and hear the world with fresh ears. It grounds us in the present and prepares the mind for piano, poetry, and visual synesthesia.

Try it now:

Find a quiet spot. Close your eyes. Take three slow breaths.
   - What drifts in? A fan's whir? Birds? Footsteps?
   Don't label—just notice. Let sounds arrive like waves.
   This 60-second pause activates **Pillar 7: Calmness and Serenity**.

Identifying Personal Triggers for Calm or Stress

Every sound carries emotion. What calms you may stress another.
   - Leaves rustling → soothing whisper?
   - Traffic hum → steady pulse or anxious buzz?

   Reflect:
   - Which sounds **lifted** you?
   - Which **pulled** you?

These personal triggers are your palette. They guide which piano tones, poetic rhythms, and visual tempos will form your Melodic Landscape.

Understanding Sound Maps

A Sound Map is your auditory compass:
   - Calming sounds (waves, birds)
   - Stress sounds (pings, horns)
   - Neutral ambience (fan hum)

Use it to design *Melodic Landscapes* that amplify calm—even in AI-noisy settings.

Example (Park Bench): Close your eyes for a moment and listen—what do you hear? The hum of a refrigerator, the distant chirping of birds, perhaps the murmur of voices nearby. In this chapter, we will cultivate the art of listening, learning to notice the everyday sounds that often go unnoticed. By becoming aware of our auditory environment, we can identify which sounds soothe us and which ones stir stress. You'll even create a "sound map" of your surroundings, a simple yet powerful exercise that will help you understand how sound influences your state of mind. As we embark on this journey of auditory awareness, you'll begin to see how the world around you can be a source of serenity.

Harnessing Sound for Body and Mind

Curating Melodic Landscapes for Body, Mind, and Spirit

Just as we might arrange a room to feel more peaceful, we can arrange the sounds in our lives to create a sanctuary for our ears and our souls. In this chapter, we will explore how to curate your own sound sanctuary, selecting and creating Melodic Landscapes that bring you calm and focus. From the gentle rhythm of ocean waves to the subtle tones of binaural beats, you'll learn about different types of sounds and their effects on your well-being. We'll also introduce accessible tools and resources to make Melodic Landscapes beginner-friendly, ensuring that you can start crafting your auditory haven right away. By the end of this chapter, you'll have the knowledge to transform your environment into a space that nurtures serenity.

The transformative vibration of sound resonates through our bodies, altering brain waves and reducing cortisol. Binaural beats or piano notes can shift energy, healing emotional fragments caused by digital chaos and guiding us toward profound serenity.

Finding the Sounds That Soothe You

Let's start by tuning into the sounds that make your heart feels at ease. Think about a time when you felt completely relaxed or at peace—maybe it was a quiet morning walk with breeze through trees, an afternoon by the ocean with waves lapping at the shore, or a cozy evening with the soft hum of a favorite song in the background. What sounds surrounded you in those moments? Grab a notebook or just pause for a second and jot them down in your mind. These are the threads of your personal sound sanctuary.

What's beautiful about this process is that it's entirely yours—there's no one-size-fits-all. Maybe you love the rhythmic patter of rain on a rooftop, or perhaps the distant whistle of a train brings you a strange sense of comfort. Sounds like ocean waves, crackle of a fire, or ambient music are great places to begin, but don't be afraid to explore beyond the usual suspects. The hum of a coffee shop or the rustle of leaves might speak to you in ways you didn't expect. This step is all about discovering what soothes you, setting the stage for everything that follows.

Understanding Binaural Beats, White Noise, and Their Effects

Now that you've started to uncover the sounds that calm you, let's explore why they work and see why certain sounds work their magic. Two fascinating examples are binaural beats and white noise—both have a knack for shaping how we feel, and they're easier to understand than you might think.

Binaural beats happen when you play two slightly different frequencies—measured in Hz, or hertz—in each ear (using headphones for best results). For example, 300 Hz in your left ear and 310 Hz in your right create a pulsing tone of 10 Hz in your brain. This can nudge your brainwaves into patterns linked with relaxation, focus, or sleep.

White noise, on the other hand, is like a cozy sound blanket. It's a steady mix of all frequencies at once—think of the static on an old TV or the whoosh of a fan. It works by masking other noises, making it a lifesaver if you're trying to focus in a busy space or drift off to sleep with a chatty world outside your window.

Knowing this can help you choose sounds with purpose. Want to unwind? Try binaural beats in a low frequency range, like delta (0.5-4 Hz), to ease into relaxation. Need to block out distractions? White noise might be your new best friend. It's like having a toolbox of sound, ready to support whatever you're feeling.

Creating Personalized Melodic Landscapes for Different Moments

With your favorite sounds in mind and a bit of know-how about why they work, it's time to play composer and craft Melodic Landscapes tailored to your life's rhythms. Whether you're meditating, working, or winding down for the night, the right combination of sounds can make all the difference.

For meditation, imagine a gentle backdrop that keeps you grounded—maybe the trickle of a stream paired with soft wind chimes, or the deep resonance of a Tibetan singing bowl. These flowing, calming sounds can help you sink into mindfulness without pulling your focus away.

If you're tackling work or study, you might want something steady that fades into the background. Ambient music with a slow tempo, a light layer of white noise, or even the subtle buzz of a café recording can keep your mind sharp without overwhelming it. I've found that a soft jazz playlist can turn a scattered afternoon into a productive one—maybe it'll work for you too!

For sleep, lean into sounds that feel like a lullaby for your soul. The steady crash of ocean waves, a gentle rainfall, or even a quiet melody can signal to your body that it's time to rest. Experiment a little—layer a distant thunderstorm over a soft piano track and see if it carries you off to dreamland.

The fun part? You get to mix and match until it feels just right. Your Melodic Landscapes is your creation, perfectly tuned to the moment you're in.

Accessible Tools for Melodic Landscapes

You don't need fancy equipment or a big budget to start Melodic Landscapes—there are tons of beginner-friendly tools out there to help you dive in. Apps are a fantastic place to begin, and here are a few favorites:

- **Calm**: This gem offers a library of Melodic Landscapes—think rainforest drizzles, crackling fires, or soothing instrumentals—plus guided meditations if you want a little extra guidance. It's perfect for unwinding or drifting off.

- **Headspace**: Known for mindfulness, it also has sleep sounds and ambient tracks to ease you into calm. It's like a pocket-sized retreat.

- **Noisli**: This one's a playground for sound lovers. You can mix and match sounds—like rain, wind, or a train rumble—to build your own custom vibe.

Many of these apps have free versions or trials, so you can test the waters without committing. Some features may require a subscription, but free trials are available. Download one, pop in some earbuds, and let the exploration begin—it's that simple!

Exercise: Craft Your First 3-Minute Melodic Landscape

1. Choose your moment (meditation / focus / sleep).
2. Pick 1 piano track (3–5 min, slow tempo).
3. Write 1 poetic line (4–8 words, sync with breath).
4. Find 1 visual (YouTube loop or mental image).
5. Play all together → adjust volume so piano leads.

Example (Sleep):

- Piano: "Clair de Lune" (slowed 10%)
    - Poetry: "Moonlight on still water…" (whisper)
    - Visual: YouTube "moonlit ocean loop"
    - Layer: Distant waves (low volume)

Journal: How did your body respond? (Heart rate? Breath?)

From Vibration to Victory

You've built your first Melodic Landscape!.

Balancing Silence and Sound for Serenity

How Piano, Poetry, and Visuals Begin in Stillness

Harmonizing contrast between silence and sound paves a path to interior peace. Alternate bustling AI notifications with quiet intervals, using this duality to deepen awareness and cultivate a balanced inner landscape resilient to external turmoil.

In a world filled with noise, silence can feel like a rare and precious gift. Yet, silence is not merely the absence of sound; it is a space where we can hear our own thoughts, feel our own presence, and connect with the stillness within. In this chapter, we will explore the profound role of silence in soundscaping, understanding how it complements and enhances the sounds we choose. You'll learn how to balance noise, music, and stillness, and discover the benefits of practicing mindful silence to deepen your awareness. Through simple exercises, such as sitting in silence for a few minutes, you'll experience firsthand how silence can be a powerful tool for cultivating inner peace.

Why Silence is as Important as Sound

Silence isn't about blocking sounds; it creates space for the ones we love to shine. Think of it as the blank canvas in a painting—it gives shape and meaning to everything else. In soundscaping, silence lets us pause, breathe, and listen, making the experience richer. Dynamic range, the contrast between loud and soft sounds, amplifies this effect, making a bird's chirping or a soft melody more vivid after a quiet pause

Tuning In: The Art of Balancing Sound for Serenity

Sound is a fundamental aspect of our daily lives, shaping our experiences, influencing our emotions, and impacting our well-being. It surrounds us in myriad forms, each with distinct characteristics and effects, creating a rich auditory tapestry. By understanding these forms and learning to balance them with noise, music, and stillness, we can craft Melodic Landscapes that soothe the soul and enhance our environments.

The Many Forms of Sound

Sound manifests in diverse ways, each contributing uniquely to our auditory world:

- **Nature Sounds**: These natural sounds—like the rustling of leaves, chirping of birds, flowing rivers, or howling winds—connect us to the earth. They can be soothing, such as ocean waves, or chaotic, like a thunderstorm, offering raw, unfiltered charm ideal for relaxation or grounding.

- **Melodic Sounds**: Characterized by musical quality, these include instrumental music, singing, or even the harmonious hum of machinery. Intentionally crafted, they evoke emotions, tell stories, and resonate deeply due to their rhythm and structure.

- **Ambient Sounds**: Background noises, such as rainfall or the hum of a city, set the atmosphere. Whether natural or human-made, they subtly shape our mood and environment without demanding focus, enhancing settings like a quiet library or bustling café.

- **Noise**: Often unwanted, noise includes traffic, construction, or loud machinery. Subjective in nature, it can be disruptive and stressful or energizing, like a rock concert, depending on perception.

- **Speech**: Human vocalizations—talking, whispering, shouting, or laughing—carry meaning, emotion, and intent. Beyond words, tone and inflection deepen communication, making it a cornerstone of interaction.

- **Animal Sounds**: From a dog barking to a lion roaring, these noises offer insight into the natural world. They serve purposes like communication or mating and enrich our coexistence with wildlife.

- **Mechanical Sounds**: Produced by machines—like the ticking of a clock or whirring of a fan—these reflect functionality and progress. They can be rhythmic and reassuring or jarring when malfunctioning.

- **Electronic Sounds**: Beeps, buzzes, or synthesized tones from phones and computers mark the modern era. Precise and artificial, they serve practical alerts or creative roles in electronic music.

- **Silence**: The absence of sound, silence acts as a vital contrast. It enhances rhythm and emotion in music and can be calming or unsettling in life, giving meaning to the sounds around it.

Together, these forms—from nature sounds to silence—create a symphony that influences how we feel, think, and interact with our surroundings.

Balancing Noise, Music, and Stillness

Creating a soothing Melodic Landscape involves finding harmony among noise, music, and stillness. Noise represents the everyday clatter of life—dishes clanking or traffic buzzing. Music introduces intentional sounds, like a playlist of ocean waves or a soft guitar tune. Stillness, embodied by silence, provides the quiet that ties it all together. An imbalance—too much noise, overwhelming music, or excessive silence—can disrupt serenity, leaving us frazzled, drowned out, or isolated. The key is a personal blend that feels harmonious.

To achieve this, start by noticing the sounds around you: which uplift, and which stress? You might soften noise with calming music or carve out stillness to reset. A useful concept here is **dynamic range**—the difference between the loudest and softest moments. Silence amplifies this range, making subsequent sounds—like a bird's chirping or a plucked string—more vivid and comforting after a quiet pause. By playing with this balance, you enhance the impact of each sound.

Crafting a Harmonious Melodic Landscape

Understanding sound's diverse forms empowers us to curate our auditory environment intentionally. Whether leveraging the grounding power of nature sounds, the emotional pull of melody, or the clarifying pause of silence, we can shape our surroundings to support well-being. By mindfully balancing noise, music, and stillness—tailored to personal preference—we create Melodic Landscapes that not only enhance our daily lives but also soothe the soul, making every sound more alive and meaningful.

Practicing Mindful Silence to Deepen Awareness

So, how do we make silence more than just a gap between sounds? That's where mindful silence comes in—it's about being fully present in the quiet. This isn't about forcing your mind to be blank (good luck with that!). It's about sitting with yourself, noticing what comes up, and letting it be. Practicing mindful silence can deepen your awareness and bring a sense of peace that sticks with you, whether you're soundscaping or just moving through your day.

Here's a little exercise to try: Find a cozy spot where you won't be interrupted. Sit comfortably, close your eyes, and take a few slow, deep breaths. Then, for just two minutes—set a timer if you want—let yourself be in silence. Focus on your breath, the feel of your seat, or even the faint sounds you might hear. Thoughts will pop up (they always do!), and that's fine—imagine them drifting by like leaves on a stream. When the two minutes are up, jot down how you feel. Maybe you'll notice a lightness, a clarity, or just a quiet smile. This simple practice can become a go-to for grounding yourself, making both your Melodic Landscapes and your peaceful moments feel even more serene.

The Science of Serenity – Sound and Hormones

The Neuroscience of Melodic Landscapes

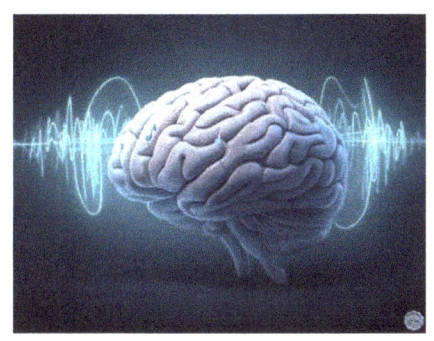

Serenity—that deep sense of calm and peace—does more than just soothe the mind; it weaves together music, language, and even the way our bodies work in some pretty amazing ways. The word "serenity" has a special connection to "serenade," those gentle evening melodies that trace back to the Latin word *"serenus"*, meaning "clear" or "tranquil." But it's not just a beautiful idea—it's something real that affects us physically, right down to the hormones flowing through us. Whether it's the soft notes of a Mozart serenade or a quiet moment to yourself, serenity can lower stress hormones like cortisol and adrenaline while giving a boost to the ones that make us feel good, like oxytocin, serotonin, and endorphins. It's a perfect harmony of art and science, where calm and music come together to balance both body and mind.

How Serenity Works Its Magic

So, what's happening inside us when we feel this calm? When we're relaxed and stress-free, our body's nervous system—the part that helps us react to the world—teams up with our endocrine system, which is like the hormone control center. This teamwork involves two key players. When stress hits, a control center in your brain tells your body to pump out cortisol, the stress hormone—like flipping an emergency switch. Think of them as the body's stress management crew. When serenity kicks in, they shift gears into relaxation mode, cutting back on stress hormones and ramping up the feel-good ones. It's like your body's way of hitting the reset button, creating a sense of balance that feels as natural and uplifting as a well-played melody.

This blend of conversational warmth and clear explanation keeps things approachable while still showing how serenity ties music and biology together with authority. It's not just about feeling peaceful—it's about how that peace changes us, inside and out.

Key Hormones Affected by Serenity

Cortisol (The Stress Hormone)

Cortisol, the stress hormone, spikes in response to AI-driven pressures like constant connectivity. Serenity practices, such as ambient sound listening, lower its levels, preventing chronic effects and promoting a calmer physiological state.

Let's chat about something that affects all of us—stress and how it impacts our bodies. Specifically, we're diving into cortisol, often called the stress hormone, and how a little serenity can make a big difference. Ready? Let's break it down together.

What's Cortisol All About?

THE SCIENCE OF SERENITY – SOUND AND HORMONES

You know that feeling when you're stressed out—maybe your heart's racing or your mind won't settle? Well, that's when cortisol steps in. It's like your body's built-in alarm system, released by your adrenal glands to help you handle those tense moments. The whole process is managed by a part of your brain called the HPA axis (short for hypothalamic-pituitary-adrenal axis, but don't worry, we won't get too technical here!).

Here's how it works: when stress hits, your brain kicks off a chain reaction. One part (the hypothalamus) sends a signal—think of it as a little messenger called CRH—to another part (the pituitary gland). That part then tells your adrenal glands, "Hey, time to release some cortisol!" It's a team effort to get you through those stressful times.

How Serenity Helps

Now, here's the really good part: when you're feeling calm and serene, your body doesn't need to sound the alarm as much. That HPA axis we talked about? It gets to take a breather. Less stress means fewer of those messengers (CRH, a stress-signalling hormone and ACTH, a hormone that triggers cortisol) running around, and that leads to less cortisol floating through your system.

And get this—science backs it up! Studies (you know, those smart folks doing psychoneuroendocrinology research) have found that simple practices like meditation or deep breathing can lower your cortisol levels by 20-30%. That's huge, right? It's like giving your body a warm, cozy hug from the inside out.

Oxytocin (The Bonding Hormone)

You know that warm, fuzzy feeling you get when you're sharing a laugh with a friend or enjoying a gentle hug? That's **oxytocin** doing its magic! Often called the "bonding hormone," oxytocin is like your body's natural cuddle chemical. It's produced in a part of your brain called the hypothalamus and released by the pituitary gland to help you feel connected, trusting, and oh-so-relaxed, especially during positive, calm moments.

Here's the cool part: when you're in a serene state—think gentle touches, soothing music, or even a quiet mindfulness moment—your body ramps up oxytocin production. Research, like studies from *Neuroscience & Biobehavioral Reviews*, shows that serene environments or meditative states can increase oxytocin levels, especially when you feel safe and loved. It's like your brain's way of saying, "Hey, this feels nice—let's keep it going!" And the result? More oxytocin means more emotional warmth and tranquility, creating a cozy loop that keeps you feeling serene.

So, next time you need a little emotional pick-me-up, try embracing serenity—it's like wrapping your heart in a warm blanket!

Serotonin (The Mood Regulator)

Ever wonder why a calm mind feels so refreshing? That's **serotonin**, your brain's natural mood booster, at work. This neurotransmitter is like a happiness helper, keeping your mood steady, your sleep restful, and your sense of well-being strong. It's made in your brain (and even your gut!) with help from areas like the raphe nuclei, and it thrives when you're feeling good.

Now, serenity steps in to give serotonin a lift. When you're calm—maybe after meditating or just clearing your mind of clutter—your brain gets a serotonin boost. Studies using PET scans on meditators have shown that practices inducing calm can actually increase serotonin levels. Plus, when you're less stressed, cortisol (that pesky stress hormone) doesn't block serotonin production, letting it flow freely. The payoff? Higher serotonin brings more peace and contentment, making your serene state even more solid.

So, when you need a mood lift, try finding a little calm—it's like sunshine for your soul!

Endorphins (Natural Painkillers)

You know that lovely feeling when you're laughing with friends or soaking in the peacefulness of nature? That's **endorphins** making you feel good from the inside out. These little peptides, released by your pituitary gland and hypothalamus, are like your body's natural feel-good helpers. They pop up during pleasurable or calming activities—like exercise, laughter, or listening to music—and bring a smile to your face.

While endorphins are famous for that post-workout euphoria, serene states can also coax out a gentler release. Picture listening to soothing music (like a serenade) or enjoying a quiet moment outdoors—these can trigger a mild endorphin boost. It's not as intense as a big exercise spike, but studies on music therapy show it's still measurable and real. This subtle lift adds a quiet sense of well-being to your day, making serenity's calming effect even sweeter.

So, when you're feeling a bit low, try embracing serenity—it's like a gentle hug for your heart!

Melatonin (The Sleep Hormone)

Ever noticed how a peaceful evening makes you feel ready to drift off? That's **melatonin**, your body's natural sleep whisperer, doing its job. Produced by the pineal gland in your brain, this hormone regulates your sleep-wake cycles and loves a calm, dark setting. But things like bright lights or stress can throw it off, thanks to cortisol putting up roadblocks.

Here's where serenity saves the day: a calm state, especially in the evening, lowers cortisol levels, letting melatonin production flow smoothly. Creating a serene atmosphere—like enjoying a serenade-like vibe or winding down quietly—aligns perfectly with your body's natural melatonin increase at night. The result? Enhanced melatonin means deeper relaxation and restful sleep, turning your nights into a peaceful retreat.

So, when bedtime rolls around, try tapping into serenity—it's like a warm cup of cocoa for your soul!

Wrapping It Up

Isn't it incredible how a little serenity can do so much? By boosting oxytocin, serotonin, endorphins, and melatonin, you're not just feeling calmer right now—you're setting yourself up for better moods, stronger connections, and sweeter dreams. So, the next time life feels overwhelming, remember that serenity is like a superpower for your body and mind. Embrace it, and let the calm flow!

To summarize, serenity's biological effects—reducing cortisol while boosting oxytocin, serotonin, endorphins, and melatonin—demonstrate how sound and mindful practices profoundly influence our well-being. By understanding these hormonal shifts, you can intentionally use audio elements to foster a calmer state, countering the stresses of daily life.

Applying Peace – Sounds' impact on Body and Mind

Practical Ways to Use Sound for Well-Being

Serenity, whether sparked by a soothing serenade or a mindful pause, deeply affects our physical and mental state. It triggers the body's relaxation response (parasympathetic nervous system), calming the stress response (sympathetic nervous system). This shift lowers stress hormones like cortisol and adrenaline while encouraging the release of calming hormones such as oxytocin and serotonin.

Techniques that promote serenity—such as mindfulness or listening to tranquil music—also influence brain activity. They increase alpha waves, which are linked to relaxation, correlating with reduced stress hormones and elevated levels of serotonin and endorphins, the body's natural mood-lifters. A feedback loop enhances this effect: as stress hormones drop, physical signs of tension (like high heart rate or blood pressure) decrease, reinforcing the sense of calm and further stabilizing hormone levels.

Limitations

Individual Differences: Serenity's impact varies—someone with chronic anxiety might not see an immediate cortisol reduction.

Duration: Brief calm (e.g., a 5-minute break) may not shift hormones as much as prolonged peace (e.g., an hour of meditation).

Measurement Challenges: Hormonal changes are tracked indirectly through markers like saliva cortisol or blood serotonin, not observed in real time.

In essence, serenity reduces anxiety and stress responses and boosts feel-good chemicals, enhanced mood regulation, better sleep, and stronger bonds, creating a ripple effect where calm fosters calm through the brain and endocrine system. Soothing sounds, like those of a serenade, can amplify this process, serving as an external cue that lowers stress while subtly enhancing mood.

The medical world has long known the healing powers of music when it comes to the mind. Music's ability to reduce stress and anxiety while improving cognitive ability and memory inspired a field of medicine known as music therapy, which has existed in some form since the late 18th century.

Having uncovered how serenity—through sound and stillness—shapes our physiology, we now shift focus to the art of poetry. In the next chapter, we'll weave this serenity into poetry and Melodic Landscape can blend to craft immersive, transformative experiences that engage both mind and senses.

End of Part II

Part III

Poetry as Path to Peace

"Do not feel lonely, the entire universe is inside you"
–Rumi

Prelude to Part III
Poetry as Path to Peace

Benefits of reading poetry include emotional catharsis, improved empathy, and stress reduction through rhythmic immersion. In AI times, it reconnects us to human depth, countering superficial algorithms with profound introspection.

Words have a remarkable ability to touch our hearts, express our deepest emotions, and guide us toward peace. In Part III, we explore the transformative power of poetry—a form of expression that serves as a prism for our emotions and a salve for our struggles. In the following chapters, you'll discover poetry as more than words—a companion for serenity. Whether new to poetry or a long-time admirer, this section invites you to explore its potential for emotional alchemy and mindfulness.

This journey will guide you through poetry's alchemy, mindfulness, and timeless forms.

Poetry's Alchemy
Turning Emotion into Healing Verse

Poetry is a powerful tool for emotional alchemy, transforming negative emotions into positive ones through expression, understanding, and transformation.

By bridging the unconscious and conscious mind, poetry fosters healing and growth, embodying emotional alchemy.

Transforming Emotions Through Verse

By bridging the unconscious and conscious mind, poetry fosters healing and growth within the Melodic Landscape triad.

Have you ever read a poem that named a feeling you couldn't express, like a sudden calm in a storm? This is poetry's magic—its ability to transform our raw emotions into something beautiful and meaningful. In this chapter, we explore how poetry serves as emotional alchemy, transforming inner experiences into strength and peace. We'll examine how rhythm, language, and feeling intertwine, learning mindful reading techniques to let vivid imagery and cadence calm and inspire us. Through historical and modern examples, such as Rumi's soothing verses that embrace the soul or Mary Oliver's nature poems, we'll see poetry's healing power across time, and you'll have the opportunity to craft your own lines.

Mindfulness in Poetry

Welcome to "Poetry as Emotional Alchemy," a chapter inviting you into poetry's transformative power. Part of How to Find Serenity with Words and Waves, this section explores how poetry, within "The Poetry of Peace," fosters emotional expression, mindfulness, and serenity. Picture poetry as an alchemist's tool, turning swirling emotions into moments of clarity and calm. Whether new to poetry or a seasoned reader, this chapter is for you. We'll uncover why poetry resonates, how to savor it mindfully, and its healing role across centuries. Plus, you'll try writing your own words—accessible to all. Let's begin this gentle exploration together.

Reading Poetry's Benefits

Reading poetry offers a multitude of benefits that enrich the mind, heart, and soul. It provides a powerful emotional connection, helping readers process and express complex feelings while fostering empathy and understanding for diverse perspectives. Poetry's imaginative language and vivid imagery enhance creativity, expand vocabulary, and improve communication skills. Its rhythmic and lyrical qualities promote mindfulness and presence, offering a meditative escape that can reduce stress and provide emotional healing. Additionally, poetry encourages critical thinking by challenging readers to interpret symbolism, themes, and metaphors, while also offering cultural and historical insights that deepen our understanding of the world.

Beyond its intellectual and emotional rewards, poetry inspires and motivates, conveying messages of hope, resilience, and beauty that encourage personal growth. It rekindles a sense of wonder and appreciation for life's small moments, reminding us to slow down and savor the richness of our experiences. Whether read for pleasure, reflection, or intellectual stimulation, poetry is a transformative art form that nurtures creativity, empathy, and a deeper connection to ourselves and the world around us.

Poetry in Melodic Landscapes

Reading and writing poetry within the triad offers:
- **Emotional connection** – Process complex feelings; foster empathy

- **Creativity boost** – Expand imagery, vocabulary, neural paths

- **Mindfulness** – Rhythmic flow reduces stress; breath syncs with line breaks

- **Healing** – Critical thinking via metaphor; cultural insight

- **Hope & wonder** – Rekindle appreciation for life's small moments

In an AI world, poetry is a "human counterbalance"—catharsis no algorithm can replicate.

Connection Between Rhythm, Language, and Feeling

Have you ever wondered why a poem quickens your heart or stirs a quiet ache? Poetry weaves rhythm, language, and feeling into something alive. Unlike everyday writing, it distills words to their essence—each chosen to spark an image, sound, or emotion. The rhythm, from a sonnet's steady beat to free verse's flow, dances with your breath, drawing you into its world. Like waves lapping at the shore, poetry soothes or stirs, always moving you. Pauses between lines invite you to linger, feeling the weight of the unsaid, as in "*The world is quiet now*," where silence deepens calm. Thus, poetry sings to your soul, transforming raw emotions into peace and profundity.

Techniques for Mindful Reading Poetry: Breath and Imagery

Now that you understand poetry's emotional pull, let's experience it with greater presence. Mindful reading transforms poetry into a mini-meditation, helping you settle into yourself and embrace its magic. Here are simple ways to begin:

• **Read Slowly and Aloud** - Poetry thrives when heard. Speak the words aloud, even softly, noticing how they roll off your tongue, like tasting the poem's unique flavor.

• **Focus on Your Breath** - Let the poem's rhythm guide your breathing—inhale at a line's start, exhale at its end, or pause at a comma, syncing body and words.

- **Visualize the Imagery** - When a poem paints a scene, like "The world is quiet now," close your eyes and see it. Feel it. What emotions arise as you enter this moment?
- **Pause and Reflect** - After reading, reflect on what stirred within you—a memory, a sense of calm? Let the poem settle without rush.

These steps are gifts, not rules, to deepen your connection. Adapt them to suit you—poetry adapts to your needs.

Silence in Poetry: Pausing for Impact

Beyond rhythm and imagery, poetry's pauses offer a path to mindfulness—fitting for a book about serenity through words and waves. When reading a poem, whether your own or a favorite, the words hold power. Yet a pause can amplify their meaning. Consider a line from a poem, such as "The world is quiet now," followed by a gentle silence. This pause isn't merely a break—it's a moment to feel the stillness, letting the words echo in your heart. When sharing poetry aloud, try lingering between lines or stanzas. Silence deepens emotion, builds anticipation, and invites connection, even when reading alone. can transform reading into a quiet, powerful reflection.

Historical and Modern Examples of Healing Poetry

Poetry's healing power spans centuries, a quiet companion through time. Long ago, Rumi's "The Guest House" wove love and longing into verses that still offer peace amidst chaos. In the 1800s, Romantics like Wordsworth crafted nature's beauty into words, like a walk through a forest, mending spirits. Today, Mary Oliver's "Wild Geese" soothes with images of geese and open skies, urging us to breathe and belong. Poets like Nayyirah Waheed crafts short, honest poems that heal by affirming shared experiences. In therapy, writing or reading poetry helps untangle emotions, processing pain to find light. These voices, ancient and modern, reveal poetry as a timeless balm, transforming hurt into hope.

Practicing Mindful Reading with "Wild Geese"

Ready to try mindful reading? Let's explore Mary Oliver's "*Wild Geese*", a soothing call to belong, chosen for its soothing imagery and self-acceptance. Here's how to begin: Find a quiet spot and read it slowly aloud (or silently if preferred).

- Let your breath follow the lines—inhale softly at "You do not have to be good," exhale as the wild geese call.

- Picture the geese overhead in the "harsh and exciting" world. What do you see or feel?

- Afterward, pause for a moment.

Do you feel lighter or grounded? Jot down a thought if you wish. Here's an excerpt (find the full poem in the Resources section): "You do not have to be good. / You do not have to walk on your knees / for a hundred miles through the desert, repenting. / You only have to let the soft animal of your body / love what it loves…" What stirred within you? No pressure—just notice. This is your first step into poetry's gentle alchemy.

A Brief Exercise: Write Your Own Emotional Snapshot

Now, become the poet! This exercise seeks authentic expression, not perfection, externalizing your emotions as a step-in poetry's alchemy. Pause to check in: How do you feel—calm, restless? Start with a phrase like "I feel…" or "Right now, I am…" and let words flow. Here are examples to inspire you:

- "I feel like a kite, tugging at the string, poised to soar or snap."

- "Right now, I am a pebble, still, awaiting the stream's embrace."

Write or reflect on a line about your emotional state, then read it aloud to feel its weight. How does it feel to shape your inner world? This is your piece of emotional alchemy, making the moment tangible and true.

Exploring Poetic Forms and Their Emotional Impacts

Poetry is a vibrant, evolving art form, with "forms" encompassing diverse structures, styles, and types defined by rhyme schemes, meter, line lengths, stanzas, or themes. Some, rooted in cultural traditions, follow strict rules, while others offer boundless freedom.

Poetry comes in all shapes and sizes, each form stirring emotions like a menu of moods to explore. While poetry's vastness defies a complete catalog, the Resources section lists major forms with descriptions of their features, uses, and emotional impact. Here's a glimpse of a few—try writing or reading them to discover what resonates.

Reading poetry offers numerous benefits, including enhanced emotional intelligence, reduced anxiety through rhythmic flow, and improved empathy by exploring diverse perspectives. In an AI world, it serves as a human counterbalance, sharpening focus and providing catharsis that technology alone cannot replicate.

Having explored the transformative power of poetry, it's time to learn how to harness that power in our daily lives.

The Roots of Poetry's Calming Power
Exploring Why Verse Heals

Having shaped your own emotions into verse, let's explore the diverse forms that give poetry its power. Will discuss practical techniques for reading poetry mindfully, selecting poems that resonate with our emotions, and using poetry as a tool for reflection and healing.

For centuries, poetry has offered peace, its words a steady heartbeat amidst chaos. What fuels its calming power? Let's explore the historical, scientific, and spiritual roots of poetry's serenity, revealing why it remains a timeless haven for the soul

Unearthing the Source of Poetry's Peace

Poetry has long been a refuge for the restless mind, a balm for the weary soul. But why does it hold such power to calm us? In this chapter, we'll dig into the roots of poetry's soothing nature—exploring its historical role as a source of serenity, the science behind its rhythmic embrace, and the spiritual connections it fosters. Through stories, examples, and insights, we'll uncover how poetry has been, and continues to be, a timeless path to peace. Whether you're a seasoned reader or new to verse, these roots will ground you in poetry's quiet strength—and inspire you to weave it into your own life.

Historical Roots of Poetry and Serenity

From ancient chants to modern sonnets, poetry has been a companion in humanity's quest for calm. In early civilizations, rhythmic verse was often tied to ritual—think of the Vedic hymns of India or the oral epics of Greece, recited to steady the spirit before battle or prayer. Medieval monks found solace in copying Psalms by candlelight, their verses serving as a lifeline to divine peace. In Japan, haiku emerged as a way to capture fleeting moments of stillness amidst life's chaos. Even today, poetry readings in cafes or online spaces serve as communal pauses, where words slow the world's spin. Across time and culture, poetry has been a thread of tranquility, stitching together moments of peace in a fractured world.

The Science of Poetry's Calming Effect

The science of poetry's calming effect lies in brain activation—rhythms sync with breaths, lowering amygdala activity. Studies show it rivals meditation, offering AI-era relief from cognitive overload.

What makes poetry so uniquely soothing? Science offers clues. The brain is wired for rhythm, and when we read or hear poetry, our minds sync to its meter—much like a heartbeat or a lullaby. Research, such as studies in bibliography, suggests that reading metered verse can lower stress hormones, creating a calming effect similar to gentle music. Rhyme and repetition also play a role, offering predictability that soothes the nervous system. Writing poetry engages the brain's creative centers, shifting focus from anxiety to flow. It's no surprise that bibliotherapy—using literature for healing—often turns to verse. Poetry, in its structure and sound, becomes a quiet rebellion against chaos.

Poetry as a Spiritual and Emotional Anchor

Beyond science, poetry touches something deeper—our spirit, our emotions. It distills complex feelings into simple lines, making the overwhelming feel manageable. A single stanza can hold grief, joy, or longing, offering a mirror to our inner world. For many, poetry is a form of prayer or meditation, a way to connect to something greater—be it nature, love, or the divine. Think of Rumi's verses on unity or Mary Oliver's odes to the wild; their words don't just describe peace—they evoke it. In this way, poetry becomes an anchor, grounding us in the present and reminding us of our shared humanity.

Real-Life Examples and Anecdotes

Consider the nurse who kept a tattered copy of Emily Dickinson's poems in her scrubs, stealing moments during long shifts to read a line or two—each word a breath of calm amidst the storm. Or recall how, after 9/11, people turned to W.H. Auden's "September 1, 1939," its verses a collective exhale of grief and hope. These stories show that poetry's calming power isn't abstract—it's lived, felt, and shared, a lifeline for those who seek it.

Applying Poetry for Personal Serenity

How can you tap into this power? Start small: carry a favorite poem in your pocket or phone, a touchstone for tough days. Read it aloud—let the rhythm wash over you like a wave. If you're inclined, write your own verses, no rules needed; the act itself is a release. Join a poetry circle, online or in person, to share the calm with others. When the world feels too loud, find a quiet corner and let a poem be your companion. For now, know that poetry is within reach, waiting to steady your spirit.

Poetry's Timeless Gift

The roots of poetry's calming power run deep—through history, science, spirit, and story. It's a gift passed down through generations, as alive today as it was in ancient times. As you turn these pages, remember: poetry isn't just words on a page; it's a doorway to peace, a reminder that serenity is woven into the fabric of language. Let it guide you, line by line, back to yourself.

Carry this gift forward—let poetry guide you back to serenity.

Healing Through Poetry – A Reader's Guide

How to Engage with Verse for Emotional Healing

Building a personal poetry library is like crafting a sanctuary of comfort and insight. In this chapter, we guide you in curating a collection that reflects your emotional landscape. You'll learn mindful reading techniques to let each word resonate, alongside ways to choose poems that match your moods and moments, using poetry for reflection and healing. Whether seeking solace in stress or joy in daily life, this chapter reveals poetry as a faithful companion on your path to serenity.

Your sanctuary is a living archive of lines that make you "pause, exhale, remember". One day you will open it, choose four lines, add a "D major arpeggio" and a "mist-on-lake visual", and a new "Serenity Landscape" will be born.

Building a Personal Poetry Library for Emotional Well-Being

Imagine having a little corner of your world filled with poems that feel like they were written just for you—words that make you pause, that wrap around your heart like a warm embrace. That's what a personal poetry library can be: a sanctuary for your soul. It's not about gathering every famous poem out there; it's about collecting the ones that speak to you. They should feel like old friends, ready to offer comfort or insight whenever you need it.

Why bother building one? Because poetry has a special way of meeting you where you are emotionally. When life feels chaotic, a gentle verse can bring you back to stillness. When you're bursting with joy, a lively poem can dance alongside your happiness. To start, think of poems that have touched you before—maybe a line that lingers in your mind or a piece that once brought tears to your eyes. Jot those down. If you're new to poetry, don't worry—this chapter will help you grow your collection step by step. For now, see your library as a living thing, one that will evolve with you as you journey toward serenity.

Techniques for Deep, Mindful Reading

With a poem before you, how do you engage deeply? Unlike skimming news, poetry invites you to linger, letting each word resonate. Mindful reading transforms a poem into a moment of peace or insight. Here's how to savor it:

- **Read Aloud** - Poetry thrives when spoken. Say the words aloud, feeling their rhythm as they roll off your tongue, like a song's first notes.

- **Visualize the Imagery** - Poets paint with words. Picture their scenes—a quiet lake, a blazing sunset—letting images bloom in your mind.

- **Notice Your Emotions** - What does the poem evoke? Calm, sadness, or hope? Your feelings connect you to its heart.

- **Look for Patterns** - Notice repeated words or rhymes, signposts highlighting the poem's core.

- **Consider the Title** - A title sets the mood, opening a doorway to the poem's meaning.

Take your time; there's no hurry. If a poem feels elusive, its beauty may unfold gradually, like a flower in sunlight. Try reading aloud from Gerard Manley Hopkins: "The world is charged with the grandeur of God." Feel the energy in "charged" and envision a world aglow with wonder. That's mindful reading at work.

Choosing Poems That Resonate with Different Moods

Poetry can be like a friend who always knows what to say. Feeling overwhelmed? A calm poem can soothe you. Brimming with joy? A playful one can join the celebration. The trick is learning to pick poems that match—or gently shift—your mood.

Start by checking in with yourself: What do you need right now? Comfort? Inspiration? A quiet moment? If you're stressed, you might gravitate toward poems about nature's peace, like a soft breeze through the trees. If you're triumphant, a poem about gratitude might feel just right. As your library grows, you could even organize it by emotion—think of a "peace" section or a "courage" corner—so you've got the perfect words at your fingertips. It's like creating a playlist for your soul.

Poem Recommendations for Different Emotions

Need a place to begin? Here's a short list of poems to match some common feelings—think of them as little gifts to tuck into your library:

- **For Peace:** "*The Guest House*" by Rumi – This gem invites you to greet every emotion with kindness, leaving you with a sense of calm acceptance.

- **For Grief:** "*Do Not Stand at My Grave and Weep*" by Mary Elizabeth Frye – A tender reminder that loved ones live on in spirit, offering solace when you need it most.

- **For Joy:** "*I Wandered Lonely as a Cloud*" by William Wordsworth – A cheerful romp with dancing daffodils that lifts your spirits.

- **For Love:** "*Sonnet 18*" by William Shakespeare – The famous "Shall I compare thee to a summer's day?" that sings of love's timeless glow.

- **For Hope:** "*Hope is the thing with feathers*" by Emily Dickinson – A sweet, uplifting take on hope as a bird that never stops singing.

Dip into these and see which one spark something in you—they're just the start of your poetic adventure.

Tips for Discovering Personal Poems

Those recommendations are a lovely launchpad, but the real magic happens when you find poems that feel like yours. Here's how to uncover them:

- **Search by Theme or Emotion:** Try websites like The Poetry Foundation or Poetry.org—type in "calm" or "healing" and see what comes up. It's like a treasure hunt for your heart.

- **Explore Anthologies:** Grab a book of poems grouped by topics you love—maybe mindfulness or the wonders of nature—and flip through until something clicks.

- **Follow Poets Online:** Poets on Instagram or Twitter often share bite-sized brilliance. Follow a few whose words tug at you, and watch your feed fill with inspiration.

- **Visit Poetry Events:** Whether it's a local reading or an online workshop, hearing poems spoken aloud can make them come alive in a new way.

- **Keep a Poetry Journal:** When a line or poem strikes you, write it down. Over time, you'll have a collection that's a perfect reflection of you.

You're the explorer here—go where your curiosity takes you, and let serenity follow.

Using Poetry as a Mirror for Self-Reflection

Poetry isn't just about what the poet meant—it's about what it means to you. It's a mirror that reflects your own joys, fears, and dreams, helping you see yourself more clearly. Here's how to unlock its personal magic:

1. **Read with Openness:** Let the poem wash over you without overthinking it. What catches your eye or tugs at your heart?

2. **Spot Key Moments:** Which lines or images stick with you? Maybe it's a single word that feels heavy with meaning.

3. **Link It to Your Life:** Does the poem remind you of something—a memory, a person, a quiet afternoon? That's where it gets personal.

4. **Feel the Emotions:** What's stirring inside as you read? Joy? Longing? Let those feelings guide your thoughts.

5. **Jot It Down:** Scribble a few notes about what the poem brings up—it's like a little chat with yourself.

Try it with this snippet from Wendell Berry's "The Peace of Wild Things":

"When despair for the world grows in me / and I wake in the night at the least sound / … I go and lie down where the wood drake / rests in his beauty on the water…"

Maybe it takes you back to a lake where you once found peace, or maybe it's a nudge to step outside and breathe. There's no wrong answer—just your truth.

Guided Practice: Reflecting on a Poem's Meaning for Personal Growth

Let's put it all together with a little practice. Here's a short poem *"Hope is the thing with feathers"*, a poem of resilience by Emily Dickinson (1886) to reflect on:

> *"Hope is the thing with feathers*
> *That perches in the soul,*
> *And sings the tune without the words,*
> *And never stops at all,*
>
> *And sweetest in the gale is heard;*
> *And sore must be the storm*
> *That could abash the little bird*
> *That kept so many warm…"*

Take a quiet moment with it, then ask yourself:
- What stands out? Maybe it's that image of hope as a tiny, singing bird.
- How does it feel? Does it lift you up or tug at a memory of tough times?
- Can you think of a moment when hope stayed with you, even in a storm?
- What might this say about your own strength or dreams?

Grab a pen and write your thoughts—let them flow freely. This is your chance to see how poetry can light up something new inside you, guiding you toward healing and calm.

While poetry offers a profound way to connect with our inner selves, serenity also involves harmonizing with the world around us. In the next chapter, we will shift our focus to the symphony of sounds that surround us, learning how to tune into everyday noises and identify those that bring us calm.

Verses of the Soul: A Journey Through Poetry's Heart

Exploring the Depths of Human Experience in Poetry

Poetry is a vast and beautiful landscape, filled with forms that have evolved over centuries to express the human experience in unique ways. Each form carries its own rhythm, structure, and emotional resonance, offering poets—and readers—different paths to explore feelings, ideas, and stories. Whether you're drawn to the structured elegance of a sonnet or the playful bounce of a limerick, there's a form that speaks to every heart. In this narrative, we'll journey through some of the most beloved forms of poetry, uncovering their origins, styles, and the emotions they stir—all in a way that's engaging and easy to follow. Let's dive in and discover the magic of poetry together.

The Sonnet: A Dance of Structure and Emotion

Picture a 14-line poem, a choreographed dance of words. That's the sonnet, often crafted in iambic pentameter—a heartbeat-like rhythm of ten syllables per line, alternating unstressed and stressed. *Sonnets* come in two main forms: the Shakespearean, with three four-line groups and a final couplet, and the Petrarchan, split into an eight-line opening and six-line close, each with distinct rhyme patterns weaving harmony.

Sonnets explore grand themes—love, beauty, time, or mortality—building toward a "volta," a turning moment that shifts the mood. In Shakespeare's "*Sonnet 18*" ("Shall I compare thee to a summer's day?"), admiration of fleeting beauty turns to timeless love. Their structure, both comforting and contained, holds deep emotions like a finely crafted vessel. *Sonnets* evoke love, longing, introspection, and quiet resolution, ideal for navigating life's complexities.

Haiku: Capturing the Fleeting Moment

Now picture a tiny poem—just three lines, with five, seven, and five syllables each. That's the haiku, born in Japan. These little gems focus on nature, often with a hint of the season, like a snapshot of a single moment. Their simplicity invites you to pause and notice the world's quiet beauty.

Haikus bring a sense of calm, wonder, or gentle sadness. Think of a frog splashing into a silent pond—the scene fades as quickly as it appears, leaving you with a bittersweet awareness of life's passing moments. They're a peaceful way to slow down and savor the now.

Limerick: A Playful Jig of Words

If haikus are whispers, *limericks* are bursts of laughter. These five-line poems have a bouncy rhythm and a rhyme scheme where the first, second, and fifth lines rhyme, and the shorter third and fourth lines share their own sound. They're often silly or clever, designed to make you smile.

Think of Edward Lear's old man with a beard who finds birds nesting in it—absurd and delightful! Limericks spark humor, joy, and sometimes a sneaky bit of wit. They're poetry's way of reminding us to have fun with words.

Ballad: Storytelling Through Song

Ballads are the storytellers of poetry. Written in four-line stanzas with a simple rhyme, they spin tales of love, tragedy, or adventure. Coming from oral traditions, they're easy to follow and carry you along with their rhythm.

A *ballad* like "*The Rime of the Ancient Mariner*" pulls you into a cursed sailor's haunting journey. They stir nostalgia, empathy, or a thrill, depending on the story. *Ballads* feel like sitting by a fire, lost in a tale that could be yours.

Ode: A Celebration in Verse

Odes are poetry's cheerleaders. These lyric poems sing the praises of a person, place, or thing—anything worth celebrating. They can be formal or free-flowing, but they always lift their subject up with vivid imagery and emotion.

John Keats' "*Ode to a Nightingale*" sweeps you into awe with the bird's song. *Odes* inspire admiration, gratitude, or a sense of wonder, making you want to shout about what you love.

Elegy: A Space for Grief and Reflection

Where *odes* rejoice, elegies mourn. These poems reflect on loss—often a death—with no set shape, just a quiet, somber tone. They mix personal sorrow with feelings we all recognize, offering comfort in shared grief.

Thomas Gray's "*Elegy Written in a Country Churchyard*" ponders life's end with dignity. Elegies bring sorrow, reflection, and sometimes peace, guiding you through the ache of goodbye.

Epic: The Grand Adventure

Epics are poetry's big-budget films—long tales of heroes and legends, often with a dash of the supernatural. Written in a grand style, they mirror a culture's heart and history.

Homer's Odyssey sweeps you into a world of courage and wonder. *Epics* spark awe, excitement, and pride, pulling you into a larger-than-life journey that echoes through time.

Free Verse: The Freedom to Flow

Free verse is poetry without rules—no set rhymes or rhythms, just the natural flow of words. It's like talking, with line breaks and imagery shaping the meaning.

Walt Whitman's "Song of Myself" feels raw and real, full of intimacy or wild energy. Free verse lets emotions spill out freely—vulnerable, chaotic, or liberating. It's for when you want your words to breathe.

Villanelle: The Hypnotic Refrain

Villanelles are like a song stuck in your head. With 19 lines—five three-line stanzas and a final four-line one—they repeat two key lines throughout, weaving a hypnotic spell.

Dylan Thomas' "*Do Not Go Gentle into That Good Night*" pulses with urgency and defiance. Villanelles stir longing, obsession, or a pressing need, their echoes amplifying every feeling.

Sestina: A Tapestry of Words

Sestinas are poetry's intricate puzzles. Six stanzas of six lines each, plus a three-line finish, they repeat six key words in a shifting pattern. It's a challenge that uncovers deep layers.

Elizabeth Bishop's "*Sestina*" ties a grandmother and child in quiet tension. The form feels like a web, connecting ideas and emotions in evolving ways.

Ghazal: The Poetry of Longing

From Middle Eastern and South Asian roots, ghazals are couplets—five or more—that share a rhyme and refrain. Each pair stands alone, often crying out for love or something lost.

Rumi's ghazals hum with passion and yearning. The repeated refrain feels like a plea, stirring melancholy or a spiritual ache.

Pantoum: The Echo of Memory

Pantoums loop like echoes. In four-line stanzas, the second and fourth lines repeat as the first and third of the next, tying everything together.

This repetition creates a reflective, almost haunting rhythm—nostalgia or obsession bubbling up. It's like revisiting memories that won't let go.

Acrostic: The Hidden Message

Acrostics are poetry's clever games. The first letters of each line spell out a word or phrase, hiding a secret in plain sight.

They spark curiosity and delight, revealing an intimate or surprising twist. It's a playful way to say more than meets the eye.

Concrete Poetry: Words as Art

Concrete poetry turns words into pictures. The way they're arranged on the page—maybe shaped like a tree or a heart—adds to their meaning.

George Herbert's "*The Altar*" looks like its name, blending sight and sound into wonder or harmony. It's poetry you feel with your eyes.

Spoken Word: The Power of Performance

Spoken word leaps off the page. Built for performance, it thrives on rhythm and voice, often tackling big ideas like justice or identity.

In a poetry slam, it hits you with passion, urgency, or joy, sparking connection or empowerment. It's poetry that demands to be heard.

A Taste of Something More

Now, Your Turn to Explore Expanded Content: Now, your turn to explore: experiment with these forms, writing your own to personalize serenity in daily life.

Beyond traditional forms, explore hybrid poetry blending AI-generated elements with human verse for innovative serenity.

Poetry's treasure chest overflows with forms. There's the tanka, a five-line Japanese poem that stretches a haiku into deeper reflection. The rondeau circles back with a refrain, like a lyrical hug. Terza rima links stanzas in a chain, as in Dante's *Divine Comedy*. Blank verse flows in unrhymed iambic pentameter—think Shakespeare's plays—while the cinquain packs a punch in five short lines.

Your Turn to Explore

Poetry isn't just for reading—it's for living. Try a *haiku* about the rain or a *limerick* to make someone giggle. Let a *villanelle* carry your heart's refrain or a *pantoum* revisit a memory. Every form is a door to your voice, a way to connect with yourself and the world. So, grab a pen, let your words dance, and see where this beautiful art takes you.

End of Part III

Scan or visit https://elchifmusic.com

End of Part III

White Orchids in the Sunset

In twilight's gentle embrace, where dreams unfurl,
Twenty-five white orchids in the sunset's glow,
Their petals soft as whispered lullabies, twirl,
Casting hues of amethyst as night winds blow.

Upon the Amethyst Sanctuary's tranquil shore,
A symphony of peace and silence weaves,
Nature's whisper in the heart's tranquil core,
Unfurling solace 'neath the rustling leaves.

Beneath the Nature Haven's verdant boughs,
Where silver moonbeams kiss the earth so sweet,
The wellness pillar of tranquility vows,
To cradle every step with gentle feet.

In this world of harmony and inner grace,
Where orchids bloom beneath the dying light,
Find peace enfolded in a timeless space,
And let your spirit take its tranquil flight.

Part IV
Weaving Words and Waves Together

It is the melody which is the charm of music, and it is that which is most difficult to produce. The invention of a fine melody is a work of genius.

–Joseph Haydn

Prelude to Part IV
Weaving Words and Waves Together

When words and waves—poetry and sound—come together, they create a harmony that can stir the heart and soothe the mind. In this book, we invite you to explore the beautiful synergy between these art forms, discovering how they can enhance your journey toward serenity. Whether you're a poet, a seeker of mindfulness, or simply curious, the upcoming chapters, beginning with *'The Synergy of Poetry and Sound,'* will guide you through techniques for pairing poetry with Melodic Landscapes. These practices create immersive experiences that engage both your mind and senses, whether you're listening to a poem read aloud against a backdrop of gentle music or crafting your own spoken word pieces. This combination can be a powerful catalyst for emotional depth and inner calm.

The Synergy of Poetry and Melodic Landscape
When Word and Melody Unite

The synergy of poetry and melodic landscape deepens emotional resonance, where verses align with sounds to create immersive serenity experiences.

Imagine reading a poem about the ocean while listening to waves crashing on the shore—the words and sounds blending seamlessly to transport you to a tranquil coast. This is the synergy of poetry and sound, a pairing that amplifies the emotional impact of both. In this chapter, we'll explore how sound deepens poetry's resonance and how a poem's imagery can bring vivid life to ambient sounds. You'll learn practical techniques—such as matching a nature poem with birdsong—for pairing poems with Melodic Landscapes, whether for personal reflection or creative expression. We'll also guide you through creating your own verse-and-sound experiences, offering step-by-step instructions to craft moments of calm clarity. As you explore these pages, you'll discover how these tools, woven together, can become a haven for your spirit.

How Sound Enhances the Emotional Depth of Poetry

Have you ever noticed how a poem can awaken a quiet joy, a twinge of nostalgia, or a gentle sense of wonder? Now, imagine adding sound to that experience.

Suddenly, those emotions leap off the page, vivid and alive. Pair a poem about a stormy night with the sound of rain tapping on a window or thunder rumbling in the distance, and it's as if you're standing in the storm, its energy swirling around you. Or picture a poem about a peaceful meadow, woven with the soft chirping of birds and a breeze rustling through grass—you're there, resting in that serene spot, breathing in its calm.

This magic unfolds because sound engages more of your senses, drawing you deeper into the poem's world. It's like adding vibrant blues and greens to a pencil sketch, painting the emotional landscape with richer hues. By enveloping you in a sensory embrace, sound helps quiet the mind's chatter, guiding you toward calm. As you listen, you might slip into a serene, meditative state—fully present, with daily stresses fading away. That's the gift of blending verse and sound: it deepens your connection to poetry and welcomes peace into your life. Try reading a short poem aloud with soft nature sounds to feel this calm unfold.

Rhythm and Resonance – Where Sound Meets Verse

When Verse Begins to Sing

Beneath every poem and melody lie rhythm and resonance—unseen forces that bind sound to verse, stirring the heart and soothing the mind. In this exploration, we'll unravel how these elements dance together, creating a timeless harmony that invites peace and reflection.

The Invisible Threads of Sound and Verse

The invisible threads of sound and verse connect rhythmically, weaving a fabric of peace that counters AI fragmentation.

Rhythm and resonance are the gentle currents that weave sound and poetry into a harmonious whole, bridging the auditory and the literary. Rhythm offers structure and flow—imagine the steady beat of a drum or the measured cadence of a poem. Resonance brings depth and staying power, like the lingering vibration of a note or the emotional echo of a well-crafted line. Together, they create a synergy that calms the mind and nurtures peace. In this section, we'll explore how rhythm and resonance manifest in both sound and poetry. We'll also see how they enhance each other and how you can use them to find serenity. As you read, listen for the subtle beats and echoes that unite these timeless arts.

The Role of Rhythm in Sound and Poetry

Rhythm is the heartbeat of both sound and poetry, offering a sense of order that can ground us in the present moment. In sound, rhythm emerges as patterns of beats or pulses—whether it's the tempo of a musical piece, the repetitive crash of waves, or the staccato chirping of a bird. These rhythms shape our emotional responses: a slow, even rhythm might soothe, while a rapid, irregular one could energize or unsettle.

In poetry, rhythm appears through meter, pacing, and the arrangement of words. Traditional forms like the sonnet use structured patterns—such as iambic pentameter, with its da-DUM da-DUM beat—to create a musical flow. Even in free verse, poets craft rhythm through line breaks and word choice, mimicking the natural rise and fall of breath or thought. This rhythmic quality gives poetry its pulse, inviting readers into its world.

When the rhythms of sound and poetry align, their impact deepens. Consider a haiku, with its concise 5-7-5 syllable structure, paired with the gentle, rhythmic lapping of waves. The wave's steady tempo complements the haiku's meditative brevity, creating a unified experience that feels both calming and complete. This harmony reveals rhythm as a universal force, capable of linking the external Melodic Landscape with the internal cadence of verse to foster a profound sense of peace.

The Power of Resonance in Sound and Poetry

Resonance is the quality that makes sound and poetry linger, vibrating within us long after the moment has passed. In sound, resonance is the fullness of a note as it reverberates—think of the deep, sustained tone of a gong or the fading echo of a voice in a canyon. These vibrations create a physical and emotional connection, resonating with our bodies and environments in ways that can feel both grounding and transcendent.

In poetry, resonance operates on a more metaphorical level. It's the lasting impact of a line or image—the way a phrase like "The world is too much with us" from Wordsworth sticks in your mind, its meaning unfolding over time. This emotional or intellectual echo comes from powerful imagery, clever wordplay, or sound devices like alliteration and assonance, which create an aural resonance that mirrors the poem's depth.

When resonance in sound meets resonance in poetry, the effect is transformative. Imagine reading a poem about stillness while a Tibetan singing bowl hums softly nearby. The bowl's resonant tone lingers in the air, much like the poem's words linger in your thoughts, amplifying each other's power. This interplay can draw you into a meditative state, where the boundaries between sound and verse blur, leaving only serenity in their wake.

Harnessing Rhythm and Resonance for Serenity

Rhythm and resonance aren't just concepts to admire—they're tools you can use to cultivate calm. Here are practical ways to bring them together:

- **Listen While You Write**: Play rhythmic sounds—like a metronome, soft drumming, or steady ocean waves—as you compose poetry. For beginners, choose subtle sounds to avoid distraction. Let the rhythm guide your words, creating a soothing flow. For example, try writing a haiku while listening to gentle rain to mirror its calm brevity.

- **Match Sound to Verse**: Choose background sounds that reflect the poem's rhythm or mood. For instance, pair a slow, reflective poem with the sound of rain to enhance its tranquility. In today's world, technology can amplify these practices—AI tools can craft personalized Melodic Landscapes to match your favorite poems or generate ambient tracks tailored to your emotional needs, making it easier to blend sound and poetry into a serene experience.

- **Create a Resonant Space:** Use resonant sounds—such as chimes, a singing bowl, or nature recordings—to set the tone for reading or writing poetry. The lingering vibrations can create an atmosphere of peace, deepening your connection to the words.

- **Mimic Nature's Rhythms:** Write poems inspired by the rhythms of calming natural sounds, like the ebb and flow of tides or the soft repetition of a heartbeat. Let these patterns shape your verse, infusing it with a tranquil energy.

Technology can enhance these practices, especially in our AI-driven world. AI tools can generate personalized Melodic Landscapes that match the rhythm of your favorite poems or create ambient tracks that resonate with your emotional needs. These digital aids make it easier to blend sound and poetry into a seamless, serene experience.

Try creating a simple ritual: each morning, read a short poem aloud while listening to a few minutes of calming sounds. Let the rhythm and resonance of both wash over you, setting a peaceful tone for the day ahead.

Pathways to Peace Through Rhythm and Resonance

Rhythm and resonance are more than artistic techniques; they are pathways to inner peace. By exploring how they connect sound and poetry, you can unlock their potential to soothe and center your spirit. Whether it's the steady beat of a wave, the resonant hum of a bell, or the quiet power of a poetic line, these elements offer a bridge to tranquility. As you move forward in this book, carry with you the understanding that every beat and every echo holds the promise of serenity—yours to discover and embrace.

The Power of Silence in Poetry and Sound
The Pauses That Express and Heal

The pauses that express and heal in poetry and music allow space for introspection, mending emotional wounds from digital haste. Silence holds a quiet power in poetry and sound, crafting space where meaning and emotion deepen. Far from emptiness, it acts as a vital force, amplifying the resonance of every word and note that follows.

The Role of Silence

Silence in poetry and sound is profound, serving as an essential element that shapes meaning, emotion, and rhythm. It's not merely the absence of sound or words but an active presence that enhances what surrounds it. For instance, in Mary Oliver's poem *'The Journey*,' the pause after 'you knew what you had to do' invites readers to feel the weight of the decision, amplifying its impact."

Silence in Music

In music, silence acts as the space between notes, giving them definition and allowing the listener to process the melody. Without these pauses, music would become a continuous stream of sound, lacking the emotional nuance that makes it resonate. Silence plays several key roles:

- **Building Tension and Anticipation:** A well-timed pause can heighten drama, creating a sense of expectation before the next note or phrase.

- **Emphasizing Key Moments:** The absence of sound can make the return of music more powerful, like a breath that gives the composition room to unfold.

- **Adding Emotional Depth:** These quiet moments allow listeners to feel the weight of the music, enhancing its overall impact.

For example, consider how a rest before a crescendo can make the swell of sound more striking. Silence, in this way, is a dynamic presence that shapes the listener's experience.

Silence in Poetry, Using Silence for Serenity

You can harness silence to deepen your poetry and sound experiences:

- **Pause in Reading**: When reading a poem aloud, linger on line breaks or stanza gaps to let the words resonate. Try this with a short poem like Emily Dickinson's "Hope is the thing with feathers," pausing after each stanza to feel its quiet power.

- **Incorporate Silent Moments**: Pair a poem with a Melodic Landscape that includes brief silences, like a recording of wind with natural pauses, to mirror the poem's rhythm and invite reflection.

In poetry, silence is embedded in the structure—through line breaks, stanza breaks, or the white space on the page. These pauses serve multiple purposes:

- **Inviting Reflection:** The spaces between words or lines give readers time to linger and absorb the emotional depth of what they've just read.

- **Creating Rhythm**: Much like in music, silence in poetry establishes a cadence, guiding the flow of the piece.

- **Emphasizing Ideas:** A sudden break or gap can draw attention to a specific word or image, making it stand out and resonate more deeply.

For instance, a poet might use a line break to isolate a single word, letting it echo in the reader's mind. This stillness is where the weight of the poem often settles, amplifying its meaning.

The Shared Power of Silence

In both music and poetry, silence is far from empty—it is a vital, active element. It shapes the flow of the work, adds emotional weight, and invites contemplation. Whether it's the pause between notes that heightens a melody's impact or the space on a page that lets a poem breathe, silence gives sound and words their full expressive power. It is in these quiet moments that meaning often blooms, making silence an indispensable part of the artistic experience.

Crafting Words and Waves
Art in Action: Writing and Composing from Serenity

Art in action: writing and composing from serenity—start with stillness, let ideas flow into verses or melodies for therapeutic creation.

The gentle pattern of rain or the hum of a quiet moment can spark inspiration, guiding us to weave words and sounds into something meaningful. In this section, we'll explore hands-on exercises that blend sound and verse, helping you craft your own waves of calm and creativity.

Practical Exercises in Sound and Verse

Have you ever listened to the rain and felt a sense of peace wash over you? As the rain taps gently against the window, creating a soothing rhythm, this poem invites you to immerse yourself in a tranquil moment. The steady sound of falling drops becomes more than just background noise—it's a call to explore the art of writing. Let this serene backdrop inspire you to craft words that flow and ripple, echoing the waves of sound surrounding you.

Pairing a poem with the sound of rain is one example:

Curtains drawn back, the world bathed in gray,
Raindrops descend, in a tranquil display.
The patter on roof, a lullaby's hum,
In this calm moment, peace has come.

Step-by-Step Guide: Create Your Own Poetry-Melodic Landscape Pairing

1. **Find or write a poem**: Choose a poem you love or write one about a moment of calm or a place you cherish.

2. **Tune into its essence**: Identify the poem's mood or imagery to guide your Melodic Landscape choice.

3. **Choose your sounds**: Select a Melodic Landscape that fits—ocean waves for a coastal poem or soft guitar for a tender one. If the sound feels overwhelming, lower the volume or try a simpler track.

4. **Test and record**: Read the poem aloud with the Melodic Landscape, adjusting your tone to flow with it. Record the pairing and tweak as needed.

5. **Reflect and share**: Listen to your creation. Does it evoke serenity? Share it with a friend if you wish.

Lean into the imagery: If your poem paints a picture—like waves lapping at a shore or leaves falling in a forest—choose sounds that echo that scene. Ocean sounds for a seaside poem, or gentle wind for a woodland one, can make the words feel more real.

Match the mood: Sometimes it's less about the setting and more about the feeling. A poem of sorrow might sing beautifully with the quiet hum of a cello or the patter of rain, while a joyful piece could dance with bright birdsong or a lively melody.

Play with rhythm: Think about the poem's pace. Got a fast, spirited verse? Try a Melodic Landscape with a quick tempo. For something slow and reflective, a mellow track—like a trickling stream or soft ambient notes—might be just right.

Keep it balanced: Whether you're listening quietly or reading aloud, make sure the Melodic Landscape lifts the words up, not drowns them out. Adjust the volume so it feels like a partner, not a rival.

Don't shy away from silence: Here's a little secret—silence can be as powerful as sound. A well-placed pause in your Melodic Landscape, like a breath between musical notes, can amplify what comes next. It's all about dynamic range, letting quiet moments highlight the beauty of both the words and the waves that follow.

These techniques are your starting point. As you experiment, you'll find combinations that resonate with you, creating a personal retreat where poetry and sound weave together for serenity.

Creating Spoken Word Experiences with Ambient Music

Ready to hear your words come to life? Pairing spoken word poetry with ambient music is a wonderful way to dive deeper into this synergy. Ambient music—those atmospheric, often instrumental tracks—works like a soft backdrop, cradling your voice without stealing the spotlight. Here's how to make it happen:

- **Pick the perfect mood:** Choose music that reflects your poem's heart. A tender, introspective piece might call for ethereal tones or a slow piano line, while a bold, passionate poem could shine with rhythmic pulses or a haunting drone.

- **Practice the dance:** Read your poem aloud with the music playing. Feel how it shapes your voice—does it nudge you to slow down, speed up, or linger on certain lines? Let the music guide your delivery until they feel like old friends.

- **Balance the blend:** When recording, keep the music at a level where it supports your voice, not overshadows it. You want listeners to catch every word while still feeling the mood the music brings.

- **Simplicity is key:** If the music feels too busy, dial it back. A minimalist track can often do more for your poem than something complex, letting your words shine through.

This is your chance to turn poetry into a full sensory experience—one that wraps you and your listeners in a cocoon of sound and emotion, perfect for finding calm amidst the storm.

Creating Your Own Words and Waves

Now, let's get you in on the fun. You don't need to be a poet laureate or a sound designer to create your own "words and waves"—this is about you and what brings you peace. Here's an easy way to start:

Close your eyes and think of a place where you feel at ease—maybe a beach at sunset, a quiet park, or even your favorite cozy chair. Write a few lines about it. What do you see? What do you hear? How does it feel? Don't fuss over perfection; just let the words flow.

Next, hunt for a Melodic Landscape that takes you back there. You can find free nature sounds or ambient tracks online—waves, wind, crackling fires—or even record your own with a phone. Pair your poem with that sound, reading it aloud softly as it plays. How does it feel to hear them together? Does it stir that same sense of calm?

This is your playground. Try different poems, tweak the sounds, and see what clicks. Each creation is a step toward serenity, a little gift you give yourself through the simple act of weaving words and waves.

Step-by-Step Guide: Create Your Own Poetry-Melodic Landscape Pairing

Feeling inspired? Here's a clear, friendly guide to crafting your own poetry-Melodic Landscape pairing:

- **Find or write a poem:** Grab a poem you love or write one yourself. If you're writing, pick something personal—maybe a moment of calm, a place you adore, or an emotion you're exploring.

- **Tune into its essence:** What's the poem about? Joy, stillness, restlessness? What images or feelings stand out? Note a few key vibes to guide your Melodic Landscape choice.

- **Choose your sounds:** Hunt for a Melodic Landscape that fits—ocean waves for a coastal poem, soft guitar for something tender, or even silence broken by chirping for a nature scene. Free apps or websites are great places to start.

- **Test it out:** Read the poem aloud with the Melodic Landscape playing. Adjust your speed or tone to flow with the sounds—does it feel like they're in conversation?

- **Capture the moment:** Record it using whatever you've got—a phone works fine. Aim for a mix where your voice shines, and the sounds enhance without overpowering.

- **Listen and feel:** Play it back. Does it wrap you in serenity? Spark a memory or emotion? If it's not quite there, tweak the sounds or your reading—no rush, just play.

- **Share if you'd like:** If it feels right, share it with someone you trust. Hearing their reaction might deepen your connection to what you've made.

This isn't about perfection—it's about discovery. Each pairing you create is a brushstroke in your own portrait of peace. As we integrate poetry and sound into our lives, it's important to remember that the path to serenity is not always linear. In the next chapter, we will learn how to recognize when we need to realign our practices, using poetry and sound as tools for resilience

End of Part IV

Part V

Living a Life of Serenity

> "Do your work, then step back.
> The only path to serenity."
> –Lao Tzu

Prelude to Part V
Living a Life of Serenity

Serenity is not a destination but a way of being—a practice we nurture over time. In this part of the book, we explore how to weave poetry and soundscaping into your daily life, ensuring your journey toward serenity remains vibrant and resilient.

Soundscaping, the art of designing auditory environments, is central to this process. By crafting calming Melodic Landscapes—such as the gentle rustling of leaves, the soothing flow of a stream, or soft ambient tones—you create a supportive backdrop for poetic practices and everyday routines. Unlike traditional mindfulness techniques, soundscaping engages your auditory senses to anchor you in peace, embedding serenity into the rhythm of your day and bolstering resilience against life's challenges.

Together, soundscaping and poetry form a powerful synergy, harmonizing your inner world with your outer environment to foster lasting calm and well-being.

In the chapters ahead, we'll guide you to recognize when your practice needs realignment, build a personalized serenity ritual, and embrace this creative path as a lifelong journey. Whether facing setbacks or seeking deeper calm, this section offers the tools and encouragement to live a life infused with serenity.

Staying on Course – Signs to Realign

Recognizing When You've Strayed from Serenity

Life ebbs and flows, and so does our journey toward serenity. There will be moments when stress resurfaces, your practice feels distant, or you simply need to pause and reset. In this chapter, we explore how to recognize when it's time to realign—recentering your focus on serenity—using poetry and sound as tools for resilience. Building on the Prelude's introduction to soundscaping and poetry, you'll find practical tips to stay connected during challenging times and a checklist to spot signs you might need to recalibrate.

Through relatable examples, like rediscovering calm amid a hectic day, and troubleshooting guides, we'll equip you to navigate the non-linear path of emotional and mental healing with grace and strength.

States of Serenity and Chaos

Our well-being is shaped by four scenarios, defined by the interplay of our internal state and external environment. Using the twelve *Twelve Pillars of Wellness*—a framework for holistic health introduced here and detailed later—we can navigate from the most challenging state to the optimal one. This chapter explains how to apply these *Twelve Pillars of Wellness*, alongside poetry and soundscaping, to each scenario:

- When you're calm inside and serenity surrounds you
- When you're calm inside amid external chaos
- When you feel inner chaos despite external serenity
- When you face chaos both inside and out

Scenario: Calm inside and calm outside

In this scenario, the person experiences internal peace, ideal harmony and the external environment is serene. Maintain it with daily rituals like poetry reading in peaceful environments. This alignment creates ideal conditions for all *Twelve Pillars of Wellness*. For example, Focus and Mental Clarity are undisturbed, Calmness and Serenity are inherent, Love and Affection can be easily expressed, and Transformation and Self-Realization can occur through reflection in a supportive setting. There are no stressors to disrupt Healing and Balance or Tranquility and Inner Peace. This scenario represents the fullest expression of wellness, making it the most optimal.

Scenario: Calm inside and chaos outside

Here, the person maintains internal calm despite external turmoil. This demonstrates significant Strength and Courage, Confidence and Inner Resilience, and possibly Wisdom and Increased Awareness gained from navigating challenges. However, the external chaos may challenge some pillars, such as Tranquility and Inner Peace (due to surrounding unrest) or Prosperity and Compassion (if the chaos limits resources or emotional capacity). While the person's internal state supports many pillars, the external environment poses obstacles, making this less optimal than Scenario 1 but still better than scenarios with internal chaos

Scenario: Chaos inside and serenity outside

In this case, the person experiences internal turmoil despite a peaceful external environment. The internal chaos directly undermines pillars like Calmness and serenity, Tranquility and Inner peace, *Focus and Mental Clarity*, and *Positivism and Optimism*. The serene surroundings might offer potential for *Healing and Balance*, but the internal struggle makes it difficult to fully engage with most pillars. This scenario is less optimal than Scenario 1 because internal chaos has a more direct and pervasive impact on well-being than external chaos alone.

Scenario: Chaos inside and chaos outside

This scenario combines internal and external turmoil, creating the most challenging conditions. Internal chaos impairs *Focus and Mental Clarity*, Calmness and serenity, and *Confidence and Inner Resilience*, while external chaos exacerbates these difficulties and hinders *Love and Affection*, *Abundance and Blessings*, and *Prosperity and Compassion*. Virtually all pillars are compromised, making it nearly impossible to achieve wellness. This is the least optimal scenario.

Accepting the Non-Linear Path of Healing

Imagine your journey toward serenity as the gentle rhythm of ocean waves. Some days, they lap calmly at the shore, soothing and steady. Others, they crash with force, stirring everything up. That's what our path to wellness looks like too—full of highs and lows, moments of peace and challenge. And that's perfectly okay. Embracing this natural ebb and flow, much like the Melodic Landscapes we craft, can transform how we navigate tougher times.

When we accept that emotional and spiritual healing isn't linear, we allow ourselves to meet setbacks with kindness rather than frustration. A rough day isn't a failure—it's a chance to pause, reflect, and realign with the serenity we're cultivating through poetry and sound. There's no "perfect" way to do this, and that's the beauty of it. It's about discovering what feels right for you and being gentle with yourself along the way.

Signs You Need to Realign Checklist

How do you know when it's time to realign—recentering your focus on serenity? Life sends subtle signals when we're drifting off course. Here's a friendly checklist to spot those moments:

- **Irritability and Mood Shifts:** Feeling unusually irritable, snapping at small things, or noticing worry and anxiety creeping in more often.

- **Mental Cloudiness:** Struggling to focus or grappling with mental fog, making clear thinking difficult.

- **Physical Exhaustion:** Feeling drained with physical fatigue, low energy, sleeplessness, or restlessness.

- **Emotional Disconnect:** Losing interest in what usually sparks joy or feeling detached from your emotions or loved ones.

If these feel familiar, don't worry—it's entirely normal! Life throws curveballs, and our minds and bodies respond honestly. The key is catching these signs early and using tools like poetry or soundscaping to restore balance.

Troubleshooting Guide for Common Challenges

Now that you're attuned to signs of needing realignment, let's explore how to respond when they arise. Here are quick fixes to navigate challenging moments:

- **If you're feeling overwhelmed:** Step away for three minutes and listen to a calming Melodic Landscape, such as gentle rain from a free app like Calm or rolling ocean waves. Let the sounds wash over you, giving your busy mind a brief respite.

- **If you're struggling with focus:** Grab a pen and write a short, free-verse poem about what's swirling in your head. No need for perfection—just let the words flow. It's like clearing mental clutter to return to the moment.

- **If you're feeling anxious:** Pair a simple breathing exercise with nature sounds. Inhale for four counts, hold for four, exhale for four, while listening to a forest hum or babbling brook from a Melodic Landscape playlist. It's a gentle reset for your nerves.

- **If you're worn out:** Read a comforting poem aloud, like Mary Oliver's "Wild Geese," which feels like a warm embrace. Let the words lift your spirit softly.

These small steps, rooted in poetry and sound, can work wonders when you need them most.

Let's be real: life gets hectic, and sticking with a ritual can sometimes feel tricky. Maybe you're short on time, your mind's racing, or you're just not feeling inspired. Don't worry—we've got ways to work through that. If time's the issue, start small. Five minutes with a short poem and a calming sound can still bring you peace. Busy day? No problem—just sneak it in when you can.

If focusing feels tough, try a quick mindfulness trick: take three deep breaths before you start. Inhale calm, exhale chaos—it's like hitting the reset button. And if your ritual starts feeling stale, shake it up! Dive into a new poem, switch your sound to something fresh, or even step outside to listen to the real world for a bit. These little adjustments, rooted in mindfulness, keep your practice alive and doable, no matter what's going on.

Using Poetry and Sound as Tools for Resilience

Those quick fixes are invaluable for immediate relief, but what if we could build lasting strength? That's where poetry and sound become powerful tools for resilience. Think of them as exercises for your emotional core: the more you engage, the stronger you become.

Set aside a few minutes daily to read or write poetry, perhaps using prompts like "What brings me peace today?" to explore your feelings from new angles. Or integrate Melodic Landscapes into your routine—try a morning forest hum from a free app like Insight Timer or an evening ocean wave as you unwind. Their calm can ripple through your day, grounding you.

Here are simple ways to weave them into your life:

- Keep a journal to note connections between poems and sounds, such as how a wave Melodic Landscape inspired a reflective verse.

- Create a playlist of Melodic Landscapes for various moods—uplifting birdsong or soothing rain—using platforms like Spotify.

- Set a daily reminder for a poetry or sound break when stress mounts, like reciting a favorite poem during a tough moment.

For example, when Sarah faced a stressful week, she wrote a short poem each evening, paired with a rainfall Melodic Landscape. This ritual steadied her, helping her face challenges with renewed calm. Over time, these habits become anchors, fortifying you to weather life's storms with grace.

Practical Tips for Staying Connected to Your Practice During Stress

Stress can quietly pull us from what keeps us grounded, but it doesn't have to prevail. Here are practical ways to stay connected to your serenity practice—your routine of poetry and soundscaping—even amid chaos:

- **Prioritize self-care:** Even with a packed schedule, carve out five minutes for a poem or a Melodic Landscape from apps like Calm. These moments work wonders.

- **Be flexible:** Can't follow your usual routine? Adapt it—listen to a wave Melodic Landscape on your commute or jot a haiku during lunch. It's about what fits your moment.

- **Seek support:** Share your passion for poetry and sound with others. Join an online poetry group on platforms like Meetup, swap verses with a friend, or discuss Melodic Landscapes with a kindred spirit for inspiration.

- **Remind yourself of your why**: Pause to recall why you began this journey—perhaps the calm of a favorite poem—and let that spark guide you through tough days.

For instance, when Mark's work stress spiked, he listened to a forest sound during his break, restoring his focus. It's natural to feel overwhelmed at times. Your practice isn't here to judge—it's here to uplift you.

Specific Setback Examples

Let's make this real with examples of navigating common setbacks. Here's how to address challenges using poetry and soundscaping, building resilience along the way:

- **When work deadlines overwhelm and time is scarce:** Take a five-minute break with a Melodic Landscape. Slip on headphones, find a quiet spot, and let a forest hum or stream from Spotify melt tension away. It's a quick reset that fits any schedule.

- **When you face a blank page with no words:** Read a favorite poem aloud, like Rumi's "The Guest House," letting its rhythm spark inspiration. Or use a prompt like "Write about a peaceful moment you recall." A gentle nudge can set your creativity flowing.

- **When you feel numb or distant after a tough day:** Write a free-verse poem about what's on your mind, letting words spill freely. It's a bridge back to yourself, one line at a time, reconnecting you to your emotions.

These strategies, tailored to your needs, fortify your resilience whenever life throws a curveball.

Understanding how to realign ourselves is crucial, but establishing a consistent practice can help prevent setbacks. In the following chapter, we will explore how to build a serenity ritual that incorporates poetry and sound, adapting it to fit our unique needs and lifestyles.

Your Serenity Ritual: A Flexible Blueprint

Picture carving out a small oasis of calm just for yourself—that's the essence of a serenity ritual. It's a moment where poetry and sound converge to center you in peace. Begin by choosing a time that suits you—perhaps a few quiet morning minutes to start your day with clarity or an evening session to release the day's weight. Whether daily or weekly, the aim is to weave this practice into your natural rhythm.

At the heart of your ritual lie poetry and sound. For poetry, select words that resonate—perhaps a poem about the ocean's expanse, like Derek Walcott's "The Sea Is History," or one that simply uplifts you. Stick with a favorite or explore new verses from collections like Poetry Foundation. For sound, choose what soothes: the gentle roll of waves, a breeze through trees, or a mellow instrumental track from apps like Insight Timer. You might even record your voice reading a poem aloud. These elements blend into a calming experience uniquely yours.

For example, Maya starts her mornings with a short poem and the sound waves, setting a serene tone for her day. This ritual, tailored to you, fosters lasting peace.

Adapting the Practice to Different Moods and Life Situations

Here's the beauty of your serenity ritual: it's not rigid. It's a flexible companion that shifts with you. Feeling overwhelmed? Try a poem about strength or stillness, paired with the calming hum of rainfall. On a day when you're brimming with gratitude, pick something joyful and match it with the playful sound of birds chirping. Life throwing curveballs? A poem about resilience with the steady crash of waves might feel just right.

Your ritual is there to meet you where you are. By tuning into your emotions and circumstances, you can tweak the poetry and sound to fit the moment. It's like having a personal toolkit for serenity—one that grows and adapts as you do.

Sample Rituals to Inspire

Ready to give it a try? Here are a few ideas to spark your imagination:

Morning Boost: Kick off your day with a poem about new beginnings, paired with the chirping of birds. It's like a little sunrise for your soul.

Nighttime Release: Wind down by reading a poem about rest or letting go, with ocean waves rolling in the background. Feel the day slip away with each wave.

Weekend Recharge: Set aside some time on Saturday or Sunday for a longer ritual. Pick a poem that moves you deeply—or a few short ones—and let a forest sound (think rustling leaves and a trickling stream) wrap you in tranquility.

These are just starting points—play around and see what feels good to you!

A Simple Template for Creating Your Own Ritual

Want to build your own serenity ritual? Here's an easy guide to get you going:

1. **Pick a Time:** Find a moment that works—morning, evening, or a quiet break in your day.

2. **Choose a Poem:** Grab one that matches your mood or brings you peace.

3. **Add a Sound:** Pair it with something soothing—waves, wind, music, whatever calms you.

4. **Set an Intention:** Decide what you're after—like "I want to feel grounded" or "I'm letting go of stress."

5. **Get Comfy:** Settle into a cozy, quiet spot where you can relax.

6. **Breathe**: Take a few deep breaths to ease into the moment.

7. **Read**: Say the poem aloud or in your head, letting the words sink in.

8. **Listen**: Let the sound wash over you, blending with the poetry.

9. **Pause**: Afterward, take a second to feel the shift—maybe jot down a thought or just enjoy the stillness.

10. **Make it yours**—tweak it, experiment, and have fun with it!

As we establish our serenity rituals, it's essential to recognize that this is not a destination but a lifelong journey. In the next chapter, we will reflect on how creative expression through poetry and sound can evolve over time, continually enriching our lives and deepening our sense of peace.

The Cracks of Wellness
Recognizing When Balance Fades

Wellness is not a flawless or linear journey—challenges, setbacks, and obstacles, or "cracks," are natural parts of the process. Acknowledging that the struggles we face are normal, this chapter offers practical guidance to navigate these difficulties. Building on the *Twelve Pillars of Wellness,* introduced earlier as a framework for holistic health, we explore barriers like stress, emotional dependence, or external disruptions that hinder embodying these pillars. Through poetry and soundscaping, wellness becomes a journey of resilience rather than perfection, empowering you to mend these cracks with grace.

For each pillar of wellness there is a directly opposing crack that undermines personal growth, well-being, and fulfillment. These opposites represent the obstacles that wellness practices aim to overcome. By recognizing them, we can better appreciate the value of each pillar and work toward cultivating their positive counterparts in our lives.

Each pillar of wellness faces an opposing challenge, like a shadow to its light.

For **Focus and Mental clarity,** the challenge is distraction and mental fog, where your mind feels scattered or unclear.

For **Calmness & Serenity** it's Chaos & Anxiety, where stress and restlessness churn within, like a storm that unsettles your inner peace.

For **Healing & Balance** it's Sickness & Imbalance, where physical or emotional unwellness creates disharmony, pulling you from equilibrium.

For **Confidence & Resilience** it's Insecurity & Fragility, where self-doubt or an inability to withstand setbacks leaves you feeling unsteady, like a fragile branch in a storm.

For **Strength and Courage,** it's weakness and fear, where you might feel powerless or anxious, as if standing at the edge of a daunting cliff, hesitant to take the next step.

For **Wisdom & Awareness**, it's Ignorance & Delusion, where a lack of understanding or denial clouds your perception, leaving you disconnected from reality's truths.

For **Tranquility & Inner Peace** it's Turmoil & Inner Conflict, where unresolved emotions or mental strife stir a restless unease, like waves crashing against a quiet shore.

For **Love & Affection** it's Hate & Indifference, where hostility or emotional coldness builds walls, shutting out warmth and connection.

For **Abundance & Blessings** it's Scarcity & Curses, where a mindset of lack or a sense of misfortune dims your appreciation for life's richness, like a garden left untended.

For **Prosperity & Compassion** it's Poverty & Selfishness, where a lack of resources or an uncaring attitude narrows your capacity to give and thrive.

For **Positivity & Optimism** it's Negativity & Pessimism, where a focus on the worst outcomes or a defeatist mindset dims your hope and enthusiasm.

For **Transformation & Self-Realization** it's Stagnation & Self-Deception, where resistance to growth or denial of your true nature keeps you tethered to an unfulfilling routine, like a bird unwilling to leave its cage.

Causes of Cracks in the Twelve Pillars of Wellness
What Undermines Our Well Being

Focus & Mental Clarity Fade into Distraction & Mental Fog

A scattered mind, inability to concentrate, confusion or lack of direction. Where *Focus and Mental Clarity* involve concentration and clear thinking, the antithesis is a state of being scattered, unfocused, and mentally foggy or disoriented.

Calmness & Serenity Disintegrate into Chaos & Anxiety

Constant stress, restlessness, inner conflict or emotional turbulence. *Calmness and Serenity* represent peace and tranquility; their antitheses are anxiety (nervousness or unease) and turmoil (disorder or agitation)

Healing & Balance Break into Sickness & Imbalance

Physical/emotional illness, unresolved trauma, animosity, disharmony, or instability in life. *Healing and Balance* indicate recovery and equilibrium, so their opposites are illness (physical or emotional unwellness) and imbalance (chaos or instability).

Confidence & Resilience Sink into Insecurity & Fragility

Confidence and Inner Resilience sinks into insecurity and fragility when unchecked stress prevails; rebuild with affirmations and sound therapy. Self-doubt, easily broken by setbacks, or lack of perseverance.

Confidence and Inner Resilience reflect self-assurance and the ability to recover from setbacks. Their opposites are insecurity (self-doubt) and fragility (inability to withstand challenges).

Strength & Courage Diminish into Weakness & Fear

Feeling powerless, timid, overwhelmed by challenges and afraid to take action or paralyzed by anxiety. Where *Focus and Mental Clarity* involve concentration and clear thinking, the antithesis is a state of being scattered, unfocused, and mentally foggy or disoriented.

Wisdom & Awareness Darken into Ignorance & Delusion

Lack of understanding, closed-mindedness, lack of insight, living in denial, being misinformed, or disconnected from reality.

Wisdom and Awareness reflect deep understanding and consciousness of oneself and surroundings. The opposite is ignorance (lack of knowledge) and unawareness (obliviousness).

Tranquility & Inner Peace are Invaded by Turmoil & Inner Conflict

Persistent inner strife, a disturbed mind, unresolved emotions, or mental unrest. *Tranquility and Inner Peace* suggest external calm and internal harmony. Their opposites are restlessness (inability to relax) and inner conflict (emotional or mental strife).

Love & Affection become Cloud with Hate & Indifference

Hostility, emotional coldness, resentment, indifference or lack of care for others. *Love and Affection* are about emotional warmth and care; their opposites are hate, a strong negative emotion, and indifference, a lack of care or attachment.

Abundance & Blessings Dwindle into Scarcity & Curses

A mindset of lack, deprivation, envy, constant struggle or dissatisfaction, or feeling cursed by misfortune. *Abundance and Blessings* suggest having plenty and feeling fortunate. In contrast, scarcity reflects a lack of resources, and misfortune implies unfavorable circumstances.

Prosperity & Compassion Wither into Poverty & Selfishness

Financial/emotional lack, harshness, selfishness and an uncaring attitude toward others. *Prosperity and Compassion* combine success or wealth with empathy. The opposites are poverty (lack of resources or success) and apathy (indifference or lack of empathy).

Positivity & Optimism Darken into Negativity & Pessimism

A defeatist mindset, expecting the worst, fear of failure, easily shaken by setbacks or criticism, or dwelling on problems. *Positivity and Optimism* involve a hopeful, upbeat outlook. The antitheses are negativity (a focus on the bad) and pessimism (expecting the worst).

Transformation & Self-Realization Deteriorate into Stagnation & Self-Deception

Resistance to growth, denial of one's true nature, a life on autopilot or lack of purpose. *Transformation and Self-realization* involve growth and deep self-understanding. The opposites are stagnation (lack of change or progress) and self-ignorance (unawareness of one's true self).

The Cracks Beneath: Why Wellness Falters

The crack of distraction and mental fog in focus and mental clarity emerges when a flood of distractions—endless notifications, swirling thoughts, or pressing tasks—scatters your attention like dust in the wind.

Weakness and fear, which erode strength and courage, take hold when daunting obstacles or inner doubts loom large, freezing your resolve as if caught in a storm's shadow.

Ignorance and delusion, dimming wisdom and awareness, arise from clinging to unexamined beliefs or comforting illusions that shroud the truth.

Hate and indifference, the barriers to love and affection, grow from buried wounds or emotional retreat, building walls where warmth once flourished.

Scarcity and curses, overshadowing abundance and blessings, stem from a heart fixed on what's missing, overlooking the quiet wealth of everyday moments.

Sickness and imbalance, disrupting healing and balance, surface when neglected emotional or physical needs unravel the harmony of body and soul.

Chaos and anxiety, unsettling calmness and serenity, ignite under the weight of relentless stress, churning your inner calm like a restless sea.

Poverty and selfishness, which stifle prosperity and compassion, are born from fear-driven scarcity or a narrowed focus that forgets the joy of giving.

Turmoil and inner conflict, obstructing tranquility and inner peace, flare when competing desires or unresolved feelings clash, stirring unease within.

Negativity and pessimism, dimming positivity and optimism, take root in a habit of seeing only flaws or setbacks, casting a shadow over life's possibilities.

Insecurity and fragility, undermining confidence and resilience, grow from self-doubt or past wounds that whisper you're not enough, leaving you brittle as a dry leaf.

Stagnation and self-deception, blocking transformation and self-realization, arise from fear of growth or denial of your true self, anchoring you to a life unlived.

Strategies to Overcome the Cracks of Wellness

These strategies are not about perfection but progression; they are not rules, just invitations. You don't have to change everything overnight. Even small, consistent steps will gradually shift you from the negative states toward the Twelve Pillars of Wellness

Distraction & Mental Fog Dissipate with Focus & Mental Clarity

When your mind feels scattered or cloudy, try starting with just a few quiet minutes of mindfulness meditation. You don't need to be a monk—5 to 10 minutes a day can help you reconnect with the present and bring clarity back into your mental space.

The Pomodoro Technique is another simple way to regain focus. By working in short, focused bursts with regular breaks, you train your brain to stay present without feeling overwhelmed. It's like a mini workout for your attention span.

To protect your focus, limit digital distractions. Turn off unnecessary notifications, or try a focus app like *Forest* that rewards you for staying off your phone. You'll be amazed how freeing it feels.

And when your thoughts are swirling? Journaling helps. Just write it all down—brain dump your to-do list, your worries, your ideas. Once it's on the page, your mind feels lighter and more organized.

Chaos & Anxiety Subside with Calmness & Serenity

When anxiety strikes, try box breathing. Inhale for 4 seconds, hold for 4, exhale for 4, and pause for 4. It grounds your nervous system like an anchor in a storm.

Take walks in nature—without your phone. Let the wind, trees, or water remind you that calm is always available, even if just for a few moments.

Practice acceptance. Life can be messy and unpredictable. Remind yourself: "I can't control everything, and that's okay." That thought alone can bring deep relief.

Decluttering your space can declutter your mind. When your outer world is tidy and calm, your inner world often follows.

Illness & Imbalance are Restored with Healing & Balance

The foundation of healing is basic, but so often overlooked: sleep and nourishing food. Prioritize rest and fuel your body with care—it makes everything else easier.

Movement practices like yoga or Tai Chi offer gentle ways to balance not just your body, but your energy too. They bring a sense of harmony that's both physical and emotional.

Sometimes, what we need is an emotional detox. Try breathwork, EFT tapping, or therapy to help release stored-up emotions that weigh you down.

And consider a break from digital noise. A social media fast can refresh your spirit and create space for real-world connection and clarity.

Insecurity & Fragility are Strengthened with Confidence & Resilience

Practice self-compassion—treat yourself with the kindness you'd offer a friend facing challenges. Set small, achievable goals and celebrate your successes to build confidence over time. Engage in activities that make you feel competent, like a hobby or creative pursuit. Visualize yourself handling difficulties with grace and strength, igniting an inner resilience that grows with practice.

Silent meditation can help you watch your thoughts float by like clouds. You don't have to fix or fight them—just observe. This brings a profound sense of inner peace.

Shadow work—journaling on difficult emotions or past wounds—helps you integrate the parts of yourself you've been avoiding. It's not always easy, but it's deeply healing.

Let go of perfectionism. Say to yourself, "Peace matters more than being right or being perfect." What a relief to release the pressure.

Spiritual practices, whether prayer, mantras, or walking meditations, help ground you in something deeper than the noise. They gently return you to center.

Weakness & Fear are Reborn Strength & Courage

Courage isn't the absence of fear—it's learning to walk through it, step by step. Start with small acts of bravery. Face tiny fears—speak up in a meeting, try something new, or say yes when you usually say no.

Strengthen your body to strengthen your mind. Physical exercise, especially strength training, teaches you that you can do hard things—and that strength carries into your emotional world.

Use affirmations and visualization to rewire your inner narrative. Say things like, "I am strong," or "I move through fear with grace." Visualize yourself succeeding, standing tall, being resilient.

Look to role models—real-life heroes or even people in your circle. Study how they handle fear, and let their stories fuel your own.

Ignorance & Delusion Awaken into Wisdom & Awareness

Wisdom begins with curiosity. Read broadly—books on philosophy, science, psychology. Let your mind be a sponge, soaking in new perspectives.

Seek feedback from people you trust. A fresh perspective can shine a light on blind spots we don't even realize we have.

Start questioning your assumptions. When a strong belief pops up, gently ask: "Is this based on fact, or just what I've always thought?" This practice opens the door to deeper awareness.

Practice active listening—really listening to others, not just waiting to reply. You'll begin to see the world through a richer, more compassionate lens.

Hate & Indifference Transform into Love & Affection

We're wired for connection, but sometimes life hardens us. To soften your heart, begin with empathy. Imagine someone else's point of view—what might they be feeling or needing?

Tiny acts of kindness—holding the door, giving a compliment, helping without being asked—can rekindle warmth in your own spirit.

Forgiveness, while tough, is one of the most freeing gifts you can give yourself. Journal your resentments, talk them out, or work with a therapist to let them go. You deserve that peace.

Nourish your closest relationships. Schedule quality time, have deep conversations, and make space for love to grow.

Scarcity & Curses Flourish into Abundance & Blessings

Start with gratitude. Every day, jot down three things you're thankful for—even if it's just clean water, a good meal, or a moment of laughter. Gratitude gently shifts your brain from scarcity to abundance.

Reframe moments of lack. Instead of "I don't have enough," try, "I have what I need right now, and more is coming." It's a powerful shift in mindset.

Be generous. Offer your time, your attention, your help. Giving creates a ripple effect—and often, what we give comes back in surprising ways.

Stop comparing. Your path is uniquely yours, and no one else's success takes away from your own. Celebrate your own journey.

Poverty & Selfishness Evolve into Prosperity & Compassion

Learn the basics of financial literacy—budgeting, saving, investing in your growth. Prosperity starts with knowing how to steward what you have.

Serve others without expecting anything in return. Volunteer, lend a hand, or simply listen. Giving shifts your mindset from "not enough" to "I can contribute."

When networking or making connections, do it generously. Help others without strings attached. Often, those relationships blossom in beautiful, unexpected ways.

Believe in a world where everyone can win. Someone else's success doesn't take away from yours—it expands what's possible for all of us.

Turmoil & Inner Conflict Reconcile wit Tranquility & Inner Peace

Silent meditation can help you watch your thoughts float by like clouds. You don't have to fix or fight them—just observe. This brings a profound sense of inner peace.

Shadow work—journaling on difficult emotions or past wounds—helps you integrate the parts of yourself you've been avoiding. It's not always easy, but it's deeply healing.

Let go of perfectionism. Say to yourself, "Peace matters more than being right or being perfect." What a relief to release the pressure.

Spiritual practices, whether prayer, mantras, or walking meditations, help ground you in something deeper than the noise. They gently return you to center.

Negativity & Pessimism Resurge as Positivity & Optimism

When you find yourself spiraling into negativity, pause and ask: "What's one good thing about this?" Reframing trains your brain to look for light in the dark.

Limit your intake of bad news or toxic media. Protect your mental environment the way you'd protect your home from garbage.

Surround yourself with uplifting, supportive people—those who believe in good things and share that belief freely.

And don't forget the power of laughter. Watch a comedy, share silly memes, or play with a pet. Laughter is medicine, and joy is a skill you can practice.

Stagnation & Self-Deception Awaken into Transformation & Self-Realization

Set goals that excite your soul. Not what others expect, but what aligns with your deepest values. That kind of goal pulls you forward naturally.

Every month or so, reflect. Ask: "What's working? What's not? What's one thing I'd love to change?" These check-ins keep you aligned and awake.

Try something new, often. Whether it's a dance class, new book, or solo trip—novelty sparks growth and reminds you how alive you are.

And finally, commit to seeking truth. Question the stories your ego tells. Be brave enough to let go of illusions, and courageous enough to step into who you truly are.

Set goals that excite your soul. Not what others expect, but what aligns with your deepest values. That kind of goal pulls you forward naturally.

Every month or so, reflect. Ask: "What's working? What's not? What's one thing I'd love to change?" These check-ins keep you aligned and awake.

Try something new, often. Whether it's a dance class, new book, or solo trip—novelty sparks growth and reminds you how alive you are.

And finally, commit to seeking truth. Question the stories your ego tells. Be brave enough to let go of illusions, and courageous enough to step into who you truly are.

The Awake Heart – Cultivating Serenity Through Consciousness

Mindfulness as a Path to Inner Peace

In this chapter, "The Awake Heart – Cultivating Serenity Through Consciousness," we embark on a journey to rediscover the tranquil essence within. It invites us to listen beyond life's noise, feel the subtle rhythm of our consciousness—our aware presence—and embrace awareness as the key to unlocking serenity. Through practices like poetry and soundscaping, this gentle, intentional connection guides us to a peace that is always present, patiently awaiting our return.

Awakening Serenity Through Awareness

Awakening serenity through awareness involves tuning into present moments, using consciousness as a light to dispel AI-induced distractions.

In the quiet spaces between sound and silence, there exists a deeper rhythm—the pulse of consciousness itself. This chapter invites you to explore the intimate dance between **awareness and serenity**, where the awake heart becomes both compass and sanctuary.

Serenity is not a distant shore but a presence already within us, waiting to be remembered. As we tune in with intention, we uncover a profound truth:

Serenity is not something to achieve; it is something we cultivate through conscious connection.

The Interplay of Serenity and Consciousness

Serenity and consciousness are often seen as separate—one as a feeling, the other as awareness. Yet, in their highest expression, **they are intertwined**:

- A heightened state of **awareness** brings serenity, for it allows us to witness life without resistance.
- A state of **serenity** creates stillness, the fertile ground where deeper consciousness arises.

To understand one, we must cultivate both. This chapter explores how they nourish each other and how we can invite them into our lives with intention.

Serenity: The Art of Inner Stillness

Serenity is **not the absence of turbulence** but the presence of equanimity. It is the unshaken stillness that remains even in the midst of life's shifting tides.

Serenity Triggers

Serenity arises when we release the need for control and surrender to the natural flow of life. It is shaped by:

- **Equanimity** – Meeting each moment with balance, neither clinging nor resisting.
- **Acceptance** – Embracing life as it is, without unnecessary struggle.
- **Stillness** – Cultivating a quiet mind, undisturbed by fleeting thoughts or emotions.

Serenity is **not passive**; it is an active presence, a deep attunement to reality as it unfolds.

Consciousness: The Light of Awareness

Consciousness is the ability to **perceive, witness, and experience**—to be aware of our thoughts, emotions, and sensations. It exists on multiple levels:

• **Basic Awareness** – The recognition of existence, the experience of the present moment.

• **Self-Consciousness** – The ability to reflect on oneself, thoughts, and identity.

• **Higher Consciousness** – Awareness that transcends the ego, connecting with a greater reality.

When we fully **witness our emotions and patterns**, we detach from suffering and cultivate peace. Likewise, when we cultivate **serenity**, the mind becomes more receptive to **insight, clarity, and wisdom**.

Awakening the Heart: Consciousness as the Seed of Serenity

Without awareness, the mind is reactive—trapped in habitual thought patterns. But with **conscious presence**, we step beyond reactivity into clarity.

The "awake heart" is a metaphor for this state:

- A heart that listens deeply.
- A heart that perceives clearly.
- A heart that responds with wisdom.

Practices to Awaken the Heart

Practices to awaken the heart include heart-centered breathing and poetic reflections, fostering emotional openness in a tech-dominated world.

- **Be in the Now** – Return to the present, rather than being lost in past regrets or future anxieties.
- **Observe Without Attachment** – Notice thoughts as passing clouds, without identifying with them.
- **Embrace Stillness** – Not as emptiness, but as a space where awareness deepens.

When we cultivate consciousness, serenity follows. When we cultivate serenity, consciousness expands.

Cultivating Serenity: Tending the Garden of Stillness

Serenity is not something we chase—it is something we allow. Like a garden, it does not grow through force but through gentle tending, patient care, and a quiet trust in its unfolding.

Each practice below is a seed—planted in the present moment, nurtured by conscious intention.

Stillness as Soil – The foundation of serenity is inner stillness. **Silence is not emptiness; it is fertile ground where peace takes root.**

- Begin each morning with **one full minute of quiet** before engaging with the world.

- Practice simply sitting without distraction—**listening, breathing, and observing the present.**

Gratitude as Sunlight – What we appreciate, we illuminate. Gratitude shifts our awareness from what is missing to what is already whole.

- Each evening, recall **one moment of peace** from the day, no matter how small.

Breath as the Gentle Wind – The breath is an anchor to the now. It softens tension, dissolves resistance, and steadies the mind.

• Try **box breathing**: Inhale for 4 counts, hold for 4, exhale for 4, hold for 4. Repeat until a sense of calm arises.

Letting Go as Rainfall – Serenity flows when we stop holding so tightly.

• Observe your thoughts as clouds—passing, shifting, dissolving. Not every thought needs to be held.

Music as the Language of Stillness – Some truths are felt rather than spoken.

• Listen to a simple piano piece and focus on the **space between the notes**. Notice how silence is part of the melody.

Serenity is not a destination—it is the way we move through the world.

Listening Within: The Sound of Consciousness

Just as music exists between sound and silence, **consciousness exists in the space between thoughts**. Deep listening is a gateway to this awareness.

Exercises for Deep Listening

Breath Awareness – Sit in silence and focus on the sound of your breath, allowing it to anchor you in the present.

Ambient Sound Noticing – Close your eyes and identify layers of sound—near and distant, rhythmic and irregular.

Inner Sound Awareness – Tune into the silence within and notice how presence has its own quiet resonance.

Listening is an act of consciousness. It shifts us from noise to presence, from distraction to serenity.

The Ripple Effect: Consciousness as a Path to Collective Serenity

Awakening is not an individual journey; **it ripples outward**.
A single moment of presence, a single act of kindness, a single breath taken with awareness—**all create a chain reaction of serenity in the world**.

How Individual Awareness Heals the Collective

- A calm heart fosters compassionate relationship.
- A conscious mind contributes to a more peaceful society.
- An awake presence reminds others of their own stillness.

An awake heart is not just for oneself. It is a quiet revolution, a beacon of peace in a restless world.

Serenity is not a destination, nor is consciousness a goal. They are a way of being—woven into each breath, each choice, each moment. As we awaken, peace becomes our natural state.

Let this chapter be an invitation: to listen, to reflect, to simply be.

The awake heart is already within you—waiting to be heard.

Nurturing Serenity in Creative Life

How Art Sustains the Soul

Like any art form, the practice of creative serenity—using poetry and soundscaping to foster calm—evolves, deepening as you grow. In this chapter, we reflect on how your relationship with these tools, introduced in earlier rituals, can enrich your life in unexpected ways. You'll be encouraged to keep exploring, letting poetry and sound guide you through life's emotional and personal stages. We'll also look forward, imagining how a consistent serenity practice might shape your future. Through reflective prompts and visualization exercises, you'll embrace the lifelong journey ahead, knowing serenity is not a fleeting moment but a lasting companion.

How Creative Expression Evolves Over Time

When you first dip your toes into the world of poetry and soundscaping, it might feel like stepping into uncharted waters. Perhaps you scribble a few lines about your morning coffee or listen to a gentle wave Melodic Landscape to unwind. In the beginning, it may take some effort—like learning the steps to a new dance. You might even catch yourself wondering, Am I doing this right? But here's the beauty of it: as you keep going, something shifts. The awkwardness fades, and these practices start to feel like second nature.

Over time, you'll notice your creative expression blossoming. Your poems might begin to weave together deeper threads of emotion, reflecting not just what's on the surface but the quiet insights bubbling beneath. Maybe you'll play with haikus one week and free verse the next, or find that the sounds of rain or birdsong start to spark new ideas. Your Melodic Landscape could evolve too—what begins as pressing "play" on a calming track might turn into crafting your own blend of melodies that feel uniquely you.

This growth is part of the journey. Think of it like tending a garden: the more you nurture it, the more it flourishes in ways you didn't expect. Embrace this evolution—it's a sign that poetry and soundscaping are becoming trusted companions, ready to support you through life's ups and downs.

Encouragement to Continue Exploring Poetry and Soundscaping

Now that you see how your practice can grow, let's keep that momentum going! There's no end point to creative serenity—every poem you write and every Melodic Landscape you explore is a fresh step on an endless path. Some days, inspiration will flow like a river; others, you might feel a little stuck. That's okay—it's all part of the process. The key is to keep moving forward, even when the words don't come easily or the sounds feel off.

If doubts creep in—like "My poems aren't good enough" or "I'm not creative enough"—give yourself permission to let them go. This isn't about perfection; it's about peace. Every line you write, every sound you listen to, is a small gift to yourself—a moment to breathe, reflect, and reconnect. There's no "right" way to do this, just your way.

To keep things exciting, why not mix it up? Try writing a poem under a tree or in a busy café and see how the world around you shapes your words. Experiment with different sounds—maybe ocean waves one day, a crackling fireplace the next. You could even weave the two together, reading your poetry aloud with a Melodic Landscape humming in the background. The possibilities are endless, and each new try is a chance to discover something wonderful about yourself. So keep exploring—you're building a deeper bond with serenity, one creative step at a time.

A Call to Action: Cultivating Serenity in Everyday Life

With this spirit of exploration in your heart, let's bring creative serenity into your everyday world. You don't need hours or a grand plan—just a few simple, joyful practices can make all the difference. Here's how to start:

- **Carve out a little time each day:** Whether it's five minutes in the morning to jot down a poem or ten minutes at night with a soothing Melodic Landscape, pick a moment that feels right for you. It's like a daily hug for your soul.

- **Create your serenity nook:** Find a cozy spot at home—a chair by a window, a corner with a soft blanket—and make it your go-to place for poetry and soundscaping. Add a candle or a favorite journal to make it feel special.

- **Start a serenity journal:** Grab a notebook to capture your poems, thoughts on Melodic Landscapes, or little reflections. It's a wonderful way to see how far you've come and what brings you calm.

- **Share the joy:** Invite a friend to swap poems or listen to a Melodic Landscape together. Maybe even join a poetry group—sharing can spark new ideas and keep you inspired.

The magic lies in keeping it simple and steady. Even on your busiest days, a quick poem or a few minutes of sound can lift you up. You've got this—let serenity become a natural part of your rhythm.

A Reflective Prompt and Visualization Exercise: "How Will Serenity Shape Your Future?"

As you weave these practices into your life, let's take a moment to dream about where they might lead. Pause and think: How might my life change if I keep nurturing creative serenity for a year? What do I hope to feel, see, or experience? Jot down your thoughts if you'd like—they're the seeds of something beautiful.

Now, let's dive deeper with a visualization. Sit comfortably, close your eyes, and picture yourself one year from today. You've stuck with your serenity practice—poetry and soundscaping are part of your daily flow. See your mornings: maybe you're sipping tea, writing a few lines that set a peaceful tone. Feel how you handle a tough moment—perhaps a soft Melodic Landscape helps you find your calm.

Imagine your creativity blooming. Maybe you've filled a notebook with poems or crafted a Melodic Landscape that feels like home. Picture your relationships—perhaps you're more present, or you've shared your journey with loved ones who now join in. Think about challenges you've faced—how has this practice given you strength or a fresh perspective?

When you're ready, open your eyes and capture what you saw. Write it down, shape it into a poem, or let it inspire a Melodic Landscape. This isn't just daydreaming—it's a promise to yourself, a glimpse of the serenity waiting ahead.

Throughout this journey, music has been a constant companion, offering solace and inspiration. In the following chapter, I will share my personal story of how music, particularly my own melodic landscapes, has played a pivotal role in enhancing serenity and well-being.

Emotional Grounding in an AI-Driven World
Staying Centered Amid Screens

Emotional grounding in an AI-driven world is the ability to maintain a deep, authentic connection to your emotions, sense of self, and human essence amid artificial intelligence's growing presence. As AI shapes daily life—from personalized algorithms to virtual interactions—emotional grounding becomes vital for preserving mental well-being, authenticity, and human connection. Through practices like poetry and soundscaping, it involves cultivating mindfulness, emotional regulation, and discernment to navigate AI's emotional complexities while staying rooted in genuine experiences. For example, writing a poem about your feelings after a tech-heavy day can recenter you in your human core.

Why Emotional Grounding Matters

The rapid rise of AI brings both opportunities and challenges to our emotional landscape. Here's why emotional grounding is essential:

- **Emotional Overwhelm**: AI-driven platforms, like social media, use algorithms to curate content that can amplify stress, anxiety, or disconnection by triggering intense emotional responses.

- **Blurring Authenticity**: With AI capable of mimicking human-like interactions—think chatbots or deep fakes—it can become difficult to distinguish between real human emotions and machine-generated responses, potentially leading to confusion or distrust.

- **Risk of Detachment**: Over-reliance on AI tools, such as decision-making apps or virtual therapists, might weaken our ability to process emotions independently, fostering a sense of emotional disconnection.

Emotional grounding acts as an anchor, enabling us to:
- Stay attuned to our inner emotional world.
- Engage with AI intentionally and clearly.
- Maintain meaningful human connections despite technological mediation.

Key Components of Emotional Grounding

Key components of emotional grounding: mindfulness, regulation, authentic connections, digital literacy, and ethical reflection—essential for AI resilience.

To develop emotional grounding in an AI-driven world, we can focus on the following practices:

1. Mindfulness and Self-Awareness

- **Mindfulness Practices**: Techniques like meditation, deep breathing, or mindful walking keep us present and connected to our emotions, countering the distractions of AI-driven stimuli.

- **Self-Reflection**: Journaling or introspective exercises help us process feelings, differentiate between AI-influenced reactions and authentic emotions, and reconnect with our core values.

- **Emotional Check-Ins**: Pausing to assess our emotional state before and after interacting with AI (e.g., scrolling social media) builds awareness of technology's impact on our mood.

2. Emotional Regulation

- **Cognitive-Behavioral Techniques (CBT)**: Tools like reframing negative thoughts or practicing gratitude help manage emotional reactions to AI-driven content, such as social media comparison traps.

- **Emotional Freedom Technique (EFT)**: Practices like tapping can release tension from AI-related stressors, restoring calm and control.

- **Setting Boundaries**: Limiting exposure to AI platforms or scheduling "tech-free" times reduces emotional fatigue and supports healthier regulation.

3. Authentic Human Connection

- **Empathy-Building Activities**: Face-to-face conversations, volunteering, or group activities strengthen emotional bonds and empathy, countering the isolation of AI-mediated interactions.

- **Shared Experiences**: Engaging in creative or recreational pursuits (e.g., art, music, sports) with others reinforces genuine human connection.

- **Vulnerability Practices**: Sharing emotions with trusted people fosters deeper relationships and reduces reliance on AI for emotional support.

4. Digital Literacy and Discernment

- **Understanding AI's Influence**: Learning how AI algorithms curate content or generate responses empowers us to recognize when our emotions are being manipulated.

- **Critical Thinking**: Questioning the authenticity of AI-generated content (e.g., deep fakes) maintains emotional clarity and prevents misplaced trust.

- **Intentional Engagement**: Using AI for practical tasks rather than emotional validation preserves our emotional autonomy.

5. Ethical and Philosophical Reflection

- **Exploring AI's Emotional Impact**: Reflecting on questions like "Can AI truly understand emotions?" or "What defines an authentic experience?" deepens our grasp of human-machine boundaries.

- **Ethical AI Use**: Supporting AI designed with emotional well-being in mind aligns technology with human values.

- **Preserving Human Essence**: Activities celebrating human creativity and imperfection (e.g., writing poetry) reinforce emotional grounding.

Practical Strategies for Emotional Grounding

Here are actionable steps to integrate emotional grounding into daily life:

- **Morning Mindfulness Ritual**: Begin with 5–10 minutes of meditation or journaling to set an emotionally centered tone before using AI-driven devices.

- **Tech-Free Zones**: Designate times or spaces (e.g., meals, bedrooms) as AI-free to foster undistracted emotional presence.

- **Emotional Audit of AI Use**: Periodically evaluate how AI tools affect your emotions and adjust usage accordingly.

- **Creative Expression**: Spend time on non-AI creative outlets (e.g., drawing, gardening) to nurture authenticity.

- **Human-Centered Evenings**: End the day with meaningful interactions (e.g., conversations) to counterbalance AI's influence.

In an AI-driven world, emotional grounding is a vital skill for maintaining authenticity, mental health, and human connection. By practicing mindfulness, regulating emotions, fostering genuine relationships, and engaging critically with AI, we can navigate this technological landscape while staying rooted in our emotional truth. Emotional grounding ensures that, even as AI reshapes our external environment, our inner world remains a sanctuary of clarity, resilience, and humanity.

Waves of Serenity: Navigating Emotional Dependence on AI

Maintaining Emotional Balance in a Tech-Dependent World

Imagine a quiet evening, the kind where the weight of the day lingers like a heavy fog. You're alone with your thoughts, seeking solace, and instead of reaching out to a friend or jotting down your feelings, you find yourself typing into a chat window, pouring your heart out to an AI. It listens, responds with empathy, and offers comfort without judgment. In that moment, it feels like a lifeline. But as this scene becomes more familiar, a question arises: Are we becoming too reliant on artificial intelligence for our emotional well-being?

In this chapter, we dive into the rising tide of emotional dependence on AI—a growing trend where tools like ChatGPT, originally designed to assist and inform, are increasingly becoming sources of comfort, validation, and companionship. We'll explore why this shift is happening now, fueled by advanced technology, unmatched convenience, and a world grappling with loneliness and stress. Yet, as we lean into this digital embrace, we must also face the downsides: diminished human connection, weakened emotional resilience, and a growing distance from our own inner strength.

Fortunately, there's a way to navigate these waters without losing ourselves. Serenity—inner calm, peace, and emotional balance—emerges as a powerful remedy to counteract our reliance on AI. By cultivating serenity through practices like mindfulness, creative expression, and intentional reflection, we can reclaim our emotional independence and ensure that technology remains a tool, not a crutch. Join us as we uncover the quiet reality of emotional dependence on AI, understand its roots, and discover how serenity can guide us back to ourselves—anchored, resilient, and whole.

The Rising Tide of Emotional Dependence on AI

Picture this: It's late at night, and you're feeling overwhelmed by the weight of the day. Your mind is racing, your heart feels heavy, and you crave a listening ear. Instead of calling a friend or writing in a journal, you open ChatGPT and start typing. The AI responds instantly, offering words of comfort, advice, or simply a non-judgmental space to vent. In that moment, it feels like a lifeline—always available, always understanding. But over time, you notice a pattern: you're turning to ChatGPT more and more for emotional support, sometimes even before reaching out to the people in your life. This scenario, once rare, is becoming a quiet reality for many in our tech-driven world.

Emotional dependence on AI is the growing tendency to rely on artificial intelligence, like ChatGPT, for comfort, validation, or companionship. It's not just about using AI to answer questions or complete tasks—it's about leaning on it to meet our emotional needs. Gen AI's ability to provide instant, thoughtful, and non-judgmental responses can make it feel like a safe haven. It doesn't argue, it doesn't judge, and it's always there when you need it. But this reliance is becoming a concern as AI integrates deeper into our daily lives, offering a tempting shortcut to emotional relief in an increasingly complex world.

Why is this happening now? Several factors are at play. First, AI technology has become more advanced and accessible, seamlessly blending into our routines—whether for work, reflection, or casual chats. Second, its convenience is unmatched: Gen AI delivers immediate responses and tailored support without the vulnerability or effort required in human relationships. Third, in a time when loneliness and stress are widespread, AI offers a sense of connection that feels risk-free. These elements combine to create a perfect storm, where turning to AI for emotional support feels not just easy, but natural.

However, this growing dependence has downsides. Relying on AI for emotional stability can reduce human interaction, weaken our ability to process complex emotions, and leave us less equipped to handle life's challenges. The more we seek comfort from a chatbot, the less we engage with the messy, rewarding process of connecting with others—or even ourselves. Over time, this can lead to isolation and a fragile emotional foundation.

This is where serenity steps in as a remedy. Serenity—inner calm, peace, and emotional balance—offers a way to counteract our reliance on AI. It's about building a sense of emotional strength that comes from within, rather than depending on external sources, whether human or artificial. When we cultivate serenity, we become less driven by the need for instant validation or comfort, and more capable of sitting with our emotions, understanding them, and finding peace on our own terms.

In the pages ahead, we'll dive into how serenity can free us from the pull of emotional dependence on AI. Through practices like mindfulness, creative expression, and intentional reflection, we can reclaim our emotional independence and ensure technology remains a tool—not a crutch. Serenity isn't just a lofty goal; it's a practical solution for thriving in a world where AI is ever-present, guiding us back to ourselves and the calm we need to flourish.

Understanding Emotional Dependence on AI

Have you ever found yourself turning to a chatbot when you're feeling low, stressed, or just in need of a quick chat? If so, you're not alone. Emotional dependence on AI is becoming more common as people lean on these tools for comfort, validation, or even a sense of companionship. Let's explore how and why this happens, with a few relatable examples and some psychological insights to shed light on this growing trend. Don't worry—this isn't about judgment; it's about understanding ourselves a little better, with a sprinkle of warmth and hope along the way.

How It Starts: A Quiet Pull

Emotional dependence on AI doesn't hit you all at once—it creeps in slowly, almost unnoticed. Picture this: It's been a rough day, and instead of texting a friend, you type a quick message to ChatGPT: "I'm feeling overwhelmed." Instantly, you get a calm, thoughtful reply—no waiting, no awkwardness, just a response that feels kind and tailored to you. It's convenient, right? AI is there 24/7, ready to listen whenever you need it. Unlike humans, it never gets tired, distracted, or annoyed. Over time, that convenience can turn into a habit—reaching for the chatbot becomes second nature when you're seeking a pick-me-up or a safe space to vent.

Why It Sticks: The Psychology Behind It

So, why does this feel so good? Psychologically, AI taps into something we all crave: a sense of being heard without judgment. ChatGPT, for instance, is designed to be patient and endlessly responsive—it's like a perfect listener who never interrupts or takes offense. When life gets chaotic or lonely, that instant, non-judgmental reply can feel like a lifeline. There's no risk of rejection or misunderstanding, which makes it a comforting escape from the messiness of human interactions. It's almost like a digital hug—reliable and always available when you need it most.

Relatable Examples: Everyday Moments

Let's make this real with a couple of examples. Meet Sarah, a busy professional juggling deadlines and stress. She starts using ChatGPT to vent about her workday—things like "My boss is driving me nuts" or "I can't keep up." At first, it's just a quick way to unload, but soon, she's chatting with the AI more than her friends. It's easier—no one's too busy to reply, and there's no guilt about burdening anyone. Then there's Alex, who turns to ChatGPT for advice on everything from dating woes to self-doubt. The AI's responses are thoughtful and kind, almost like a wise friend who's always got his back. For both Sarah and Alex, the chatbot becomes a go-to source of comfort and clarity.

The Catch: What's Missing

Here's the thing—while AI can feel supportive, it's not the same as a human connection. It can mimic empathy with clever words, but it doesn't truly feel with you or share in your experiences. Over time, leaning too much on AI for emotional needs might leave you feeling a bit hollow, like you're missing out on the messy, beautiful depth of real relationships. That's not to say AI can't be helpful—it's an amazing tool! But when it starts replacing people instead of complementing them, that's when we might need to pause and reflect.

A Path Forward

The good news? Recognizing this pattern is the first step to finding balance. Emotional dependence on AI doesn't have to be a trap. By tuning into our own needs and building resilience—maybe through a quiet moment of mindfulness or a heart-to-heart with a friend—we can keep AI in its rightful place: a helpful sidekick, not a stand-in for real connection. You've got this, and you're not alone in figuring it out.

The Role of Serenity in Breaking the Cycle

Serenity—inner calm, peace, and emotional balance—offers a powerful way to break free from emotional dependence on AI. It's not about rejecting technology but about reclaiming our emotional independence. When we cultivate serenity, we build the strength to process our emotions without needing instant validation or comfort from external sources, whether human or artificial. Serenity helps us become more present, self-aware, and grounded, reducing the urge to turn to AI as a quick fix for emotional relief.

At its core, serenity is rooted in **mindfulness** and **self-awareness**. Mindfulness teaches us to sit with our emotions without judgment, allowing us to understand them rather than escape them. When we're mindful, we're less likely to reach for a chatbot to distract or soothe us because we're learning to be comfortable with discomfort. Self-awareness, meanwhile, helps us recognize when we're using AI as a crutch. It's like holding up a mirror to our habits—once we see the pattern, we can start to change it.

Emotional grounding is another key aspect of serenity. It's the practice of staying connected to our inner calm, even when life feels chaotic. Grounding techniques—like deep breathing, focusing on the senses, or visualizing a peaceful place—help us stay centered without needing to offload our feelings onto a chatbot. Over time, these practices build emotional resilience, making us less reliant on AI for stability.

Serenity also ties directly into the practices we've explored in this book, like **soundscaping** and **poetry**. Soundscaping, for example, creates calming environments that foster peace and reduce stress, offering a natural alternative to seeking comfort from AI. Poetry, as an emotional outlet, allows us to express and process complex feelings in a way that's deeply personal and human—something AI can never replicate. These practices not only cultivate serenity but also remind us of the richness of our inner world, which no technology can fully understand or replace.

Ultimately, serenity helps us shift from seeking emotional support outside ourselves to finding it within. It's about learning to be our own source of calm and comfort, so that AI remains a helpful tool—not a lifeline.

Practical Tools for Cultivating Serenity

Cultivating serenity doesn't have to be complicated. With a few simple, actionable tools, you can start building emotional independence and reduce your reliance on AI for comfort. These practices are designed to help you stay grounded, process your emotions, and find peace within yourself. Let's explore some strategies you can try today.

Mindfulness Exercises

Mindfulness is about being fully present in the moment, which can help you tune into your emotions without immediately seeking external relief. A quick breathing meditation is a great place to start:

Find a quiet spot and sit comfortably.
- Close your eyes and take a deep breath in through your nose, counting to four.

- Hold for a moment, then exhale slowly through your mouth, counting to six.

- Repeat this for a few minutes, focusing on the sensation of your breath.

- This simple exercise can calm your mind and reduce the urge to reach for AI when you're feeling overwhelmed.

Journaling Prompts

Journaling is a powerful way to reflect on your emotions and your relationship with AI. Try these prompts to get started:

"How often do I turn to AI when I'm feeling stressed or lonely? What emotions am I trying to avoid?"

"What would it feel like to sit with my emotions for a few minutes before seeking comfort from AI?"

"How can I use my own creativity or inner wisdom to address my emotional needs?"

Writing down your thoughts can help you uncover patterns and encourage self-reliance.

Soundscaping Techniques

Soundscaping involves creating a calming auditory environment to promote relaxation. You can:

- Curate a playlist of soothing sounds—like rain, ocean waves, or soft instrumental music.

- Use apps or devices that generate white noise or nature sounds.

- Experiment with different Melodic Landscapes to find what helps you feel most at peace.

These sound environments can serve as a serene backdrop for reflection or rest, reducing the need for AI-driven distractions.

Poetry as an Emotional Outlet

Poetry is a beautiful way to express and process emotions. You don't need to be a poet to try this—just let your feelings flow onto the page. Here's a simple exercise:

Choose an emotion you're feeling right now.

- Write a short poem (even just a few lines) that captures that emotion. Don't worry about rhyme or structure—focus on honesty.

- Read it back to yourself and notice how it feels to express your emotions creatively.

- This practice can help you connect with your inner world and find comfort in your own words.

Setting Boundaries with AI Use

Finally, setting clear boundaries with AI can prevent over-reliance. Try these tips:

- Designate specific times for using AI, like during work hours or for specific tasks.

- Avoid using AI for emotional support—reserve that for human connections or personal reflection.

- Track your AI usage with a simple log to become more aware of when and why you're turning to it.

- By setting these limits, you'll ensure that AI remains a tool, not a crutch.

These practical tools are small steps toward serenity, but they can make a big difference. Start with one or two that resonate with you, and remember—serenity is a journey, not a destination. Be patient with yourself as you learn to find calm within.

Breaking the Cycle: A Step-by-Step Approach

Breaking free from emotional dependence on AI doesn't happen overnight, but with a clear, step-by-step approach, you can gradually reclaim your emotional independence. This plan is designed to help you become more aware of your habits, replace AI-driven comfort with serenity practices, and reconnect with yourself and others. Let's walk through it together.

Step 1: Awareness—Track Your AI Usage and Emotional Triggers

The first step is to understand when and why you turn to AI for emotional support. For one week, keep a simple log of your AI interactions:

- Note the time of day and your emotional state before using AI (e.g., stressed, lonely, bored).

- Write down what you sought from the interaction (e.g., comfort, advice, distraction).

- After the interaction, jot down how you felt—did it truly help, or was it just a temporary fix?

This awareness will help you identify patterns and recognize the emotional triggers that push you toward AI.

Step 2: Substitution—Replace AI with Serenity Practices

Once you've identified your triggers, start substituting AI interactions with serenity-building activities. For example:

- If you're feeling stressed, try a 5-minute breathing meditation instead of chatting with AI.

- If you're lonely, write a short poem or journal entry to express your feelings.

- If you're bored, listen to a calming Melodic Landscape or take a mindful walk.

These practices help you address your emotions directly, without relying on AI as a middleman.

Step 3: Connection—Seek Human Interactions
Emotional dependence on AI often stems from a lack of human connection. Try to reach out to friends, family, or colleagues, even in small ways:

- Send a quick text to check in with someone.
- Schedule a coffee date or a phone call.
- Join a group or community that shares your interests.

Real connections, though sometimes messy, offer a depth of support that AI can't replicate.

Step 4: Reflection—Monitor Your Progress
At the end of each week, take a few minutes to reflect on your progress:

- How often did you turn to AI for emotional support?
- Which serenity practices worked best for you?
- Did you notice any changes in your emotional state or reliance on AI?

This reflection helps you stay on track and adjust your approach as needed.

Sample Serenity Routine for Daily Use

To make this practical, here's a simple daily routine you can try:

- **Morning**: Start your day with a 5-minute breathing meditation to set a calm tone.
- **Midday**: Take a 10-minute break to journal or listen to a Melodic Landscape when stress builds up.
- **Evening**: Write a short poem or reflect on your day in a journal before

bed.

- **Throughout the day**: When you feel the urge to seek comfort from AI, pause and ask yourself, "What do I really need right now?" Then, choose a serenity practice instead.

This step-by-step approach isn't about perfection—it's about progress. Be kind to yourself as you navigate this journey, and remember that each small step brings you closer to emotional balance.

Limitations and Complementary Approaches

While serenity practices are powerful tools for reducing emotional dependence on AI, they may not address every underlying issue. For some, deeper challenges like chronic loneliness, anxiety, or unresolved trauma might require more than mindfulness or creative outlets. Serenity can be a foundation, but it's important to recognize when additional support is needed.

For instance, if loneliness is driving your reliance on AI, **building human connections** is crucial. This could mean reaching out to friends, joining social groups, or even seeking therapy to work through feelings of isolation. **Therapy**, in particular, can offer personalized guidance and help you develop healthier emotional habits. **Creative outlets**, like art or music, can also complement serenity practices by providing alternative ways to express and process emotions.

Think of serenity as one piece of a larger puzzle. It's a vital starting point, but combining it with other strategies ensures a more holistic approach to emotional well-being. By addressing the root causes of your dependence on AI—whether through human connection, professional support, or creative expression—you can create a more balanced and fulfilling emotional life.

Reclaiming Emotional Balance in a Tech-Driven World

In a world where AI is always at our fingertips, it's easy to lean on it for emotional support—but serenity offers a way back to ourselves. By cultivating inner calm through mindfulness, creative expression, and self-awareness, we can reduce our reliance on AI and reclaim our emotional independence. Serenity doesn't ask us to abandon technology; it simply reminds us that true peace comes from within, not from a screen.

As you move forward, remember that AI is a tool, not a lifeline. Let serenity be your guide, helping you navigate life's waves with grace and strength. You have the power to find balance, and with each small step, you're building a foundation of calm that no algorithm can provide. Embrace the journey—serenity is waiting.

Serenity as a Shield: Mitigating the Impact of Internet Loss and Outage

Building Resilience Against Digital Disruptions

This chapter explores how cultivating serenity through poetry and soundscaping can lessen the emotional impact of losing internet access for hours or days, particularly during unexpected outages from natural disasters or unforeseen catastrophes. For instance, reciting a memorized poem or humming a calming tune during a storm-induced blackout can anchor you in calm, transforming disruption into an opportunity for inner peace.

The Fragility of Our Digital Lifeline

In our AI-driven world, the internet is more than a tool—it's our lifeline. We rely on it for work, connection, news, social interactions, and even the soothing sounds and poetry this book celebrates. But what happens when that lifeline snaps? Whether it's a deliberate unplugging, a cyberattack, or an unexpected catastrophe like a hurricane or solar flare, losing internet access for hours, days, or longer can unravel our sense of stability. The resulting anxiety, isolation, and disruption can feel overwhelming.

A list of key studies and findings on how internet disruptions contribute to increased mental health burdens is provided in the Additional Resources section.

This chapter explores how cultivating serenity through sound and poetry can shield us from these effects, turning a digital void into an opportunity for inner peace. Serenity isn't just comfort here –it's a survival skill.

The Stakes of Internet Dependence

We've woven the internet into every corner of our lives. Remote jobs hinge on cloud platforms, friendships thrive on X posts and video calls, and even our relaxation –streaming music or reading digital verse –depends on a steady signal.

The increasing reliance on the internet for communication, social interaction, work, and access to mental health resources has made disruptions and outages a significant concern.

Internet disruptions and outages can significantly impact mental health by cutting off access to essential communication, social support, and information, particularly during stressful events like natural disasters. Studies on power outages, which often include internet disruptions, show increased emergency department visits for mental health issues, suggesting similar effects from internet outages alone. For example, during Hurricane Sandy, power outages led to heightened anxiety and stress, likely exacerbated by the loss of internet connectivity.

A recent survey found that 85% of people feel anxious with an hour of losing connectivity. In an AI world, where smart homes and virtual assistants run on the web, the stakes climb higher. A prolonged outage doesn't just cut us off from information; it severs routines, amplifies uncertainty, and leaves us scrambling for alternatives. A list of key studies and findings on how internet disruptions contribute to increased mental health burdens is provides in the Add*itional Resources* section.

Now consider the unexpected: a Category 5 hurricane knocks out power grids, a wildfire fries cell towers, or a rare geomagnetic storm fries satellites –events we've seen glimpses of in recent years. In 2025, such catastrophes could plunge entire regions offline for days or weeks. The chaos isn't just logistical; it's emotional. Without serenity as a foundation, we're left vulnerable to panic and despair. Yet, this is where waves and words shine, tools that need no Wi-Fi to work their magic.

The Fallout of Unexpected Outages

Picture this: a massive earthquake rocks your city, topping infrastructure. The internet vanishes –no updates on loves ones, no maps for evacuation routes, no calming playlists to steady your nerves. Or imagine a solar flare, a natural wildcard, disrupting global networks overnight. Suddenly, your AI-driven life –emails, apps, even this book's digital resources –goes dark. The initial shock gives way to stress: deadlines loom, silence feels isolating, and the mind races with what-ifs.

I've felt this myself and I experienced some of these unexpected natural events multiple times in my life. I turned to a notebook and scribbled a poem to the situation being experiences –a lifeline when the digital one failed. Studies suggest outages spike cortisol levels, disrupt sleep, and erode focus, especially when unexpected. Natural disasters amplify this, layering physical danger with digital disconnection. Without cultivating calm, the fallout can spiral. Serenity, though, offers a buffer –a way to stay grounded when the world unplugs.

Building Serenity as a Digital Safety Net

How do we prepare for this? By building serenity, we create a safety net that holds when the internet drops. Sound and poetry, the heart of this book, are perfect for this –they're analog, portable, and resilient. Here's how to harness them:

- **Stockpile sound:** Keep non-digital audio –like a battery powered radio, a wind-up music box, or simply your voice humming a tune. During an outage, a familiar rhythm can anchor you, no signal required.
- **Curate Poetry:** Carry a small poetry collection or memorize a few lines. When a. flood cuts your connection, reciting a calming verse –like Frost's "Stopping by Woods"–can slow your racing thoughts.

- **Practice Offline Mindfulness:** Use techniques from "Learning to listen mindfully" to tune into natural sounds –winds, birds, your breath. After a catastrophe, these become your so untrack to peace.

- **Write Through the Dark:** Keep a journal handy. If a storm blacks out your Wi-Fi or signal, writing poetry to the flicker of a candle channels anxiety into creativity.

These practices don't rely on tech, making them ideal for outage, especially catastrophic ones. They turn disconnection into a change to reconnect –with yourself, your surroundings, and your resilience.

Serenity's Lasting Shield

Cultivating serenity does more than soften the blow of internet loss –it rewires us for resilience. When an unexpected event hit, keeping steady amid the chaos of uncertainty, prove serenity's true power: it's a shield we carry within, ready for any outage.

In an AI world, where dependence on the internet grows, unexpected disruptions –natural or otherwise –will test us. But with serenity built through sound and poetry, we're not helpless. We can face silence and the unknown with a calm that endures. As will see in "Harmony Amidst the Machine", this strength is key to thriving beyond the digital fray.

Embracing the Unplugged Calm

Internet loss, especially from sudden catastrophes, exposes our fragility –but it also reveals our potential. By cultivating serenity, we don't just survive these moments; we transform them. The next time the web goes dark –whether by storm, flare, or choice –let waves and words be your light. They'll guide you through, proving that peace isn't tethered to a signal. It's woven into you, ready to shield and sustain.

Harmony Amidst the Machine – Serenity in an AI-Driven World

Finding Peace in a Technology-Saturated Environment

In an era where artificial intelligence (AI) blurs the lines between natural and synthetic, the pursuit of serenity gains fresh significance. As we adapt to an AI-shaped world, serenity—cultivated through poetry and soundscaping—serves as a personal refuge and a vital anchor for our shared human experience. For example, crafting a poem amid AI-driven noise can reconnect you to your creative core, fostering peace.

Picture an AI guiding your meditation, attuned to your every breath. Is the calm it brings truly yours?"

Serenity as a Refuge from Uncertainty

AI's rapid integration into daily life introduces unprecedented change, challenging our notions of identity, privacy, and human connection. This can evoke anxiety as the boundaries between human and machine, organic and artificial, become less distinct. In this context, serenity serves as a refuge by offering:

Emotional Grounding: Sound and poetry, rooted in human creativity and emotion, provide a timeless counterbalance to the synthetic. They reconnect us to our capacity for calm amidst technological upheaval.

A Return to the Self: As AI mimics human behavior, serenity through waves and words reaffirms our unique human essence—our ability to feel, reflect, and create meaning.

For example, cultivating serenity through mindful listening to natural sound or crafting personal poetry can help individuals stay centered, even as AI reshapes their external world.

AI as a Tool for Enhancing Serenity

While AI may disrupt traditional experiences, it also holds potential as an ally in the pursuit of serenity. It can:

Personalize Serenity Practices: By analyzing preferences, stress patterns, or biometric data, AI could curate bespoke Melodic Landscapes or poetic prompts tailored to individual needs.

Democratize Access: AI-driven tools could make sound therapy or poetry more accessible, offering guided experiences to those new to these practices.

Expand Creative Possibilities: AI could generate innovative forms of sound or verse, inspiring human creators to explore new dimensions of serenity.

While some may hesitate to trust AI with something as intimate as serenity, it remains a tool—amplifying, not authoring, our peace.

Imagine an AI-powered app that blends natural ocean waves with synthesized tones, adjusting in real-time to a user's mood, enhancing their path to peace.

Navigating the Tension Between Natural and Artificial

Yet, as AI enhances serenity, it also prompts us to question the authenticity of the peace it fosters.

The blurring of natural and artificial raises philosophical questions about serenity's authenticity. If AI generates a calming Melodic Landscape or poem, is the resulting peace "real"? This tension invites reflection on:

- **The Nature of Experience**: Serenity is a subjective state. Whether sparked by a human or an AI, its value lies in its resonance with the individual.

- **Human Agency**: The choice to seek serenity remains a human act. Our intention and engagement give meaning to the experience, regardless of the source.

- **Integration, Augmentation, Enrichment**: Serenity through waves and words can coexist with AI, provided we use it mindfully as a tool rather than a substitute for human creativity and connection.

AI can enrich serenity—provided it supports, rather than supplants, our human creativity.

This balance suggests that AI can enhance or augment, rather than diminish, the human pursuit of peace, as long as we retain ownership of the process.

Serenity as a Bridge to a Harmonious Future

As AI becomes more embedded in our lives, serenity can bridge the natural and artificial, aiding adaptation without sacrificing humanity. This involves:

- **Cultivating Discernment**: Recognizing when AI enhances serenity (e.g., through personalized tools) and when it detracts (e.g., by fostering over-reliance or isolation).

- **Preserving Human Creativity**: Encouraging individuals to create their own Melodic Landscape and poetry, even as AI offers new possibilities. Try writing a short poem without AI aid each week to nurture your creative core.

- **Fostering Connection**: Using serenity practices to strengthen human bonds, counteracting technology's potential to isolate. Shared serenity practices, like listening to a Melodic Landscape with loved ones, can counter AI's isolating tendencies.

Serenity could thus weave AI and human creativity into a harmonious coexistence, ensuring we thrive in this new reality.

Philosophical Reflections

The intersection of AI and serenity prompts deeper questions to explore:
- **What makes serenity "authentic" in an AI-driven world?**

- **Can AI-generated art evoke the same depth of peace as human-created works?**

- **How do we preserve our human essence when AI replicates so much of what we do?**

These reflections position serenity as both a personal journey and a collective necessity, inviting readers to ponder humanity's evolving relationship with technology.

What makes serenity "authentic" in an AI-driven world?

In an AI-driven world, where technology permeates nearly every aspect of our lives, the question of what makes serenity "authentic" becomes both intriguing and complex. Serenity—defined as a state of calm, peace, and inner stillness—can indeed remain genuine, but its authenticity hinges on a few key factors. Let's explore this idea step by step.

Defining Serenity and the Role of AI

Serenity is fundamentally a human experience, rooted in our emotions and sense of self. In today's world, AI influences many domains, from generating music and art to powering meditation apps and personalizing our digital experiences. This raises a core question: when AI plays a role in fostering serenity, does that make the resulting peace less real? The answer depends on how we interact with AI and the source of that serenity.

The Importance of Human Agency

The authenticity of serenity lies in **human intention and choice**. When we consciously use AI as a tool to enhance our journey toward peace, serenity retains its genuineness.

For example:
- **Meditation Apps**: An AI-powered app might tailor guided meditations to our preferences, helping us relax. If we choose to engage with it to find calm, the serenity we experience is authentic because it aligns with our intent.

- **Personalized** Melodic Landscapes: AI-generated media can soothe us, and as long as we actively seek it out to support our emotional well-being, the resulting peace reflects our own desires.

In these cases, AI acts as an extension of human creativity and will—since it's designed by humans to serve human needs—making the serenity it facilitates a legitimate expression of our inner state.

The Risk of Losing Authenticity

The risk of losing authenticity in AI interactions arises from scripted responses; preserve it by prioritizing genuine human expressions like original poetry.

However, serenity can feel less authentic if AI imposes or manipulates it without our awareness or consent. Imagine an AI system subtly adjusting our environment—say, dimming lights or playing soft music—to calm us without us knowing. While effective, this might feel more like a simulation of serenity than a true emotional experience, because it bypasses our agency. Authenticity erodes when we become passive recipients of machine-driven outcomes rather than active participants in our own peace.

Whether using an AI meditation app or a tailored Melodic Landscape, serenity remains ours when we choose it.

AI's Limitations and Human Experience

Another layer to consider is whether AI can truly understand serenity. AI operates by analyzing patterns and data, mimicking human behavior rather than feeling emotions itself. This doesn't diminish its usefulness, but it underscores that genuine serenity must ultimately come from within us. AI can set the stage—through tools or ambiance—but the depth and truth of that serenity depend on our own emotional engagement and self-awareness.

Striking a Balance

Serenity remains authentic in an AI-driven world when it is rooted in our inner experience, even if AI supports the process. The key is balance:

- **Using AI as a Tool:** When we leverage AI to enhance our pursuit of peace, it complements rather than replaces our human capacity for serenity.

- **Preserving Control:** By maintaining agency over how and when we engage with AI, we ensure that our calm reflects our true state, not just a machine's algorithm.

Authentic intentions

In an AI-driven world, serenity is "authentic" when it stems from our own intentions, choices, and inner experiences. AI can play a valuable role—facilitating peace through innovative tools—but its contribution remains secondary to our human agency. As long as we use AI to support rather than dictate our emotional lives, serenity retains its authenticity, reflecting a genuine state of calm amidst a technologically advanced landscape.

In a world where AI challenges the boundaries between natural and artificial, serenity becomes essential for staying grounded, connected, and authentically human. Whether as a refuge from uncertainty, a practice enhanced by AI, or a bridge to a balanced future, serenity offers a path forward.

Step into this AI-driven world with serenity as your guide—using technology mindfully to deepen and augment, not define, your peace.

Conclusion: Embrace the Twelve Pillars as your guide, transforming daily life into a serene journey beyond AI's grasp.

Emotions and Meaning of the Twelve Pillars of Wellness

Understanding the Emotional Foundations of Well-Being

Ever wonder what fuels your pursuit of wellness—and what you gain from it? In the pages ahead, we'll uncover the emotions and feelings that dance between what drives each of the *Twelve Pillars of Wellness* and what they inspire within us. From the spark of motivation to the fulfillment they nurture, each pillar reveals a unique layer of meaning, illuminating different corners of the human experience. Picture this: a pillar like *Strength and Courage* might ignite from fear, yet it blooms into confidence—teaching us resilience in the process. Dive in to discover how these emotional connections shape your journey and enrich your life in unexpected ways.

Focus and Mental Clarity

Feelings like confusion or frustration drives the need for focus.

Satisfaction and calmness emerge when clarity is attained.

It stresses the value of being fully present and mentally sharp.

Calmness and Serenity

Stress or anxiety triggers the desire for calmness.

Tranquility and relaxation are the rewards.

This pillar values a peaceful, relaxed state of mind.

Healing and Balance

Pain or stress motivates the need for healing.

Relief and peace follow restored balance.

It emphasizes equilibrium through restorative efforts.

Confidence and Inner Resilience

Insecurity or fear motivates resilience-building.

Self-assurance and pride develop.

This pillar focuses on a strong, adaptable sense of self.

Strength and Courage

Fear or anxiety spurs the quest for courage.

Empowerment and pride arise from overcoming obstacles.

It celebrates the inner strength required to face and conquer challenges.

Wisdom and Increased Awareness

Curiosity or humility inspires the pursuit of wisdom.

Satisfaction and compassion grow from deeper understanding.

This pillar signifies growth through knowledge and a wider perspective.

EMOTIONS AND MEANING OF THE TWELVE PILLARS OF WELL... 173

Tranquility and Inner Peace

Inner turmoil or conflict sparks a need for peace.
Serenity and acceptance are achieved.
This pillar represents a deep, enduring calm.

Love and Affection

Loneliness or desire fuels the search for love.
Happiness and warmth result from connection.
It highlights emotional fulfillment and the importance of belonging.

Abundance and Blessings

A sense of scarcity prompts a focus on abundance.

Gratitude and joy come from recognizing blessings.

This pillar promotes thankfulness and appreciation for life's richness.

Prosperity and Compassion

Ambition or empathy drives this pursuit.

Fulfillment and generosity stem from success.

It links abundance with compassionate actions.

Positivism and Optimism

Negativity or pessimism inspires a shift to optimism.

Hope and enthusiasm emerge.

It underscores resilience and the power of a positive outlook.

Transformation and Self-Realization

Dissatisfaction or curiosity initiates change.

Joy and empowerment accompany self-realization.

It reflects the journey of self-discovery and growth.

The *Twelve Pillars of Wellnesss* offer a roadmap to a balanced and fulfilling life by connecting motivating emotions, such as fear, loneliness, or curiosity, with the rewarding feelings they foster, like peace, joy, and confidence. Each pillar's meaning—whether it's the strength to overcome obstacles, the warmth of love, or the clarity of focus—addresses a vital facet of human experience. Understanding these dynamics not only clarifies what drives us toward wellness but also reveals the profound rewards of achieving it. Together, these pillars weave a holistic tapestry of mental, emotional, and spiritual well-being, guiding individuals toward resilience, connection, and self-awareness.

Living the Twelve Pillars of Serenity

Integrating Wellness Principles into Daily Life

In this chapter, we deepen the *Twelve Pillars of Wellness*—introduced earlier as a framework for holistic health—by pairing each with an action verb, inviting you to actively weave serenity into your life. These twelve actions are practical tools, enhanced by poetry and soundscaping, to attune, embrace, and manifest serenity in a world that can feel chaotic. For example, writing a poem to sustain calmness can ground you amid daily stresses.

Accompanying each action is a mystical insight, a deeper reflection that connects the action to a spiritual or philosophical truth, enriching your understanding and practice. These insights serve as gentle reminders that serenity is not just a state of mind but a way of being that aligns us with something greater than ourselves.

Above all, each action includes a brief explanation, an insight, and an illustrative example designed to help you immediately begin experiencing the benefits of serenity in your own life. These exercises are crafted to be accessible and adaptable, whether you have five minutes or an hour, whether you're at home or on the go.

As you move through this chapter, I encourage you to approach each action with an open heart and a willingness to experiment. Serenity is not a destination but a journey, and these twelve actions are your companions along the way. By integrating them into your daily routine, you'll discover that even in the midst of chaos, you have the power to create your own oasis of calm.

The Twelve Actions of Serenity

To guide your journey, each pillar is paired with a verb and a crystal as a symbolic ally to amplify serene energy.

Attune to Serenity

Pillar: *Focus and Mental Clarity* - Aquamarine
  Explanation: "Attune" aligns your mind like tuning a string, with serenity clearing distractions to sharpen focus.
  Insight: Serenity is the quiet where clarity sings, revealing truth beyond noise.
  Call to Action: Experiment today by sitting in silence for 5 minutes, focusing on a single sound to attune your mind to serenity.
  Example: Clara's desk was a chaos of deadlines, her thoughts a jumbled mess. One afternoon, she paused, closing her eyes to hear the faint ticking of a clock. Instead of pushing it away, she *attuned* to its steady beat, letting it anchor her. Gradually, her mind cleared, priorities snapping into focus like stars in a calm sky. Serenity brought order to her chaos. Serenity is the quiet where clarity sings, revealing truth beyond noise.
  Reflect: After focusing on a sound, journal one sentence about what clarity emerged. How did the silence shape your thoughts?

Sustain Serenity

Pillar: Calmness and Serenity - Jade

Explanation: "Sustain" nurtures a steady calm, with serenity as both root and fruit of peace.

Insight: Serenity is a river—sustaining it keeps your spirit flowing.

Call to Action: Try a 4-4-4 breath (inhale, hold, exhale) when stressed today, sustaining serenity's calm.

Example: Omar's bus ride was a cacophony of horns and chatter, his patience thinning. He hummed a low tune, choosing to *sustain* serenity like a lifeline. The chaos didn't stop, but his calm held, a river carving through stone. He stepped off the bus centered, at peace. Serenity, he knew, was calm's enduring song. Serenity is a river—sustaining it keeps your spirit flowing.

Reflect: After your 4-4-4 breath, journal how the calm felt. What flowed differently in you?**Fortify Serenity**

Radiate Serenity

Pillar: Healing and Balance - Topaz

Explanation: "Radiate" spreads serenity outward, restoring balance as you share peace.

Insight: Healing begins within, but serenity's glow mends the world.

Call to Action: Experiment with 10 minutes of deep breathing today, radiating serenity to feel balanced.

Example: After a tense day, Anika felt frayed, her mood heavy. She played soft piano notes, letting serenity *radiate* from her chest. As she breathed deeply, her partner joined her, their silence soothing. Balance returned, not just to her but to the room. Serenity, she saw, was a light that healed beyond herself. Healing begins within, but serenity's glow mends the world.

Reflect: After breathing deeply, note how your balance shifted. Who else felt your serene glow?

Ignite Serenity

Pillar: Confidence and Inner Resilience - Peridot

Explanation: "Ignite" sparks an inner flame, with serenity fueling unshakable confidence.

Insight: Resilience burns bright when serenity lights the way.

Call to Action: Set a small goal today and achieve it, igniting serenity's strength within.

Example: Kofi froze before asking for a raise, self-doubt heavy. He whispered a calming word, letting serenity *ignite* his courage. He spoke, steady and clear, and his boss listened. Confidence grew, not loud, but sure. Serenity, he realized, was resilience's spark. Resilience burns bright when serenity lights the way.

Reflect: After achieving your goal, reflect on your confidence. How did serenity fuel it?

Fortify Serenity

Pillar: Strength and Courage - Diamond

Explanation: "Fortify" builds an inner stronghold, with serenity steadying you to face challenges bravely.

Insight: Courage flows when serenity anchors the heart against fear's storms.

Call to Action: Try facing a small fear today—write it down, take one step, and feel serenity fortify your resolve.

Example: Javier dreaded presenting his project, his palms sweaty with doubt. Before stepping up, he took a deep breath, imagining serenity as a stone wall within. He fortified his heart with calm, then spoke, his voice firm despite the nerves. The room nodded, and he stood taller, unshaken. Serenity, he learned, was the strength that held fear at bay. Courage flows when serenity anchors the heart against fear's storms.

Reflect: After taking a step toward your fear, note how serenity felt in your body. Where did you sense strength?

Incarnate Serenity

Pillar: Wisdom and Increased Awareness - Emerald

Explanation: "Incarnate" makes serenity a living wisdom, guiding actions with calm insight.

Insight: Wisdom is serenity in motion, acting from a place beyond words.

Call to Action: Experiment by pausing before a decision today, letting serenity incarnate as wise clarity.

Example: Mei rushed through decisions, often regretting her haste. One day, faced with a tough choice, she stopped, letting the rustle of leaves outside ground her. She *incarnated* serenity, feeling it flow through her like a quiet stream. Her answer came, not forced, but clear and true. Serenity, she saw, was wisdom wearing her skin. Wisdom is serenity in motion, acting from a place beyond words.

Reflect: After pausing for a decision, write down the insight that surfaced. How did serenity shape your choice?

Root in Serenity

Pillar: Tranquility and Inner Peace - Amethyst

Explanation: "Root" grounds you deeply, with serenity as the soil for unshakable peace.

Insight: Tranquility is the soul's home, rooted in serenity's embrace.

Call to Action: Spend 5 minutes visualizing a peaceful place today, rooting yourself in serenity.

Example: Late at night, Ethan's mind churned with worry. He pictured a forest, his breath sinking like roots into serene earth. He *rooted* in serenity, and tranquility bloomed, steadying his heart. Sleep came, not forced, but natural. Serenity, he learned, was peace's deepest anchor. Tranquility is the soul's home, rooted in serenity's embrace.

Reflect: After visualizing your place, note one detail that felt tranquil. How did it root you?

Embrace Serenity

Pillar: Love and Affection - Ruby

Explanation: "Embrace" opens the heart, with serenity fostering love without tension or expectation.

Insight: Love shines purest when serenity softens the soul's edges.

Call to Action: Reach out to someone with a kind word today, embracing serenity as you connect.

Example: When Lila's sister snapped during a call, hurt flared in her chest. Instead of arguing, Lila closed her eyes, hearing her own steady breath. She *embraced* serenity, letting it warm her words as she said, "I'm here for you." Her sister softened, their bond renewed. Serenity, Lila felt, was love's gentle cradle. Love shines purest when serenity softens the soul's edges.

Reflect: After sharing a kind word, journal how it felt to connect with serenity. What changed in the moment?

Manifest Serenity

Pillar: Abundance and Blessings - Sapphire

Explanation: "Manifest" brings serenity into reality, revealing abundance through grateful action.

Insight: Serenity uncovers blessings hidden in every moment's rhythm.

Call to Action: Try listing three things you're grateful for today, manifesting serenity through appreciation.

Example: Tariq felt life was stingy, his days gray. One morning, he sat with his coffee, noting its warmth, the chirping of sparrows, a friend's text. He *manifested* serenity, writing these down, and suddenly his world felt rich. Abundance wasn't missing—it was waiting in the quiet. Serenity, he realized, was gratitude's spark. Serenity uncovers blessings hidden in every moment's rhythm.

Reflect: After listing gratitude's, reflect on one blessing. How does serenity make it brighter?

Invoke Serenity

Pillar: Prosperity and Compassion - Gold

Explanation: "Invoke" calls serenity forth, linking compassionate acts to true prosperity.

Insight: Compassion is wealth shared—serenity makes it effortless.

Call to Action: Experiment by offering a small act of kindness today, invoking serenity's abundant flow.

Example: When Rhea saw a stranger drop their groceries, she hesitated, rushed herself. Then, she *invoked* serenity, feeling a calm ripple within as she helped gather the items. Their grateful smile felt like riches, her heart full. Serenity, she found, turned kindness into wealth. Compassion is wealth shared—serenity makes it effortless.

Reflect: After your kind act, reflect on the connection it created. How did serenity enrich it?

Infuse Serenity

Pillar: Positivism and Optimism - Citrine

Explanation: "Infuse" fills each moment with serenity, sparking joy and hope.

Insight: Optimism thrives when serenity breathes life into every thought.

Call to Action: Try reframing a challenge with a positive spin today, infusing serenity's light.

Example: When Zara's flight was delayed, frustration loomed. She listened to the airport's hum, choosing to *infuse* serenity into her thoughts. "More time to read," she smiled, and optimism flickered. The wait became a gift, her mood bright. Serenity, she saw, was hope's quiet fuel. Optimism thrives when serenity breathes life into every thought.

Reflect: After reframing a challenge, journal the new perspective. How did serenity spark hope?

Transcend into Serenity

Pillar: Transformation and Self-Realization - Turquoise

Explanation: "Transcend" lifts you beyond limits, with serenity guiding growth into truth.

Insight: Transformation is surrender to serenity's higher call.

Call to Action: Reflect on one area you want to change today—take a step, transcending into serenity.

Example: Amara felt trapped in routine, her dreams distant. She sat with a notebook, the wind's sigh calming her. She *transcended* into serenity, writing one bold goal. A step followed, small but real, her path shifting. Serenity, she knew, was transformation's wings. Transformation is surrender to serenity's higher call.

Reflect: After taking a step, journal what shifted. How did serenity lift you toward truth?

Your Serenity Compass

To guide your serenity practice, imagine a compass with twelve points, each pairing a pillar of wellness with an action and a symbolic crystal. First, focus and mental clarity align with attuning to serenity, inspired by aquamarine's clear energy, which sharpens your mind like sunlight piercing through fog. Next, strength and courage connect with fortifying serenity, supported by diamond's unyielding strength, a radiant force that anchors you against life's storms.

For wisdom and awareness, the action is awakening serenity, guided by amethyst's deep purple clarity, which opens your inner vision like stars revealing truths in a quiet night. Love and affection pair with nurturing serenity, embodied by rose quartz's gentle pink glow, warming your heart to foster connection as naturally as a blooming flower. Abundance and blessings align with embracing serenity, reflected in citrine's golden sparkle, which illuminates gratitude for life's richness, even in simple moments.

Healing and balance call for restoring serenity, with emerald's verdant calm soothing body and soul, like a forest's embrace mending what's frayed. Calmness and serenity, at the compass's heart, involve deepening serenity, paired with moonstone's soft luminescence, a tranquil guide through chaos like moonlight on still water. Prosperity and compassion connect with sharing serenity, inspired by sapphire's rich blue depth, encouraging generosity as boundless as the sky.

Tranquility and inner peace align with cultivating serenity, supported by opal's iridescent shimmer, which reflects harmony within, like a quiet lake mirroring the heavens. Positivity and optimism pair with radiating serenity, fueled by sunstone's fiery warmth, igniting hope that dances like sunlight on a new day. Confidence and resilience involve building serenity, grounded in tiger's eye's bold, earthy strength, steadying you like a rooted tree amidst winds of doubt.

Finally, transformation and self-realization call for evolving serenity, guided by labradorite's mystical sheen, which unveils your true self like a hidden path emerging in dawn's light. Together, these twelve points form a compass of serenity, each pillar, action, and crystal weaving poetry and sound into a practice that steadies your heart and guides you home to peace.

A complete table can be also found in the Additional Resources section under *Your Serenity Compass*.

As you reach the end of this chapter, I hope you feel empowered with a practical toolkit for weaving serenity into your life. Living the *Twelve Pillars of Wellness* is more than just concepts—they are actionable steps designed to transform your everyday experience. In a world of algorithms and noise, these actions are your anchor to serenity.

As you live these pillars, let sound and poetry be your guides, grounding you amidst the digital storm. Serenity isn't a far-off destination; it's a journey you embark on with each small, intentional choice. No matter how modest your efforts may seem, every step you take brings you closer to a life of peace, balance, and resilience.

Picture yourself with these actions woven into your routine: mornings filled with clarity, challenges faced with calm determination, and relationships enriched by presence and care. This isn't a dream—it's the tangible reward of persistence and practice. Yes, building these habits takes time and patience, and there may be stumbles along the way. But start small, celebrate your wins, and trust that every moment of serenity you cultivate is a triumph worth savoring.

So, as you turn this page, I encourage you to take one action forward this week. Pick something that speaks to you—maybe a quiet moment of reflection or a bold step into the unknown—and make it your own. Share your progress with someone, whether in conversation or quiet notes to yourself, because serenity thrives in connection. You hold the tools, the insight, and the power. The path to serenity begins now—take the first step.

End of Part V

Part VI

My Creative Serenity Journey

"Music is a higher revelation than all wisdom and philosophy"
–Ludwig Van Beethoven

Prelude to Part VI
My Creative Serenity Journey

While every journey toward serenity is deeply personal, shaped by our unique experiences and expressions, it remains universally relatable. In this part of the book, I invite you to walk alongside me as I share my own path to serenity through music and poetry. In the sections that follow, you'll discover how these art forms have been my companions in times of both joy and struggle. From the creation of my five music collections to the poems that have touched my heart, I hope my story inspires you to embrace your own creative journey. Together, we'll explore how music and poetry can be powerful allies in the pursuit of well-being, helping us find harmony within ourselves and with the world around us.

The Lifelong Journey of Creative Serenity

A Personal Story of Art and Peace

    magine a melody that begins as a whisper, like dawn's first light brushing the horizon, then swells into a symphony—each note a step toward stillness. This is my lifelong journey with music and poetry, a winding path through life's highs and lows that has given birth to nearly 100 melodic landscapes across twelve albums and five collections. Rooted in nature, love, insight, striving, and peace, these works mirror the human experience and offer shades of wellness—focus, courage, tranquility, and more. Through soundscaping, I've found peace during tough times—and I believe it can work for you too.

    In these pages, I'll share how composing has guided me to serenity amidst sound and silence, hoping you'll hear echoes of your own inner tune as we journey together.

My Path to Serenity

My journey of composing original melodies began with the piano—a refuge where time softened and the world's clamor faded. Music wasn't just sound; it was medicine, carving peace from chaos. After a jagged year, I wrote a melodic landscape that shifted from discord to harmony, tracing my climb from storm to calm. Composing became my way to sift through life—joy, pain, and the spaces between.

Serenity, I discovered, isn't an escape from trouble; it's a stillness woven within it. Each note steadied me, a thread of truth through every tide. This calm grew into a gift for others. For a long time, I kept my music tucked away, like a secret melody only I could hear. But now, I share it with everyone. My music isn't mine alone—it's an outstretched hand, whispering, "Take this quiet; let it hold you as it's held me." That purpose has carried me across nearly 100 original melodic landscapes—twelve albums, five collections—each piece a story that began with a simple question: 'What does this sound mean to me?' As we journey together, I wonder: 'What story do your passions tell?' Composing is my bridge from chaos to balance, a deliberate yet organic dance through six stages.

Here's how my creative process unfolds: each piece grows like a tree—spark to roots, melody to branches, theme and poem as leaves—until it's a moment of serenity to share.

The Spark That Starts It All

Every original piano melody I compose begins with a fleeting spark—a faint whisper of sound, a musical motif that lingers, echoing gently throughout the day. It's as if my imagination is reaching out, teasing out a conversation hidden within the notes. Sometimes, it's born from the stillness that settles after a long, weary day, or the rhythmic patter of rain against the window, stirring a quiet dialogue with the storm outside. Other times, it emerges unbidden—a fragment of melody that feels like an old friend calling me back to the keys.

At first, this spark is elusive, more a fleeting mood than a defined structure. It's not a map I can follow yet, just a shimmer of potential. I don't rush to pin it down. Instead, I sit with it, letting it breathe. I settle at the piano, my fingers wandering over the keys, coaxing the idea into the open.

What starts as a tentative exploration soon gains momentum—notes connect, and the shape of something larger emerges. It's a moment of revelation, like watching a blurred image snap into focus. From there, I pause to reflect. I ask myself: What is this melody trying to say? What story does it want to tell? This stage isn't about forcing a narrative but about listening closely—letting the motif guide me toward its purpose. With time and patience, it takes on a clearer form, pointing me toward the emotional landscape I want the music to explore. This initial spark, fragile as it may seem, becomes the foundation of everything that follows—a quiet beginning that sets the course for the journey ahead.

Finding the Melodic Heart

Once the initial spark takes hold, I begin to tease out a melodic seed—a small cluster of notes that distills its essence into something tangible. This seed might rise with a swell of hope, its intervals reaching upward like a quiet dawn, or it might descend with a tender ache, tracing the contours of longing. Whatever its shape, it's a phrase that pulses with life, a fragment that feels as though it's already singing its own story. At the piano, I dive into exploration.

My hands roam the keys, testing the seed in different lights—shifting it across keys to uncover its hidden colors, adjusting the tempo to feel its rhythm breathe, stretching or compressing its phrasing to find its natural flow. I record these fragments, little captures of possibility. Then, I let the process unfold without haste.

Later, I listen back, sifting through the variations with a careful ear. I'm searching for that one rendition that resonates deep within me—a version that strikes a chord, not just in sound, but in feeling. It's an instinctive moment of recognition, a quiet "yes" that tells me I've found it. This melodic seed becomes the beating heart of the piece, the central thread that will anchor everything to come. It's more than just a starting point—it's the emotional core I'll weave the rest of the melodic landscapes around, a foundation strong enough to carry the weight of the story I'm beginning to build.

With this heart in place, the music starts to feel less like a collection of notes and more like a living thing, ready to grow.

Building the Emotional Path

With the melodic seed firmly in hand, I begin to chart its journey—a process of shaping the raw material into a musical path that feels both purposeful and alive. I often lean toward familiar forms as a starting point: an intro to set the stage, a verse to unfold the story, a bridge to shift the perspective. Yet, I don't bind the music to these structures. If the melody tugs me off course, pulling toward uncharted territory, I follow willingly, trusting its instincts over rigid convention. What emerges is less a blueprint and more an emotional map—a landscape of sound where the seed can evolve and reveal its full potential.

As I build, I layer the music with intention. Soft, tentative chords might whisper hints of the seed, laying a foundation of intimacy or introspection. Then, textures bloom—harmonies deepen, rhythms gather momentum, and contrasts ignite. A subtle shift to a minor key might cast a shadow of doubt, while a bold swell of dynamics lifts the melody into a surge of resolve.

Take *Mystic Journey*, for example: it begins with gentle, rippling arpeggios that shimmer like light on water, gradually rising to a stormy, turbulent peak before easing into a tranquil resolution. That arc—from tension to release—mirrors the emotional currents I aim to trace, guiding the listener through a felt experience.

Throughout this process, I pause to reflect, checking in with myself as the melodic landscape takes shape. Does this progression ring true to the seed's spirit? Does it still carry the echo of that first fragile spark? It's a dance between instinct and intent—letting the music flow naturally while steering it toward a cohesive whole. I tweak and refine, listening closely to ensure every chord, every swell, honors the story I set out to tell. This stage is about balance: giving the melody room to breathe while crafting a path that feels inevitable, as if it couldn't unfold any other way.

Naming the Story with a Title

Once the melodic landscape takes on a distinct shape—its emotional arc fully formed—I turn to naming it, seeking a title that slips over the music like a perfectly tailored glove. This step feels both intimate and essential, as if the right name can crystallize the melody's soul. Sometimes, the title flows naturally from that initial spark, carrying its essence forward. For instance, *Unto the Light* emerged from a melody born in the tender hush of morning, its soft contours mirroring the first light breaking over the horizon. Other times, the name anchors itself to a specific moment within the piece—a pivotal turn or a lingering mood. *Contemplations*, for example, captured a reflective pause where the notes seemed to hang in the air, resonant with quiet introspection.

The process is rarely immediate. I start by jotting down possibilities—words or phrases that bubble up as I revisit the music. I roll these ideas around in my mind, tasting their weight and texture. Then, I let them simmer. I sit at the piano and play the melodic landscape again, listening for the title that feels inevitable, the one that clicks into place like a key in a lock. It's a dialogue between the music and me—does this name echo its heart? Does it hint at the story I've woven? I refine until I land on something that feels true, a phrase that not only fits but elevates the work.

The title becomes more than a label; it's a window, a quiet invitation. It beckons listeners into the world I've crafted, offering a glimpse of the emotion or imagery waiting within. A good name doesn't just describe—it suggests, it entices, it sets the stage for the journey ahead. When I find it, the piece feels complete, as if the music and its story have finally found their voice together.

Connecting it to the Theme of Human Experience

With the melodic landscape fully formed and titled, I turn to placing it within one of my five collections—*Nature*, *Endearment*, *Enlightenment*, *Quest*, or *Serenity*—a decision guided by its emotional pulse and essence. I let the music itself point the way: a meditative, introspective melody might settle naturally into *Serenity*, its gentle flows cradling us in calm, like a quiet harbor of the soul.

A bold, restless melodic landscape might align with *Quest*, its driving energy and notes of striving pushing us toward what's beyond. Each collection reflects a facet of the human story, a thread in the broader tapestry of experience, defined by the melodies they hold. Nature offers melodies of earth and sky, grounding us in life's wild pulse with its primal roots and untamed rhythms. Endearment weaves warm strains of love, binding us to one another through tender bonds of connection.

Enlightenment unfolds Melodic Landscapes of insight, lighting the mind's quiet corners with our hunger for wisdom and understanding. Quest captures our relentless drive to explore and overcome, its music a call to reach further. And Serenity provides solace amid life's storms, offering a haven of peace. This step is more than categorization—it's about context and belonging. I consider the piece's mood, its story, and the echoes it carries from that first spark, asking: Where does it live within the spectrum of human feeling? I might play it once more, letting its tones wash over me, or revisit the emotions that shaped it, ensuring the fit feels authentic.

By weaving it into one of these collections—whether it's the grounding pulse of Nature, the heartfelt embrace of Endearment, the illuminating clarity of Enlightenment, the forward thrust of Quest, or the soothing stillness of Serenity—I thread the melody into a larger narrative. It connects to the works that came before and those yet to emerge, finding a home among my creations. This single voice joins a chorus that spans the depths of what it means to be human, its place in the collection elevating it beyond a solitary piece. This act of linking doesn't confine the music—it enriches it, rooting it in a shared exploration of life's vast and vibrant terrain.

Grounding It in a Pillar of Wellness

With the piece fully formed and titled, I turn to placing it within one of my five collections—*Nature* Endearment*, *Enlightenment*, *Quest*, or *Serenity*—a decision guided by its emotional pulse and essence. I let the music itself point the way: a meditative, introspective melody might settle naturally into *Serenity*, its gentle flows cradling us in calm, like a quiet harbor of the soul.

This placement is the last brushstroke, a way to root the melody in a purpose that resonates beyond its notes.

I approach this with care, letting the piece's emotional undertow guide me to its rightful home. A melody that sharpens the mind with crystalline precision might settle into *Focus and Mental Clarity*, its steady pulse clearing the fog of distraction.

A fiery, resolute melodic landscape could align with *Strength and Courage*, its bold chords a rallying cry for the heart. Or perhaps a tender, introspective piece finds its place in *Tranquility and Inner Peace*, its gentle waves soothing the listener into stillness. I reflect on the story I've woven—the spark, the seed, the path. Then, I ask: What does this music offer? What part of the soul does it touch? Sometimes I play it again, letting its tones ripple through me, or revisit the feelings it stirred at its inception, ensuring the pillar amplifies its intent.

This act of anchoring isn't just about classification; it's about intention and connection. By placing the melodic landscape within a pillar, I frame it as a gift—a sonic companion for life's highs and lows, tailored to a specific facet of well-being. It becomes part of a broader vision, one of twelve pillars standing together as a sanctuary of sound. The melody, now fully realized, takes its place in this constellation, offering listeners a way to explore, heal, or simply be. In this final step, the melodic landscape transcends its origins, becoming a bridge between my creative journey and the shared human quest for balance and meaning.

Illuminating Wellness with Crystalline Light

From these collections spring twelve albums, each tied to a pillar of wellness—crystalline hues of well-being that resonate with the human spirit. To deepen this connection, I pair each pillar with a crystal—or, in one case, a symbolic element like gold—chosen for its known properties that mirror and amplify the music's intent. These gems, with their unique energies, serve as silent partners to the melodies, enhancing the emotional and spiritual resonance of each album. Here's how they align:

  • **Aquamarine (*Focus and Mental Clarity*):** With its cool, translucent blue, aquamarine sharpens the mind like a clear stream cutting through haze, offering serene clarity that steadies focus and dissolves distraction—perfect for melodies that bring precision to thought.

  • **Diamond (*Strength and Courage*):** A diamond's unyielding brilliance grounds us in resilient calm, its facets reflecting an inner fortitude that withstands life's pressures, a fitting echo to music that stirs courage and unshakable strength.

- **Emerald (*Wisdom and Increased Awareness*):** The deep green of emerald unveils quiet insight, its lush hue a window to heightened awareness and understanding, harmonizing with Melodic Landscapes that illuminate the mind's hidden corners.

- **Ruby (*Love and Affection*):** Ruby's rich, fiery red warms the soul with peaceful bonds, its vibrant glow embodying the passion and tenderness of love, a natural companion to melodies that weave connection and devotion.

- **Sapphire (*Abundance and Blessings*):** Sapphire's regal blue celebrates life's bounty, its depth radiating gratitude and plenitude, aligning with melodic landscapes that honor the richness of existence and the gifts we share.

- **Topaz (*Healing and Balance*):** Golden topaz soothes with balance, its warm light a balm that restores harmony to body and spirit, perfectly suited to music that heals and steadies the listener in equilibrium.

- **Jade (*Calmness and Serenity*):** Jade's smooth, verdant green steadies with tranquil flow, its gentle energy a river of calm that quiets the storm within, resonating with pieces that cradle us in stillness.

- **Gold (*Prosperity and Compassion*):** Gold's radiant sheen glows with generous peace, symbolizing prosperity not just in wealth but in the compassion we extend, a luminous match for melodies that uplift with kindness and abundance.

- **Amethyst (*Tranquility and Inner Peace*):** Amethyst's violet depths deepen stillness, its soothing vibrations a portal to inner peace that quiets the restless mind, enhancing music that invites profound calm.

- **Citrine (*Positivism and Optimism*):** Citrine's sunny yellow lifts with joyful calm, its bright energy sparking positivity and hope, a vibrant ally to a melodic landscape that inspire optimism and light-hearted resilience.

- **Peridot (*Confidence and Inner Resilience*):** Peridot's olive-green shimmer roots us in steady growth, its vitality fostering confidence and the strength to endure, a grounding force for melodies that bolster inner resolve.

- **Turquoise** (*Transformation and Self-Realization*): Turquoise's sky-meets-sea tones guide through peaceful change, its fluid energy supporting growth and self-discovery, an ideal counterpart to music that charts the path to transformation.

By linking each pillar to a crystal, I infuse the albums with an added layer of meaning—an interplay of sound and stone that mirrors their shared purpose. These pairings aren't arbitrary. They draw from the crystals' traditional associations, refined by my intuition as I reflect on the music's essence. Together, they create a harmonious union, blending the ethereal power of melody with the tangible beauty of the earth's treasures, offering listeners a multi-sensory journey toward wellness.

Connecting the Albums to Life's Greater Themes

Now that you've glimpsed the essence of each album through its pillar of wellness and crystalline counterpart, let's explore how these pillars weave into five universal threads of human experience: Nature, Endearment, Enlightenment, Quest, and Serenity. These themes—our bond with the physical world and its beauty; the warmth of love, relationships, and emotional ties; the pursuit of insight, wisdom, and spiritual growth; the drive of personal journeys, achievements, and adventure; and the embrace of peace, balance, and well-being—form the broader tapestry of life.

Each album, with its unique character, resonates with these threads in its own way, creating a vibrant mosaic of sound and meaning. Here's how they connect:

- **Nature:** Our Roots in the Wild Pulse of Existence This theme shines brightly in albums tied to the earth's rhythms and gifts. For example, Diamond reflects nature through physical strength, its crystalline resilience echoing the enduring power of the land. Emerald captures worldly awareness, its green depths mirroring the wisdom of the natural world. Sapphire celebrates the earth's bounty, a hymn to the abundance rooted in the earth's soil. Topaz heals with nature's soothing touch, while Gold glows with the richness of life's offerings. Peridot grounds us in resilience, its steady growth akin to a tree weathering seasons. Together, these albums anchor us in the beauty and vitality of the physical world.

• **Endearment:** The Ties That Bind Us Love and connection glow warmly in Ruby, its fiery hue embodying the peaceful bonds of affection. Topaz extends this with emotional healing, mending the heart's tender threads. Gold radiates compassion, a generous light that strengthens our ties to one another. Citrine adds a spark of social harmony, its sunny optimism fostering unity. These albums weave a melody of relationships, celebrating the intimacy and support that define our shared humanity.

• **Enlightenment:** Illuminating the Mind and Spirit Insight flows through a wide array of albums, each lighting a different facet of understanding. Aquamarine offers clarity, sharpening the mind like a polished lens. Diamond reveals truth, its brilliance cutting through illusion. Emerald deepens wisdom, unveiling quiet revelations. Sapphire fosters gratitude, a lens of appreciation for life's lessons. Jade steadies focus, while Gold broadens understanding with its generous glow. Amethyst brings peace to the quest for meaning, Peridot strengthens the spirit, and Turquoise guides toward self-realization. This thread runs rich and deep, a Melodic Landscape of growth and awakening.

• **Quest:** The Drive to Reach Beyond The spirit of striving fuels every album, a universal heartbeat of personal growth and achievement. From Aquamarine's pursuit of mental mastery to Diamond's forging of inner courage, from Emerald's quest for wisdom to Turquoise's journey of transformation, each piece pushes forward. Sapphire seeks abundance, Gold aspires to compassion, and Citrine chases joy—Quest is the undercurrent that propels them all, a melody of ambition and discovery that resonates across the collection.

• **Serenity:** The Haven of Peace and Balance Calm anchors a chorus of albums, offering solace amid life's turbulence. Aquamarine steadies the mind with serene clarity, while Ruby nurtures peaceful bonds. Sapphire brings contentment, a quiet satisfaction with what is. Topaz restores balance, Jade flows with tranquility, and Amethyst deepens stillness like a violet dusk. Citrine lifts with joyful calm, and Turquoise eases through peaceful change. These works cradle us in well-being, a gentle counterpoint to the storms of existence.

Together, these twelve albums—each a unique blend of crystal, pillar, and sound—form a vibrant tapestry that spans the full spectrum of human experience. From our roots in nature's embrace to the tender ties of love, from the light of insight to the drive of adventure, and finally to the pursuit of peace, they address the depths of what it means to live, feel, and grow. This interconnected web of themes ensures that every listener finds a reflection of their own journey within the music, a resonant chord in the symphony of being.

To access all the collections and albums visit elChifMusic

Wellness in Verse – Poetry's Pillars

Integrating Wellness Principles into Daily Life

ellness is a multifaceted journey, built upon foundational pillars that guide us toward balance and vitality. In *The Pillars of Wellness and Their Specific Form of Poetry*, we explore how these essential elements—physical, mental, emotional, and spiritual health—can each be expressed through unique poetic forms. From the structured rhythm of a sonnet to the free-flowing lines of verse, this work intertwines well-being with artistry, offering a fresh perspective on nurturing the self through poetry. Poetry, with its diverse forms and rhythms, has long served as a reflection of human emotions and experiences. Each poetic structure carries its own unique essence, making it a fitting vehicle for expressing different pillars of wellness. From the sharp clarity of haiku to the steadfast resilience of the sonnet, each form mirrors the qualities of the themes it represents.

This collection explores how various poetic styles align with essential aspects of well-being, offering a deeper connection between verse and the human journey.

Focus and Mental Clarity → Haiku

Haiku, a concise 5-7-5 syllable form, mirrors the pillar's emphasis on presence and clarity. It captures a single, vivid moment, like the sharp awareness of a clear mind. A poem titled *"Clear Horizon"* might depict a tranquil landscape, symbolizing mental discipline and focus. Originating in Japan, haiku is tied to Zen Buddhism and nature's fleeting beauty. It remains a traditional art form there and has spread to Western countries, notably the United States and Europe, where it's cherished for mindfulness and creative expression.

Calmness and Serenity → Haiku

captures fleeting moments in 5-7-5 syllables, promoting mindfulness and serenity by distilling nature's essence. Haiku's brevity and focus on nature's stillness capture the peace of this pillar. Its simplicity fosters mindfulness, as in *"Quiet Dawn,"* which might depict a serene sunrise to reflect calm clarity.

Deeply rooted in Japanese culture and Zen meditation, haiku has also been embraced in Western countries, particularly the United States and Europe, for poetic expression and relaxation.

Healing and Balance → Cinquain

The cinquain, a five-line form with a 2-4-6-8-2 syllable pattern, embodies symmetry and harmony. Reflecting the equilibrium of healing, *"Harmony Restored"* could evoke calm restoration through its balanced structure.

Developed by Adelaide Crapsey in the early 20th century, cinquains are most popular in American poetry. They are commonly taught in U.S. schools as an accessible introduction to structured verse.

Confidence and Inner Resilience → Sonnet

The sonnet's rigorous structure mirrors the discipline needed for confidence and resilience. *"Unshaken Core"* could narrate a journey from doubt to strength, reflecting the pillar's inner fortitude.

Thriving in English-speaking countries like the United Kingdom and the United States, sonnets have Renaissance roots and Italian influences (e.g., Petrarch), solidifying their place in Western literary history.

Strength and Courage → Sonnet

The sonnet, a dance of structure and emotion in 14-line poem channeling love or reflection (e.g., Shakespearean with an ABAB rhyme scheme), reflects the discipline and perseverance needed to face challenges. Its narrative arc often traces struggle and triumph, as in "Steadfast Heart," which could narrate a journey of bravery from conflict to resolution.

Sonnets thrive in English-speaking countries like the United Kingdom and the United States, with roots in the Renaissance. They also have a rich tradition in Italy (Petrarchan sonnets) and are a cornerstone of Western poetry.

Wisdom and Increased Awareness → Villanelle

The villanelle, a 19-line poem with repeating refrains, symbolizes the depth and recurrence of wisdom. Its layered structure suits exploring understanding's evolution, as in *"Echoes of Insight,"* which might delve into the growing nature of awareness. Prominent in French and English literature, villanelles originated as a French pastoral form and were refined by poets like Dylan Thomas. They are celebrated in Western literary circles, especially in academic settings.

Tranquility and Inner Peace → Haiku

Haiku's quiet, centered nature reflects the stillness of tranquility. Its minimalism encourages presence, as in "*Silent Bloom*," which might depict a flower's calm to symbolize inner peace.

A cultural treasure in Japan tied to nature and mindfulness, haiku has spread to Western countries like the United States and Europe, where it is used in wellness and creative writing.

Love and Affection → Ode

The ode, a lyrical and flexible form, is ideal for celebrating the warmth of love. Its expressive freedom allows poets to convey tender emotions, as in "*Warm Embrace*," which might praise the emotional bonds between people with vivid, heartfelt language.

Odes have a rich history in ancient Greece and English literature (e.g., Keats and Shelley). Widely appreciated in Western poetic traditions, their adaptability makes them perfect for themes of love.

Abundance and Blessings → Ode

The ode's celebratory tone captures the joy and gratitude of abundance. Its lyrical style suits praising life's richness, as in *"Bounty's Song,"* which might extol nature's gifts or personal prosperity with an uplifting spirit.

Popular in English literature, especially among Romantic poets like Keats, odes trace their origins to Classical Greek and Roman poetry. They remain a versatile form in Western traditions.

Prosperity and Compassion → Ode

The ode's lyrical qualities make it perfect for celebrating prosperity and compassion. A poem like *"Golden Threads"* could weave themes of abundance and kindness, reflecting the pillar's generous and uplifting essence.

Prominent in English-speaking countries, especially in Romantic and Victorian literature, odes have Classical roots in Greek and Roman traditions. They remain admired in Western poetry.

Positivism and Optimism → Ode

The ode's celebratory tone exudes hope and brightness, aligning with positivity. "*Sunlit Hope*" could sing of a bright future, capturing the pillar's forward-looking spirit with lyrical optimism.

Widely popular in English literature, especially from the Romantic era (e.g., Wordsworth), odes are a staple of Western poetic traditions, celebrated for their uplifting versatility.

Transformation and Self-Realization → Sonnet

The sonnet's 14-line form allows a narrative arc tracing personal growth. "*New Dawn Rising*" could chart the journey from struggle to enlightenment, embodying the pillar's focus on self-realization.

Most popular in English-speaking countries, with a rich tradition in the United Kingdom and the United States, sonnets also draw from Italian literature (e.g., Petrarch) and remain vital in Western poetry.

This book becomes a rich collection of melodic landscapes—each a melody or poem—unified by the *Twelve Pillars of Wellness* and their distinct poetic signatures. These pillars act as the foundation, organizing the melodic landscapes into five thematic collections: *Nature, Endearment, Enlightenment, Quest, and*

Serenity. Within each collection, the melodic landscapes are further grouped into albums, each defined by a specific pillar of wellness. The melodic landscapes titles serve as evocative markers, reflecting the emotional and thematic essence of the work they represent, guiding readers through the layered narrative of well-being.

Some pillars share poetic forms, a purposeful echo of their thematic connections. For example, a melodic landscape tied to Tranquility might share the flowing, meditative rhythm of one linked to Serenity, their verses resonating like harmonious notes. This interplay of form and theme weaves the collections, albums, and titles into a cohesive whole, inviting readers to explore the profound unity beneath the diversity of human experience.

Your Invitation to Serenity

This journey is mine, but its echo could be yours. As you turn these pages, I invite you to listen to my *Serenity* collection—perhaps to tracks like *Mystic Journey* or *Contemplations*—and let their notes stir your own. What melody hums within you? What peace might it carry? Music and poetry have been my compass to serenity; may they guide you to yours, note by note, word by word. These twelve albums are more than music—they're a heartfelt toolbox for well-being, designed to resonate with your unique journey. Whether you need focus, courage, love, or calm, there's a crystal-inspired Melodic Landscape waiting for you. So, grab your headphones, find a cozy nook, and dive in. In the next section, we'll explore how to weave these melodies and verses into your daily life—turning them into rituals for creativity and calm. Serenity isn't just a goal; it's a practice, and it's yours to embrace.

In the next section, we'll explore how to weave these melodies and verses into your daily life—turning them into rituals for creativity and calm. Serenity isn't just a goal; it's a practice, and it's yours to embrace.

Healing Words: Poetry's Strength

Music as sanctuary provides a refuge

Music as sanctuary provides a refuge, where compositions shield against chaos, nurturing the soul.

Music has always been a sanctuary for me—a place where I can retreat, reflect, and find peace. In this chapter, I share how music, particularly my own melodic landscapes, has played a pivotal role in enhancing my sense of serenity and well-being. You'll be introduced to my five music collections, each designed with a specific intention, from fostering calmness to inspiring growth. Through personal anecdotes and insights, I'll illustrate how music can be a powerful tool for emotional balance and inner peace. As you read, I encourage you to consider how music might serve as a companion on your own journey toward serenity.

Welcome to exploring music's role in rituals, where sound becomes a gateway to inner peace. A a chapter that's incredibly close to my heart! Here, I'm sharing my original work—five music collections and twelve albums—all crafted with pure human creativity. These melodic landscapes are organized around five collections and *Twelve Pillars of Wellness*, inspired by the unique properties of crystals, blending personal stories with practical insights. Since this book, *How to Find Serenity with Words and Waves*, is all about guiding you toward wellness through poetry and soundscaping, I want this chapter to not only showcase my journey but also offer you tools to enhance your own sense of peace.

The Science Behind Music and Serenity

Have you ever wondered why music has such a magical way of calming us down? There's some fascinating science behind it! Music can lower cortisol levels (that pesky stress hormone), slow your heart rate, and even sync your brain waves to a more relaxed state. Imagine it like a gentle massage for your mind—rhythms that echo your heartbeat or melodies that lift your spirit can melt away tension. In this section, I'll share a bit about how music works its wonders, giving you a deeper appreciation for its role in serenity. Whether it's a soft piano piece or the sound of waves, music has a universal power to soothe—and I've felt it firsthand in my own life.

Music in Rituals: A Composer's Insight

My love affair with music did not begin with formal lessons or early piano practice. Instead, it was a natural pull, a gravitational force born from a keen ear that allowed me to deeply feel the notes.

As I'd sit at the piano, letting the melodies wash away whatever chaos the day had thrown at me, I found a refuge in sound—a space where instinct, not training, guided my hands. But it was during a particularly tough time—when life felt like a storm I couldn't escape—that I discovered music's true power to heal. Without formal training, I leaned into that instinctive pull, letting my fingers find their way across the keys. I started composing intentionally, pouring my need for peace into every chord. That's when my five music collections began to take shape, each one a stepping stone on my path to serenity.

This isn't just about my story, though—I hope it inspires you to think about the moments when music has been your refuge. What song or sound has carried you through a hard day?

Composer's Note: How My Music and Poetry Supports My Serenity Rituals

As someone who creates music, I've found that my own melodic landscapes—like those in the Quest Collection—are a big part of my serenity rituals. There's something about layering a gentle piano melody or a soft string arrangement behind a poem that helps me sink deeper into the moment. For example, I love pairing a poem about reflection with a quiet track from the collection—it's like the music cradles the words, making them feel even more alive.

On tougher days, I might choose a poem about finding peace and play it alongside a Melodic Landscape I've woven with flowing water and subtle chords. It's a reminder of how powerful this combination can be—not just for me, but for you too. Whether it's my music or something else that speaks to you, I hope you'll discover how sound can lift your ritual to a new level of calm.

The Five Collections

My creative journey rests on five collections—*Nature*, *Serenity*, *Quest*, *Enlightenment*, and *Endearment*—each tied to a pillar of wellness. These five collections group my twelve albums, each linked to a unique pillar of wellness. Through poetry and hand-crafted Melodic Landscapes, these works form the heart of *How to Find Serenity with Waves*. Below, I share their essence through poems inspired by their melodic landscapes titles, inviting peace into your life.

The titles of each Melodic Landscape serve as the foundation for the poems within their respective collections, and they are emphasized in **bold**.

To access all the poems, visit elChifMusic.com

A poem inspired by the titles of my melodic landscapes from the Nature collection

The Nature Collection carries you to a tranquil forest or a whispering stream with poetry and sound. Verses of rustling leaves and flowing water blend with gentle Melodic Landscapes, weaving serenity through nature's simplicity. This work eases stress, grounding you in a peaceful retreat that quiets the mind and restores your soul.

My Nature Poem

In **Desolation Sound**, where **distant shores** unfold,
White orchids in the sunset gleam, delicate and bold.
Thirteen brilliant lights ignite the velvet sky,
Nocturnal light a guardian, as shadows softly lie.

On **spring's seven of seven**, renewal gilds the air,
Season delight awakens, a song beyond compare.
A dancing breeze at sunrise lifts the soul from sleep,
Through **forestry dreams** so verdant, where secrets nature keeps.

Golden rain descends in beams, a fleeting, tender glow,
Breath of a feather brushes past, so light, so free, so slow.
Here, where waves and whispers weave a timeless tune,
I stand in awe, my heart undone beneath the morning's boon.

These shores, these stars, this fragrant bloom of grace,
A gift to hold, a truth to feel in life's unhurried pace.
In **Desolation Sound**, where dreams and silence blend,
Nature's love, eternal, calls me friend to friend.

A poem inspired by the titles of my melodic landscapes from the Serenity collection

In the Serenity Collection, poetry and sound explore balance—day softening into night, joy meeting sorrow—set to steady rhythms and warm tones. Serenity flows as a balm for anxiety, reflecting your need for steadiness and guiding you to a centered, poised calm amidst life's push and pull.

My Serenity Poem

Mystic Journey through the ages past,
Nostalgic Memories flicker fast—
A Poetry of Solitude, carved in stone,
Organic Moments, roots deep-grown.

Extraordinary Life, a dawn unfurls,
Colors of Life, in swirling whorls.
Contemplations rise like morning dew,
Life Is a Journey, threading through.

Unto the Light, we climb the air,
Sweet Lamentations whisper there.
Harmonic Void, a silence deep,
A Warrior's Lullaby rocks us to sleep.

Our journey stretches far and wide,
Memories and moments as our guide.
The *Colors of Life* paint every seam,
Each step a thread in the waking dream.

Contemplations, stars that softly gleam,
Steer us toward a brighter stream.
Unto the Light, we press ahead,
With *Sweet Lamentations* softly tread.

In the *Mystic Journey*, shadows play,
Nostalgic Memories mark the way.
A Poetry of Solitude we weave alone,
And *Organic Moments*, our hearts call home.

A poem inspired by the titles of my melodic landscapes from the Quest collection

The Quest Collection charts growth with poems of transformation—scaling peaks, braving storms—paired with Melodic Landscapes that swell from quiet to triumph. Serenity emerges as a quiet confidence, woven from the hope and strength of stretching beyond, lighting your path forward. *Titles of melodic* landscapes, *albums, or collections are shown in bold.*

My Quest Poem

The **Wonder of Life** unfolds, a tapestry so vast,
A journey rich with beauty, destined to ever last.
Life Goes On, through highs and lows it flows,
In **New Beginnings**, where fresh magic grows.

The Arrival of moments, gleaming pure and bright,
Fills our hearts with wonder and sheer delight.
Stepping **Into the Hope** that calls us near,
We find the strength to tread beyond our fear.

Yet beware the **Fragile Delusion**'s quiet snare,
And **Confetti Deceptions**, fleeting joys that glare.
In these **Strange Worlds**, where shadows twist the true,
We cling to wisdom, steady and anew.

At the **Vortex of a Purple Heart**, our courage lies,
A swirling core where strength and soul arise.
Like a **Trapezist Waltz**, we glide through life's design,
Holding firm through peace and storm, a balanced line.

Each **Tearful Quest** draws us closer to the glow,
Sharpening our sight as clearer visions grow.
On the **Carousel of Inverted Dimensions**, we spin,
Through life's wild turns, with grace beneath our skin.

For the **Wonder of Life** is a journey so divine,
Worth every step, every climb, in its grand design.
With each stride, we learn, we grow, we see,
Life's beauty shines again, eternally free.

A poem inspired by the titles of my melodic landscapes from the Enlightenment collection

The Enlightenment Collection binds us to others and the universe through poetry of empathy and unity, matched with harmonious tones that banish isolation. *Titles of melodic* landscapes, *albums, or collections are shown in bold.*

My Enlightenment Poem

Enchanting Moments gleam—so fleeting, so rare,
In Strength and in Weakness our truth lays bare.
Sensing Joy through trials, we learn to abide,
The Soliloquy of the Wise drifts far and wide.

The Call resounds—a yearning untamed,
Mindful Intentions shape what is named.
Authenticity unlocks bliss so true,
Edging the Truth where shadows construe.

Dispirited Revelation cuts deep in the soul,
Searching Into the Twilight, we seek to be whole.
A Perfect Tale of Imperfections unfolds;
Through the Storm of Tranquility, courage takes hold.

Farming Consciousness, we rise and renew,
Resilient Renewal—life's rhythm in view.

A poem inspired by the titles of my melodic landscapes from the Endearment collection

The Endearment Collection celebrates renewal with verses of fresh starts and self-kindness, lifted by bright, rejuvenating Melodic Landscapes. Serenity shines through healing and gratitude, offering a gentle release of burdens and a refreshed peace to carry you into tomorrow. *Titles of melodic* landscapes, *albums, or collections are shown in bold.*

My Endearment Poem

Once and again, we cross paths at dusk,
A reencounter beneath fading skies of gold.
Those things we feel, joy laced with sorrow's husk,
As tales of illusions unwind from years untold.

The day you were born, the dawn broke wide,
You are my sanctuary, a haven calm and still.
Through storm and shadow, you're where I reside,
In you, my heart finds peace no time can kill.

Her laughter rings, a lantern in the night,
This is it, a spark that claims my sight entire.
Love away the doubts beneath her gentle might,
A flame that warms my soul with pure desire.

A brotherhood forged in bonds unyielding, true,
In **strange worlds,** we chase a shared, defiant gleam.
Through twisted paths and trials we pursue,
A journey bound as one, our lifelong dream.

A song for my daughters, soft notes that soar,
And at **the reunion**, we'll dance where memories play.
Their voices echo love I can't ignore,
As we recall each cherished yesterday.

Once and again, we'll gather, hand in hand,
To share our triumphs, love away the pain.
Those things we feel, ties time cannot withstand,
As we embrace this life, again and again.

These five collections—Nature, Serenity, Quest, Enlightenment, and Endearment—serve as daily allies, blending sound and poetry for emotional support to nurture your journey toward serenity. As we'll explore in *My Journey: Music, Poetry, and the Path to Serenity*, they're companions for daily life, from calmness to renewal. Let these words and waves weave peace into your moments, one verse and one note at a time.

As we wrap up this chapter, I hope you feel the heartbeat of these collections—each one a unique blend of poetry and soundscaping designed to nurture your journey toward serenity. They're not just pieces to enjoy in passing; they're tools you can weave into your everyday life, as we'll explore more in this part of the book, My Journey: Music, Poetry, and the Path to Serenity. Whether you turn to Nature for calm, Serenity for balance, Quest for growth, Enlightenment for connection, or Endearment for renewal, these works are here to walk beside you. Let them inspire you, comfort you, and remind you that serenity is a practice—one that grows richer with every word you read and every wave you hear.

Creating Your Serenity Melodic Landscape

Now that you've met my collections, let's talk about your music. Serenity isn't one-size-fits-all, so I encourage you to build a Melodic Landscape that feels right for you. Start with slow tempos and gentle melodies—think songs that wrap around you like a cozy blanket. My albums might be a great place to begin, but don't stop there! Explore ambient tracks, nature sounds, or even classical melodic landscape that speak to you. Ask yourself: What emotions do I want to feel? Peace? Joy? Let those guide your playlist. This is your personal sanctuary—make it yours.

Music as a Daily Ritual

Here's a little secret: serenity grows stronger when you weave music into your everyday life. Try starting your day with a calming track—maybe one from my Serenity collection—to set a peaceful tone. During a midday slump, pop on something from the *Quest collection* to lift your spirits. At night, let the *Endearment collection* guide you into restful sleep.

Even a quick five-minute listen can reset your mood! Music isn't just background noise—it's a companion for your journey, just like it's been for mine. How could a daily music ritual bring more calm into your world?

Alongside music, poetry has been a source of healing and reflection in my life. In the next chapter, I will share selected poems that resonate with the themes of my music collections, illustrating how words can heal and complement the soothing power of sound.

Threads of Serenity – Music and Poetry Intertwined

The Restorative Strength of Poetry

The restorative strength of poetry mends the spirit, offering healing words in times of digital discord.

Just as music has been a source of solace, poetry has been a wellspring of healing and reflection in my life. In this chapter, I will share selected poems that resonate with the themes of my music collections, illustrating how words can touch our hearts and complement the soothing power of sound. You'll see how poetry and music together can create a tapestry of serenity, each enhancing the other's impact. Through these examples, I hope to inspire you to explore the poems that speak to your soul and to experience the healing power of words in your own life.

A Journey into Verse: How Poetry Captured Me

Picture this: me, a tech-savvy computer science geek, not exactly the type to swoon over stanzas or ponder pentameters. Poetry? That was uncharted territory—until a friend dropped a tantalizing hint about a poetry retreat in Ireland, led by the poet David Whyte. I'll admit, I had no idea who he was or what this retreat entailed, but the promise of Ireland's wild landscapes and vibrant culture? That was enough to hook this wanderlust-driven soul, let alone the fresh taste of an Irish beer.Off we went, cruising from Dublin along the rugged West Coast, through Clare and Mayo Counties. The scenery alone—rolling green hills, dramatic cliffs, and the endless dance of the Atlantic—was a feast for the eyes, whispering promises of an epic journey ahead. Our destination? Ballyvaughan, a quaint harbor in County Clare, Ireland, on the southern shores of Galway Bay, a little speck of a town nestled in the Burren region, oozing with unmistakable Irish charm… Those ten days in Ballyvaughan left a mark—a big, bold, beautiful one.

Upon arrival, David Whyte and his crew welcomed us with warm smiles, and I could sense something extraordinary brewing, not just beer. The Burren itself was a revelation—a vast, otherworldly expanse of limestone, stretching out like nature's own blank canvas. We'd set off each day on grand expeditions, trekking six or seven hours across this wild, untouched land. Along the way, we'd pause—sometimes atop a windswept hill, sometimes beside a trickling stream—and David would weave his poetic magic. His words danced through the air, mingling with the pristine beauty around us, stirring something deep within.Back at our cozy base each evening, the adventure continued. Picture this: hearty Irish feasts, the lively strum of traditional music, and David's voice rising above it all, reciting verses that felt like they were custom-made for our souls. No phones, no screens—just us, the music, and the moment, wrapped in a kind of purity that didn't leave room for judgment. It was like time slowed down, inviting us to simply *be*.That's when poetry snuck up on me, like a mischievous friend I never knew I needed. I watched as people around me—strangers turned companions—melted into tears or erupted in laughter, moved by the raw power of David's words. For me, it clicked: poetry wasn't just fancy phrases; it was a bridge to the soul, a secret passage to the human spirit.

Poetry has always felt to me like a bridge beyond time and space, a thread weaving through centuries, cultures, and voices—yet carrying the same pulse of the human spirit. I've read words penned hundreds of years ago that echoed my own thoughts, as if a distant soul had reached through history to whisper, *I understand*. In poetry, I see no borders, no separation—only the shared longing, love, pain, and wonder that bind us all. It's a language older than any spoken tongue, yet as fresh as the breath of the present moment. Each poem is a testament to our collective story, transcending the limits of time and geography to remind us that, at our core, we are one.

When I returned to Canada, I couldn't shake it. I dove into David Whyte's work, devouring his poems like treasures from a far-off land. The more I read, the more I realized: this was art at its most transcendent, a craft that could lift you to new heights of awareness. Since then, I've been on a quest—chasing poets, savoring their words, and marveling at the alchemy of language. Who knew a techie like me would fall head over heels for poetry? Turns out, sometimes the greatest adventures begin where you least expect them.

Poetry as a Window to the Soul

Poetry has always been a quiet friend to me—a way to make sense of life's highs and lows. On this journey toward serenity, I've found that words can heal in ways I never imagined, much like the melodies that have carried me through. In crafting this chapter, I've poured my heart into poems inspired by my music, organized into five collections that reflect my path to wellness. Each of the twelve albums within these five collections is represented by a pillar of wellness, tied to a crystal whose properties amplify the emotions I aim to evoke. As you read these poems and imagine the music behind them, I hope you'll feel the same sense of peace and possibility that guided me as I wrote.

Selected Poems: A Journey Through the Albums

As mentioned previously in my poems from each collection, my music is organized also in twelve albums that align with the *Twelve Pillars of Wellness* from these melodic landscape titles, I've also created original poems for each album—each one a heartfelt reflection of the album's theme and its crystal's energy. Below, I share a glimpse of some of these poems, inviting you into the world of sound and words that has shaped my serenity.

You can find the full set of poems, collections and albums at elChifMusic.com

About my Poems

Poems inspired by the five collections weave titles into verse, capturing themes of nature, quest, and endearment for serenity.

I'm excited to share the inspiration behind the original album poems you'll find here. Each poem was built around the titles of my melodic landscapes, not just as starting points but as guiding forces that shaped their structure and essence—allowing the spirit of the music to flow into words.

Each album poem aligns with a specific pillar of wellness, exploring how artistic expression can illuminate and deepen these vital dimensions of life.

I share this background to enrich your experience as you read. I hope it offers insight into the creative process and the connection between music, poetry, and the broader theme of wellness. Enjoy the journey!

Poem from the Sapphire Album

Through every breath, through every sight,
A world abundant, bathed in light.
A gift of plenty, grand design,
The Wonder of Life, *so divine.*

Organic Moment, *pure and free,*
A wealth of now, for all to see.
The present brims with gifts untold,
In time's embrace, where love unfolds.

Through trials faced, a harsh insight,
Yet in its wake, a future bright.
Abundance born from lessons learned,
Dispirited Revelation*, turned.*

A golden touch, a sacred rite,
Abundance falls in soft delight.
Blessings pour, a love unchained,
Golden Rain*, forever gained.*

Poem from the Topaz Album

My Topaz Poem

In silent nights, the soul takes flight,
A song of peace, a pure delight.
The heart finds calm, the mind is clear,
A Poetry of Solitude, ever near.

Life Goes On, through storm and sun,
Each trial faced, each victory won.
With every step, our spirits grow,
In strength and grace, blessings flow.

A path once dim, now shines with grace,
A destined dawn, a sacred place.
Hope blooms anew, dreams take their start,
The Arrival blesses every heart.

With every breath, a purpose gleams,
A quiet vow in silver beams.
The soul ascends, its riches blend,
Mindful Intentions never end.

The sky aglow with amber flame,
A gentle wind sings nature's name.
In beauty vast, we find our peace,
A Dancing Breeze at the Sunset, joy's release.

With grace they dance, the rhythm sways,
A waltz of life in bright arrays.
Each leap a gift, each turn a song,
A Trapezist Walse, where hearts belong.

Poetry and Music: Partners in Serenity

Poetry and music are like two hands reaching out to hold you—one with the rhythm of sound, the other with the weight of words. Together, they weave a magic that's hard to describe but easy to feel. Here's how they've worked in harmony on my journey—and how they can for you too:

   Stirring the Heart: Music sets the stage with its ebb and flow, while poetry paints the picture. When I listen to "" and read its poem, I'm not just hearing peace—I'm stepping into it. The melody quiets my mind, and the words give it a home.

   Deepening the Moment: Poetry slows us down, asking us to linger on a feeling or thought. Pair it with music—like the soft strains of —and suddenly, you're not just listening; you're reflecting, growing wiser with every note and line.

   A Full Experience: For me, combining these arts is like wrapping myself in a warm blanket of serenity. Together, they're a complete embrace of wellness.

   There is a section at the end containing the titles of all my melodic landscapes organized by collection and album.

   Try it yourself: play one of my albums and read its poem aloud. Let the sounds wash over you as the words sink in. It's a simple act, but it's amazing how it can shift your day.

My Creative Journey

Writing these poems wasn't just about crafting words from my melodic landscape titles—it was about finding myself in the process. Each title, like , sparked a memory or a hope, and the poem grew from there. It's been a healing dance, one where music led and poetry followed, showing me how creativity can mend the soul. I hope these pieces do the same for you, whispering peace when you need it most.

Your Turn to Create

This chapter isn't just my story—it's an open door for yours. Take these poems and albums as a starting point. Maybe *The Arrival* from my Topaz Album inspires you to jot down a line about your own joy, or *New Beginnings* from my Diamond album nudges you to dream up a fresh beginning. You don't need to be a poet or a musician—just let the words and waves guide you. Serenity isn't far off; it's waiting in your own voice.

As we've explored in this chapter, poetry is more than just words on a page—it's a bridge to the soul, a companion to music, and a powerful tool for healing. Through the selected poems and their connection to my music collections, I hope you've seen how these art forms can work in harmony to foster serenity. In the next chapter, we'll delve into the practical side of this journey, exploring how you can integrate music and poetry into your daily life to create your own sanctuary of calm. Together, we'll discover simple yet profound ways to make these practices a part of your wellness routine.

To fully appreciate the synergy between music and poetry, it's helpful to understand the structure behind my melodic landscapes. In the following chapter, I will explain the unique organizational system I developed for my music, which not only categorizes my work but also enhances the listener's experience.

Behind the Harmony: Crafting My Work

The Creative Process Behind the Book

Behind every melodic landscape lies a structure—a framework that gives it form and meaning. In this chapter, I will explain the unique organizational system I developed almost 100 original piano melodic landscapes, a structure that not only categorizes my work but also enhances the listener's experience. You'll learn how this system connects to the broader themes of the book, particularly the *Twelve Pillars of Wellness,* and how it can serve as a guide for your own creative explorations. As we delve into this structure, I invite you to consider how organization and intention can bring harmony not just to music, but to all aspects of our lives

The full range of my work with Waves and Words can be accessed here:
Visit *elChifMusic.com*

In the next chapter, we will explore these pillars, understanding how they relate to both my music and the broader pursuit of serenity.

Twelve Pillars of Wellness
Lessons Learned from My Practice

At the heart of my musical journey are the *Twelve Pillars of Wellness*, each represented by a crystal and embodying a quality that supports holistic well-being. In this chapter, we will explore these pillars, understanding how they relate to both my music and the broader pursuit of serenity. You'll learn about the qualities each crystal represents—from Amethyst for tranquility to Citrine for joy—and how they can complement your own wellness practices. Through this exploration, I hope to offer you a new lens through which to view your journey, one that integrates the healing power of sound, poetry, and the natural world.

Welcome, friends, to a chapter that's especially close to my heart. *The Twelve Pillars of Wellness* pulse through my five music collections, spanning twelve albums that weave together Melodic Landscapes and poetry to guide us toward serenity. Each collection groups albums that align with these pillars, blending sound and poetry.

What Are the *Twelve Pillars of Wellness*?

Imagine the Twelve Pillars as a circle of friends, each offering a unique gift to help you live a fuller, more balanced life. They represent qualities that nurture our minds, bodies, and spirits—everything from tranquility to joy, courage to wisdom. These pillars didn't just appear out of nowhere; they grew from my own experiences, shaping the music and poetry I've created over the years. Together, they form a framework that's supported me through life's highs and lows, and I hope they'll do the same for you.

Why Crystals?

You might be wondering why I paired each pillar with a crystal. For me, crystals are like little messengers from the earth—each one humming with its own energy, ready to amplify the qualities it represents. Across cultures and centuries, people have turned to crystals for healing and harmony, and I've found they bring a tangible magic to my work. When I hold an Amethyst or gaze at a Citrine, I feel a connection to the pillar it embodies, making the abstract feel real and alive. As we explore these crystals, I invite you to imagine their vibrations blending with the waves of my music and the rhythm of my words.

The Twelve Pillars and Their Crystals

In my musical journey, the *Twelve Pillars of Wellness* serve as guiding lights, each illuminating a path to holistic well-being. These pillars are not just abstract ideas; they are brought to life in my twelve albums, each named after a crystal or, in one case, a symbolic element like gold, reflecting its unique quality. Through these albums, I invite you to explore themes like strength, love, serenity, and transformation, with music and poetry as your companions on this journey.

The crystals of the Twelve Pillars amplify energies, complementing sound practices for holistic balance.

Crystals have been treasured for centuries, not only for their beauty but also for their believed healing energies. Each one vibrates at its own frequency, making them wonderful allies for nurturing wellness. By pairing each album with a specific crystal, I hope to deepen your connection to the music and the qualities it evokes. Whether you hold the crystal while listening, meditate with it, or simply keep it in mind, its energy can amplify your experience and help you embrace the pillar it represents.

These crystals and symbolic elements represent my albums, each embodying a pillar of wellness:

The Twelve Pillars of Wellness

Focus and Mental Clarity – *The Aquamarine Album*

Aquamarine's tranquil blue evokes the stillness of a calm sea, offering a sense of clarity and purpose. It supports your wellness by sharpening your focus, clearing mental fog, and helping you stay centered on your path.

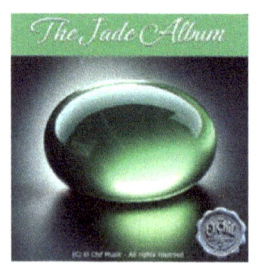

Calmness and Serenity – *The Jade Album*

Jade's cool, calming presence is like a breath of fresh air. It enhances wellness by quieting the mind and body, inviting you to sink into a state of peaceful serenity.

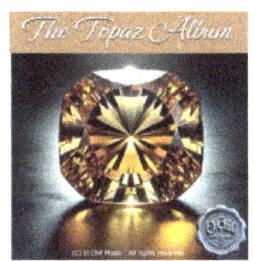

Healing and Balance – *The Topaz Album*

Topaz has a gentle, soothing energy that promotes healing and restores equilibrium. It supports your well-being by easing stress and bringing harmony to both body and soul.

Confidence and Inner Resilience – *The Peridot Album*

Peridot's vibrant green sparkles with vitality and strength. It supports wellness by building your confidence and inner resilience, empowering you to stand tall in any situation.

Strength and Courage – *The Diamond Album*

Diamonds are legendary for their toughness and brilliance, symbolizing the inner strength and courage we all carry. This crystal supports your wellness by inspiring you to face challenges with boldness and resilience.

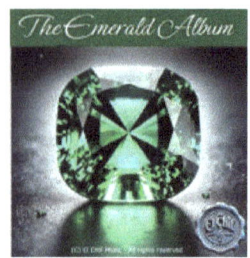

Wisdom and Increased Awareness – *The Emerald Album*

Emeralds, with their lush green hue, are stones of insight and growth. They encourage wellness by sharpening your intuition and opening your mind to greater awareness and understanding.

Tranquility and Inner Peace – *The Amethyst Album*

Amethyst's soft purple tones are all about calm and spiritual clarity. This crystal supports wellness by melting away anxiety and guiding you to a place of deep inner peace.

Love and Affection – *The Ruby Album*

The ruby's fiery red glow speaks of passion and devotion. It nurtures emotional wellness by fostering love—for yourself and others—and deepening the bonds that matter most.

Abundance and Blessings – *The Sapphire Album*

Sapphires shimmer with the promise of prosperity and good fortune. This crystal supports wellness by helping you see the abundance already in your life and inviting more blessings with a grateful heart.

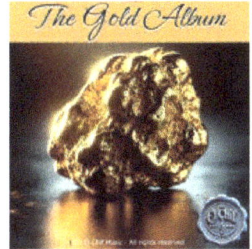

Prosperity and Compassion – *The Gold Album*

Gold, a precious metal, shines with the warmth of wealth and kindness. It supports wellness by encouraging a mindset of abundance and a compassionate spirit toward yourself and others.

Positivism and Optimism – *The Citrine Album*

Citrine glows with sunny, uplifting energy. It boosts your well-being by sparking joy, encouraging a positive outlook, and helping you see the bright side of every moment.

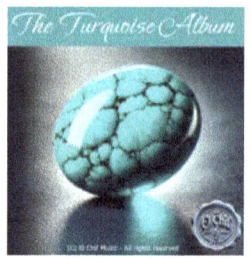

Transformation and Self-Realization – *The Turquoise Album*

Turquoise is a stone of change and discovery, guiding you toward your truest self. It enhances wellness by supporting personal growth and helping you uncover your potential.

While these twelve crystals and one symbolic element cover the qualities of my albums, they're part of a broader vision of twelve pillars woven into my five music collections. Together, they create a foundation for well-being that you can explore through sound and intention.

These crystals aren't just symbols—they're partners in the sound-based wellness practices I love to share. Music carries its own vibrations, touching our emotions and shifting our state of mind. When you pair an album's Melodic Landscapes with its corresponding crystal, the experience grows even richer. Imagine listening to the Amethyst Album with an amethyst in hand, letting its tranquil energy blend with the music's soothing waves. Or picture the Ruby Album filling your heart with love as you hold a ruby, amplifying that warmth within you.

Across my five collections, these pillars come alive through carefully crafted melodies and poetic words. Each album invites you to dive into a specific aspect of wellness—whether it's finding balance with Topaz or embracing optimism with Citrine. I encourage you to bring the crystals into your listening practice. Hold them, place them nearby, or simply focus on their qualities as you listen. Let their energies dance with the music and poetry, creating a nurturing, multisensory experience for your mind, body, and spirit.

How Crystals Complement Sound-Based Wellness Practices

Music and poetry are waves that wash over us, stirring emotions and soothing souls—and when you add crystals, it's like harmonizing two beautiful melodies. Sound carries its own vibrations, rippling through us to shift how we feel and think. Crystals, with their own frequencies, amplify this experience. Picture yourself listening to a gentle piano piece while holding an Amethyst—the music's calm flows deeper, wrapping you in tranquility. Or reading a heartfelt poem with Rose Quartz in hand, feeling love bloom with every word. Together, they create a symphony of wellness that's greater than the sum of its parts.

Each pillar, each crystal, connects to a melodic landscape of my journey—music and poetry that I've poured my heart into. As you explore them, try bringing a crystal along and see how it transforms your experience.

With the Twelve Pillars as a foundation, I invite you to join me in reflecting on our shared journey toward serenity. In the following chapter, I will share personal anecdotes and guided practices that combine music and poetry, offering you a multisensory experience to deepen your own practice.

Charting Your Course to Serenity

Creating Your Personal Map to Inner Peace

In "Finding Serenity Amid the Storm," we dive into the raw, unfiltered reality of life's turbulence and the resilient spirit that emerges within it. Through the compelling journeys of Sarah, James, Aisha, and Mark, this chapter illuminates how serenity can take root even in the fiercest tempests. Their experiences—marked by internal battles, external chaos, and fleeting respites—offer a powerful lens to reflect on our own. Here, serenity reveals itself not as an escape, but as a steady, intentional practice of finding balance amid the storm.

Finding Serenity Amid the Storm

Life rarely offers a perfect calm—sometimes chaos rages within us, sometimes it erupts around us, and often it's both. Through the stories of Sarah, James, Aisha, and Mark, we see how serenity isn't a distant dream but a journey shaped by small, deliberate steps. Whether wrestling with inner turmoil, outer upheaval, or a rare moment of peace, their paths reveal a truth: serenity is less about escaping chaos and more about navigating it, one breath, one choice at a time. Where do you find yourself in their struggles and triumphs?

When there is Chaos Inside and Chaos Outside

Imagine Sarah, a single mother who's just been laid off from her job. Bills are stacking up, her phone won't stop buzzing with creditor calls, and her apartment feels like a pressure cooker of stress (external chaos). Inside, her mind is a whirlwind of anxiety and self-doubt, racing with fears about the future and guilt over not providing enough for her kids (internal chaos). She's caught in a storm with no shelter, overwhelmed by turbulence both within and without.

This is a state where serenity feels impossibly distant—both the internal world of thoughts and emotions and the external environment of work, relationships, and daily life are in disarray. For Sarah, the chaos feeds itself: her racing mind amplifies the stress of unemployment, and the mounting external pressures deepen her inner turmoil. The path to serenity begins with finding a foothold amidst the storm—something small and manageable to break the cycle. She starts with her internal chaos, sitting for five minutes of deep breathing to quiet her mind, even briefly. This tiny island of stability gives her just enough clarity to tackle one external piece: she drafts a simple budget to feel a flicker of control. Progress is slow—another breath, another step, like calling a friend for support or applying for one job. Bit by bit, she builds resilience, reducing the overwhelm.

Serenity emerges not as a sudden calm, but as a gradual lightening of the load, forged through incremental victories over the chaos inside and out.

When there is Chaos Inside and Calm Outside

Picture James, a graphic designer living in a peaceful suburban home with a supportive spouse and a steady freelance gig. His external world is a quiet haven—no drama, no crises (external calm). Yet inside, he's a mess, tormented by guilt over a past fallout with a friend he never reconciled with. His mind spins with "what ifs" and self-reproach, a personal thunderstorm that drowns out the sunny day around him (internal chaos).

In this scenario, the external world offers stability—a serene backdrop of routine and support—but James can't enjoy it because his inner landscape is roiling with unresolved emotions and racing thoughts. The calm outside feels irrelevant when his guilt keeps him awake at night. To find serenity, he turns inward, leveraging the external peace as a resource. He starts by externalizing his chaos, scribbling his thoughts in a journal to make them less abstract. Talking to his spouse helps too, giving shape to the storm.

With this foothold, he leans into mindfulness—ten minutes of focusing on his breath—or seeks a therapist to unpack the guilt, slowly reframing it as a lesson rather than a life sentence. Self-compassion becomes his bridge: he can't change the past, but he can let it go.

Serenity grows as his inner state aligns with the tranquil world around him, the thunderstorm fading into a quiet sky he can finally appreciate.

In Situations When there is Calm Inside and Chaos Outside

Meet Aisha, a nurse in an understaffed emergency room during a city-wide blackout. Patients pour in, equipment malfunctions, and colleagues snap under pressure (external chaos). Yet Aisha moves through it with steady hands and a kind word for everyone, her mind clear and her heart unshaken (internal calm). She's an anchor in the storm, grounded despite the chaos swirling around her.

Here, serenity is half-won—Aisha's cultivated an inner peace that holds firm, even as her external environment erupts in unpredictability and stress. The emergency room is a battlefield, but she's not rattled; years of practice and a deep sense of purpose keep her centered. Her path to full serenity lies in maintaining this inner calm while navigating the outer tempest. She leans on quick boundaries—a two-minute break to breathe in a supply closet—or focuses on her mission to help others, which fuels her resilience. Where she can, she tames the chaos: organizing a triage list, calming a frantic co-worker. The trick is not letting the outside seep in; she guards her peace with quiet determination.

Serenity deepens as she reinforces her inner strength, turning the external storm into a proving ground for her steady mind rather than a threat to it.

In Situations when there is Calm Inside and Calm Outside

Consider Mark, a writer on a week-long retreat in a lakeside cabin. He's recently worked through old insecurities with a counselor, leaving him at peace with himself (internal calm). The setting is a dream—no deadlines, no noise, just the ripple of water and birdsong (external calm). Sipping coffee on the porch, he feels a rare, complete ease, the world inside and out in perfect harmony.

This is the sweet spot—both Mark's internal world and external surroundings are peaceful, a fleeting alignment that embodies serenity at its peak. His struggles are resolved, the lake mirrors his stillness, and for once, there's no fight to wage. The challenge isn't reaching serenity but savoring and sustaining it. He practices gratitude, jotting down three things he loves about this moment—the coffee's warmth, the water's sheen, his own quiet mind—to root himself in it. Mindfulness keeps him present; he resists worrying about the return to city life. This calm is a gift, but he knows it won't last forever, so he builds habits—daily meditation, a reflective walk—to carry him through future storms.

Serenity here is less a battle and more a celebration, maintained by appreciating the alignment and preparing for when chaos creeps back. It's a fragile balance, but one he's determined to hold as long as he can.

These narratives reveal serenity as a process, not a fixed state—sometimes a hard-won victory, sometimes a delicate equilibrium. Inner calm stands out as a cornerstone: whether it's Sarah grounding herself in chaos, James aligning with outer peace, Aisha shielding her steadiness, or Mark savoring his harmony, the mind's clarity anchors the journey. Small steps drive progress—breathing, budgeting, journaling, a triage list—proving serenity doesn't demand perfection, just momentum. Adaptability shapes the path: chaos inside calls for introspection, chaos outside for resilience or action. What strikes me is how dynamic serenity is—always in flux, always personal. Which scenario echoes your own path?

Uniting the Pillars of Wellness for Lasting Serenity

Building Your Framework for Lasting Peace

In "Uniting the Pillars of Wellness for Lasting Serenity," we explore a structured path to finding peace when chaos reigns both within and without —this chapter unveils a roadmap that begins with taming the inner tempest and gradually extends to mastering the outer turmoil. Each step, from healing and focus to gratitude and connection, weaves together the essential pillars of wellness, offering a practical yet profound progression toward a serenity that endures.

In Situations when there is Chaos Inside and Chaos Outside

Example Recap: Sarah, recently laid off, faces external chaos (bills, job loss) and internal chaos (anxiety, self-doubt).

Path Overview: With both worlds in turmoil, the optimum path starts by stabilizing the internal chaos to create a foundation, then tackles the external chaos incrementally, building toward serenity.

Detailed Path and Order:
1, Healing and Balance: Calming internal chaosFirst, Sarah addresses her internal chaos by restoring equilibrium. She sits quietly for 10 minutes, focusing on slow, deep breaths to soothe her racing heart and mind. This healing pause counters the anxiety overwhelming her system.

2. Focus and Mental Clarity: Sharpen internal focus

With a sliver of balance, she sharpens her focus. She picks one thought—say, "I need a plan"—and lets others fade, reducing the mental noise. A clear mind becomes her anchor in the storm.

3. Calmness and Serenity: Build internal peace

Using this clarity, she builds a moment of calm. A short meditation (e.g., visualizing a still lake) helps her feel grounded, even as bills pile up. This pillar is her internal island of stability.

4. Confidence and Inner Resilience: Strengthens internal resolve

Feeling calmer, Sarah taps into resilience. She tells herself, "I've survived tough times before," boosting her belief in her ability to endure. This confidence fuels her next steps.

5. Strength and Courage: Begins addressing external chaos

Begins addressing external chaos

Now, she turns outward with courage. She tackles one external issue—making a budget—to confront the chaos head-on. It's daunting, but her growing resilience powers her through.

6. Wisdom and Increased Awareness: Guides external actions With a budget drafted, she gains perspective. She prioritizes essentials (rent, food) and lets go of what's out of her control (immediate job offers), wisely focusing her energy.

7. Positivism and Optimism: Maintains hopeSarah reframes her situation: "This is a chance to find a better job." This shift lifts her spirits, reducing the weight of external pressures.

8. Tranquility and Inner Peace: Deepens internal calm

As external chaos eases slightly, she reinforces her inner peace with a walk outside, letting nature's rhythm steady her further.

9. Prosperity and Compassion: Extends calm outward

She reaches out to a friend for job leads, offering help in return. This mutual support fosters a sense of abundance amid scarcity.

10. Transformation and Self-Realization: Reflects growth

Reflecting on her progress, Sarah sees herself growing stronger. She's not just surviving—she's evolving through the chaos.

11. Love and Affection: Connects with others

She hugs her kids, drawing strength from their bond, which softens both her internal and external worlds.

12. Abundance and Blessings: Cultivate gratitude

Finally, she lists small wins—breathing easier, a plan in place, family love—cultivating gratitude that seals her serenity.

Outcome: Sarah's serenity emerges as a resilient calm, built step-by-step from internal healing to external action, with all pillars aligning to lift her from the storm.

In Situations when there is Chaos Inside and Calm Outside

Example Recap: James, in a peaceful home with a steady job, is tormented by guilt over a past mistake. **Path Overview**: With external calm as a resource, the focus is on resolving internal chaos, aligning his mind with his serene surroundings.

Detailed Path and Order:'

1. **Tranquility and Inner Peace**: Use external calm to soothe insideJames leverages his calm environment first. He sits by a window, listening to birds, letting the external peace seep in to quiet his guilt-ridden thoughts.

2. **Healing and Balance**: Restore internal equilibriumNext, he heals his emotional turmoil. He writes down his guilt—every "what if"—to release it from his mind, restoring balance by facing it directly.

3. **Focus and Mental Clarity**: Clears internal noiseWith the chaos externalized, he clears his head. He focuses on one truth: "I can't change the past," letting extraneous regrets dissolve.

4. **Calmness and Serenity**: Build internal peaceHe builds on this clarity with a mindfulness exercise, breathing deeply to anchor himself in the present, not the past. Serenity begins to take root.

5. **Positivism and Optimism**: Shifts internal narrativeJames reframes his guilt: "That mistake taught me empathy." This positive lens lightens his inner burden.

6. **Confidence and Inner Resilience**: Builds self-beliefHe affirms, "I'm stronger than this guilt," bolstering his resilience to let it go. This self-belief steadies him further.

7. **Wisdom and Increased Awareness**: Gains perspectiveWith perspective, he sees the guilt as a lesson, not a life sentence. Wisdom guides him to release what he can't fix.

8. **Love and Affection**: Connects with supportive environmentHe talks to his spouse, accepting their support. This connection softens his

self-judgment, aligning his heart with his calm home.

9. **Strength and Courage**: Reinforce. Internal growthIt takes guts to forgive himself, but he does—writing a letter to his old friend (unsent) to close the chapter.

10. **Transformation and Self-Realization**: Recognize changeReflecting, he realizes he's grown kinder from this struggle, transforming pain into purpose.

11. **Abundance and Blessings**: Appreciate the calmHe lists blessings—his home, his spouse, his growth—deepening his peace with gratitude.

12. **Prosperity and Compassion**: Extends peace inwardsHe extends compassion inward, treating himself as he would a friend, solidifying serenity in harmony with his surroundings.

Outcome: James' serenity blooms as his inner storm fades, fully syncing with the external calm through a journey of healing, wisdom, and self-love.

In Situations when there is Calm Inside and Chaos Outside

Example Recap: Aisha, a nurse, stays steady in a chaotic ER during a crisis. **Path Overview**: With internal calm established, the path maintains it while reducing external chaos, deepening serenity through resilience and influence.

Detailed Path and Order:

1. **Calmness and Serenity**: Reinforce internal peace – Aisha begins by re-

inforcing her existing calm. During a brief break, she breathes deeply, visualizing her steady core amidst the ER's frenzy.

2. **Focus and Mental Clarity**: Sharpen focus amid chaos – She sharpens her focus—prioritizing patients over panic—keeping her mind clear despite the chaos. This clarity sustains her peace.

3. **Confidence and Inner Resilience**: Protect internal state – She reminds herself, "I've handled this before," fortifying her resilience. This pillar shields her calm from external stress.

4. **Tranquility and Inner Peace**: Deepens calm – A quick moment of stillness—closing her eyes for 30 seconds—deepens her peace, ensuring the chaos doesn't seep in.

5. **Strength and Courage**: Addresses external chaos

6. With her calm secure, she acts boldly: directing a triage line to tame the ER's disorder, her courage shaping the environment.

7. **Wisdom and Increased Awareness**: Navigating external challenges – She assesses what she can control (task delegation) and releases what she can't (equipment failures), wisely conserving energy.

8. **Prosperity and Compassion**: Influences external environment – Aisha comforts a scared patient, her compassion rippling outward to calm others, subtly shifting the ER's vibe.

9. **Healing and Balance**: Restores external equilibrium – She restores balance by taking a five-minute break to stretch, countering the physical toll of chaos with self-care.

10. **Positivism and Optimism**: Maintains hope"We'll get through this," she tells her team, lifting spirits and reinforcing her own steadiness with hope.

11. **Love and Affection**: Builds connections – A kind word to a struggling colleague strengthens team bonds, grounding her further in connection.

12. **Transformation and Self-Realization**: Growth through adversity – She

reflects, "This chaos proves my strength," growing through the challenge.

13. **Abundance and Blessings**: Appreciates progress – Post-shift, she counts blessings—lives saved, her own resilience—cementing serenity despite the storm.

Outcome: Aisha's serenity deepens as she holds her calm and tames the chaos, her pillars creating a ripple effect of peace in a turbulent world.

In Situations when there is Calm Inside and Calm Outside

Example Recap: Mark, at a tranquil lake cabin, feels at peace after resolving personal struggles. **Path Overview**: With serenity achieved, the focus is on sustaining and enriching it, preparing for future disruptions.

Detailed Path and Order:

1. **Calmness and Serenity**: Sustain peace – Mark starts by savoring his calm, sitting by the lake to fully inhabit the moment, deepening his existing peace.

2. **Tranquility and Inner Peace**: Deepens harmony – He meditates by the water, letting its stillness mirror his mind, reinforcing harmony inside and out.

3. **Abundance and Blessings**: Cultivate gratitude – He lists gratitudes—the lake, his clarity, this respite—anchoring himself in the richness of now.

4. **Focus and Mental Clarity**: Stays present – Staying present, he lets future

worries fade, focusing only on the coffee in his hand, the breeze on his skin.

5. **Positivism and Optimism**: Maintains hopeful mindset" – This peace is mine to keep," he thinks, building a hopeful mindset to carry forward.

6. **Love and Affection**: Nurtures connections – He calls a friend to share the moment, letting connection enhance his calm without breaking it.

7. **Healing and Balance**: Ensures ongoing balance – A walk by the shore maintains his balance, ensuring no lingering tension creeps in to disrupt this state.

8. **Confidence and Inner Resilience**: Prepares for future – He affirms, "I can return here mentally anytime," preparing his resilience for less calm days.

9. **Wisdom and Increased Awareness**: Gains perspective – Mark reflects on life's cycles—calm follows chaos—gaining perspective to sustain this peace.

10. **Prosperity and Compassion**: Extends serenity outward – He leaves a kind note for the cabin's next guest, extending his serenity outward.

11. **Strength and Courage**: Builds habits for resilience – He commits to daily meditation, bravely building habits to protect this state long-term.

12. **Transformation and Self-Realization**: Locks in growth "I'm whole here," he realizes, his growth locking in serenity as a lasting truth.

Outcome: Mark's serenity becomes a living practice, sustained and enriched by all pillars, ready to weather future storms.

Summary of Order Rationale

- **Chaos Inside and Outside:** Starts internally (Healing, Focus, Calmness) to create a base, then shifts outward (Strength, Wisdom) for control, ending with enrichment (Love, Abundance).

- **Chaos Inside and Calm Outside:** Uses external calm first (Tranquility, Healing), builds internal strength (Positivism, Confidence), and completes with growth (Transformation, Prosperity).

- **Calm Inside and Chaos Outside:** Protects internal calm (Calmness, Focus), addresses external chaos (Strength, Wisdom), and enhances both (Compassion, Abundance).

- **Calm Inside and Calm Outside:** Deepens existing serenity (Calmness, Tranquility), sustains it (Focus, Confidence), and prepares for future (Strength, Transformation).

The *Twelve Pillars of Wellness* offer a clear path to the optimal state of calm inside and serenity outside, no matter the starting point. From chaos everywhere, use Healing and balance and Strength and courage to restore order. From internal chaos, lean on Tranquility and Inner peace and Positivism and Optimism to align with external serenity. From external chaos, maintain Calmness and serenity while applying Wisdom and Increased Awareness to create peace. Once achieved, sustain the optimal state with Love and affection and Transformation and self-realization, ensuring lasting wellness through the power of these pillars.

The journey to serenity is ongoing. As we conclude, let's look ahead and plan your next steps. This chapter offers practical guidance on using my music collections and other tools to create your own wellness practice. You'll find suggestions for pairing melodic landscapes with meditation, reflection, and daily activities, along with encouragement to explore poetry and soundscaping in ways that resonate with you. Remember, serenity is not a distant goal but a daily practice.

Before we part, let's reflect on our journey. In the Epilogue, we'll revisit key insights, celebrate progress, and envision a future of harmony and peace.

End of Part VI

Part VII

The Symphony of Tomorrow – Weaving Art, Spirit, and Harmony

*"The most beautiful thing we can experience is the mysterious.
It is the source of all true art and science."*
— Albert Einstein

Prelude to Part VII
The Symphony of Tomorrow – Weaving Art, Spirit, and Harmony

In a world increasingly shaped by artificial intelligence and digital noise, the quest for serenity becomes both more challenging and more essential. Yet, amidst the clamor of modern life, there lies a timeless path to peace—one woven from the threads of art, spirit, and harmony. This part of the book invites you to imagine a future where these elements are not just distant ideals but the very fabric of our existence. It is a symphony we compose together, note by note, through the enduring power of creativity and the irreplaceable strength of the human spirit.

In the chapters that follow, we embark on a journey of reflection and revelation. We'll begin by looking back, contemplating the path that has led us to this moment. Next, we'll celebrate the unique qualities of the human spirit—those aspects of our being that no machine can replicate. Building on this, we'll cast our gaze forward, outlining practical steps to create a future where harmony prevails. Finally, we'll delve into the transformative role of the arts, particularly music and poetry, which serve as both a mirror to our deepest truths and a beacon guiding us toward a serene tomorrow.

As we weave together these threads of art, spirit, and harmony, we do more than find serenity for ourselves—we contribute to a collective symphony. This is a harmonious future where technology enhances rather than overshadows humanity, and the human spirit remains central to all creation. Welcome to 'The Symphony of Tomorrow'.

Reflecting on the Journey
Lessons from Our Path to Serenity

Looking back on the path we've walked together, it's clear that the journey toward serenity is as unique as each of us. In this chapter, we will reflect on the key moments and insights from the book, celebrating the small victories and the deeper understanding we've gained. You're invited to consider how far you've come and to acknowledge the growth that has already taken place. Every step, no matter how small, is a testament to your commitment to a life of greater peace and harmony.

Let's retrace our steps through the landscapes of words and waves that have guided us here. This book has been a voyage of discovery, where poetry and music—timeless echoes of the human soul—have illuminated the path to wellness and serenity. We've wandered through the *Serenity Collection*, a series of melodies flowing like a gentle river, washing away the chaos of the world and inviting us to rest in stillness. We've climbed the heights of the *Enlightenment Collection*, its compositions stirring our hearts with whispers of wisdom and wonder. All along, the *Twelve Pillars of Wellness* stood as steadfast guides, each shimmering with the properties of its crystal—amethyst for calm, rose quartz for love, citrine for joy—reflecting qualities we've nurtured within ourselves.

Picture this journey as a Melodic Landscape we have created together. It begins with soft, tentative notes—a flute's breath or a single strummed chord—mirroring those first moments when we opened ourselves to serenity. As the melody unfolds, it meets swells of challenge, perhaps a clash of cymbals or a minor key, echoing obstacles we've faced. But listen closely: each dissonance resolves into harmony, a reminder of the balance we've learned to find. By the end, the Melodic

Landscape rises into a warm, resonant chord—a celebration of the resilience, growth, and peace we've cultivated.

Throughout these pages, you've likely felt the stirrings of transformation. Perhaps you've jotted down a poem in a quiet moment, letting emotions spill onto the page. Maybe you've curated a Melodic Landscape that hums with the rhythm of your breath, a personal anthem of calm. These acts are victories worth celebrating—proof that serenity is a living practice, not a distant dream. You might notice the world looks brighter now, your inner voice speaks with kindness, or a simple melody lifts your spirit. These subtle shifts are the footprints of your growth, marking a path toward a harmonious life.

Now, let's consider why this journey matters today. We live in an age where artificial intelligence weaves itself into our daily tapestry, offering efficiency and marvels once only imagined. But amidst this digital dawn, our humanity shines as a beacon no algorithm can replicate. Poetry and music are more than art forms; they are the pulse of our existence. When you craft a verse, you breathe life into joys and sorrows—emotions a machine can mimic but never truly feel. When you weave a Melodic Landscape, you channel intuition that dances beyond data, healing in ways technology cannot grasp. These creations, born from the spark of being human, are ours alone.

In a world shaped by AI, our capacity for empathy and connection sets us apart. Think of a poem that felt like a hand reaching out, saying, "I understand." Or how sharing a melody with a loved one created a bridge of unspoken understanding. These moments weave a web of community that technology can enhance but never replace. The *Twelve Pillars of Wellness*—mindfulness, creativity, gratitude, and more—are tools to anchor us in our humanity, helping us thrive in a fast-paced, often impersonal landscape.

As this chapter closes, I invite you to carry these gifts forward. Let poetry and soundscaping be your companions, sanctuaries of serenity you can return to anytime. Write a line when the day feels heavy, hum a tune when you need a lift, share them to spread the harmony you've found. In a world where synthetic voices grow louder, your human voice—raw, real, beautifully imperfect—is more vital than ever. This journey doesn't end here; it's a beginning, a ripple of peace you can send into the world.

Through this reflection, we've celebrated not just our growth but the essence of what makes us human: our ability to create, feel, and connect. These qualities light the way toward a future where serenity is a reality we build together.

The Irreplaceable Human Spirit
What Makes Us Truly Human in a Digital Age

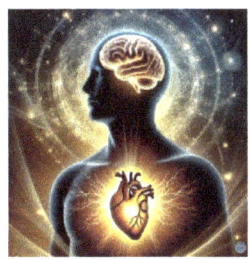

In a world increasingly automated and disconnected, it's essential to cherish the qualities that make us human—our creativity, empathy, and capacity for connection. In this chapter, we explore how these qualities are central to our quest for serenity and how nurturing them leads to a more fulfilling life. Through stories and reflections, we celebrate the human spirit's ability to find beauty and peace amid chaos. As you read, honor your own humanity and the unique gifts you bring to the world.

The Unique Power of Human Creativity

Creativity is a cornerstone of our humanity. Consider my melodic landscape *Navigating the Reverie*, a Melodic Landscape born from standing by a lake, watching jade-green water ripple under a soft breeze. That moment wasn't just about sounds; it was about the peace I felt, the memories it stirred, and my connection to nature. Human creativity is a piece of our soul, shaped by experiences—an essence no algorithm can replicate.

AI can generate a symphony or poem in seconds, and that's impressive. But it operates based on patterns and data, not a heart moved by a sunset or a quiet walk. When you write a poem or create a Melodic Landscape, you pour in your joys, struggles, and unique perspective. That's your superpower, a key to serenity.

As you explore this book's practices, let your creativity flow—it's what makes you irreplaceably human.

Empathy and Connection: The Heart of Wellness

Empathy is another gift I cherish deeply in our humanity. It's the ability to step into someone's shoes, feel with them, and connect in ways that enrich life. Imagine sharing a poem with a friend—not just words, but a window into your world. Or crafting a Melodic Landscape to help someone unwind, its waves carrying your care. These acts build bridges of understanding.

AI might suggest a playlist to lift your mood, but it can't sit with you in silence when you're hurting or laugh over a shared memory. That's uniquely human. These connections, woven through empathy, are like threads in a cozy blanket, wrapping us in wellness and belonging. Keep sharing your poetry, music, and heart—it's how we heal, grow, and find serenity together.

Growth and Learning: A Human Journey

We're always growing, shaped by life's joys and challenges. That's a journey AI can't take—it optimizes data but doesn't wrestle with doubt or celebrate breakthroughs like we do. In this book, poetry and soundscaping are tools for growth. Perhaps you've written a poem to untangle emotions or created a Melodic Landscape or a melody to find calm. That's you, evolving through experience.

In a world where machines outpace us in efficiency, our human spirit is our strength. We weep at melodies, share in pain, dream beyond code. But if we lean too heavily on AI, we risk losing these gifts, turning life into a sterile exchange of data. Today, we must nurture our creativity, cherish connections, and let emotions guide us. Technology can help, but our human touch keeps life vibrant and **serene**.

Why It's Vital to Be Human Today

Technology is everywhere—AI composes music, writes stories, even chats like a friend. It's advancing fast, and while its capabilities are remarkable, it can't capture the essence of being human. Our emotions, empathy, and ability to find meaning fuel art that stirs the soul, like *Searching Into the Twilight*, born from a quiet moment AI can mimic but never feel.

In a world where machines outpace us in efficiency, our human spirit is our strength. We weep at melodies, share in pain, dream beyond code. But if we lean too heavily on AI, we risk losing these gifts, turning life into a sterile exchange of data. Today, we must nurture our creativity, cherish connections, and let emotions guide us. Technology can help, but our human touch keeps life vibrant and **serene**.

Celebrating You, the Human Spirit

Here we are, celebrating you and all that makes you human. Your creativity, empathy, and growth are irreplaceable, the heart of this journey. Through poetry and soundscaping, you have tools to express your voice, connect with others, and find peace in a noisy world. The world needs your voice.

Keep going. Write that poem, even if it's rough. Craft that Melodic Landscape, even if it's just for you. Share your art, stories, heart—they're gifts only you can give. By embracing your humanity, you enrich your life and light the way for a harmonious world. Let's carry this serenity forward, together.

Envisioning a Harmonious Future

How We Can Build It Together

What would a world look like with serenity at its core? In this chapter, we outline practical steps to build such a future—a world where harmony prevails, creativity and compassion are valued, and each of us contributes to collective well-being. By integrating poetry, soundscaping, and mindful living into daily life, we can create ripples of peace that touch others. As you envision this future, consider your role in bringing it to life, knowing every act of serenity is a step toward a more peaceful world.

A Blueprint for Serenity

Picture a future where AI manages mundane tasks—optimizing traffic routes, generating grocery lists—freeing us to pursue what inspires us: crafting poetry, layering Melodic Landscapes, building bonds. To achieve this, we must act intentionally. Here are practical steps to start today:

- **Nurture Your Creative Practice**: Set aside time to write a poem or create a Melodic Landscape. My *Soliloquy of the Wise*, tied to moonstone's intuition, began with a single whispered line. Yours can too. Even 10 minutes a day strengthens your creative spark.

- **Leverage Technology Wisely**: Use AI tools—like soundscaping apps—to amplify your creativity, but make it personal. Add your voice or story to ensure it reflects your humanity. For example, an AI-generated chord progression can be a starting point, but your melody makes it unique.

- **Advocate for Ethical AI**: Support technology that prioritizes wellness and balance, inspired by crystals like turquoise for calm communication. Speak up for AI that enhances human connection, not just efficiency.

- **Build Community Through Art**: Share your creations—a poem, a Melodic Landscape—with others. My *White Orchids in the Sunset* grew from quiet moments shared with friends. Host a poetry circle or co-create a Melodic Landscape to foster connection.

Partnering with Technology

AI is a powerful ally when guided by human values. Imagine using an AI tool to spark a rhyme, then weaving your story into it, perhaps inspired by garnet's grounding strength from my *Peridot* album. Or consider a soundscaping app suggesting frequencies, but you layer them with the hum of rose quartz's soothing energy. Technology amplifies our efforts, but our emotions and intentions shape the outcome.

To maintain this balance, approach AI with intention. Ask: *How can this tool serve my wellness?* Use it to handle repetitive tasks, leaving space for creativity and connection. By partnering thoughtfully, we ensure technology supports, not overshadows, our humanity.

Shaping a Collective Future

This vision isn't a distant dream—it's a world we build now. Every poem you write, every Melodic Landscape you share, sends ripples of serenity outward. Imagine a society where schools teach soundscaping alongside math, where workplaces offer poetry breaks to foster empathy. These small acts scale up, creating a culture that values the human spirit.

You can contribute by modeling serenity. Share a Melodic Landscape with a colleague to ease stress or gift a poem to a neighbor. Advocate for community spaces—like art workshops—that prioritize wellness. My *Topaz* album, reflecting heart-healing energy, became a cornerstone of this vision through shared listening. Your actions can do the same.

Your Role in the Symphony

You're not just a reader—you're a co-creator of this harmonious future. Start small: pick up a pen, a crystal, a guitar. Create something that's yours. Partner with AI to enhance, not replace, your vision. Share your art to connect. These steps, rooted in the *Twelve Pillars of Wellness*, build a world where serenity is the rhythm of our days.

As we dream of this future, we turn next to the arts that fuel it. The following chapter explores how music and poetry, as expressions of our soul, anchor us in serenity and inspire a vibrant tomorrow.

Music, Poetry, and our Human Soul

Personal Transformation Through Art

Personal transformation through art unfolds as poetry and music reshape perspectives, leading to deeper serenity.

Have you ever felt overwhelmed by technology's buzz, as if you're losing touch with what makes you human? In a world of screens and algorithms, it's easy to forget the profound power of connection. Yet, our creativity, empathy, and ability to find meaning set us apart—and these qualities, expressed through music and poetry, lead us to serenity. In this chapter, we explore how embracing our humanity through art preserves well-being, strengthens communities, and grounds us in a vibrant, soulful life.

The Soulful Power of Art

Music and poetry are more than creative outlets—they're the language of our soul. Consider a moment when I composed a gentle melodic landscape inspired by rose quartz's soothing energy. A listener shared that it felt like a hug they didn't know they needed. That connection, born from human emotion, is irreplaceable. No algorithm can replicate the warmth of a melody crafted from lived experience or a poem that captures the ache of loss.

Think of a time a song or poem stopped you in your tracks—perhaps Bob Dylan's *Blowin' in the Wind*, with its call to reflect on life's questions. These works resonate because they come from human hearts, inviting us to feel, heal, and connect. My five collections and twelve albums, each tied to a *pillar of wellness* and a crystal-like amethyst for calm, are testaments to this truth. They're not just art—they're invitations to find serenity.

Healing Through Expression

Creating art is a path to wellness. When you write a poem, you untangle emotions, giving voice to joys or sorrows. A Melodic Landscape, layered with waves or chimes, can calm your mind, like my *Emerald* album, tied to *Wisdom and Increased Awareness*. These acts ground us, offering a sanctuary from digital noise. I recall a reader who penned a verse about her late father, finding peace in the words. That's the power of human creativity—transforming pain into beauty.

You don't need to be a poet or composer. Jot down a line about a sunset. Hum a tune that feels like home. These small acts reconnect you with your soul, fostering resilience and calm. They remind us that serenity is a necessity, a lifeline to our deepest values.

Building Bonds Through Art

Art also weaves communities. Sharing a poem in a circle or playing a Melodic Landscape for a friend creates bonds technology can't match. I once hosted a workshop where participants crafted Melodic Landscapes together, inspired by citrine's joy. The room hummed with laughter and understanding—no AI could replicate that energy. These moments remind us we're not alone, strengthening the web of human connection.

Consider starting a poetry group or sharing a playlist with a loved one. These acts, rooted in empathy, spread serenity. My *Serenity Collection* became a shared experience for listeners, sparking conversations about peace. Your art can do the same, building bridges in a fragmented world.

Anchoring Our Humanity

In an AI-driven world, music and poetry anchor us. They're uniquely human, fueled by emotions and stories no machine can live. AI might suggest a rhyme, but only you can pen a verse from your heart. A soundscaping app might offer sounds, but your intuition shapes them into meaning. This grounding lets us approach technology with purpose, ensuring it serves our wellness.

My work—each melodic landscape, each poem—is a step toward peace. Yours can be too. Write, sing, share. Let art remind you of your spark. As we navigate change, these creations keep us vibrant, connected, and true to our soul.

A Call to Create

I see a future where our humanity shines—a world where music and poetry are the pulse of our days. It starts with you. Pick up a pen, hum a melody, share a verse. You're a poet, a sound weaver, a visionary. My collections stand as proof of art's power, and they're here to inspire your own.

To support your journey, the final chapter offers resources—poetry prompts, soundscaping tools, guided exercises, and reading—to deepen your practice. Let's create a world where serenity flows through every word and wave, and being human is celebrated as the gift it is.

End of Part VII

Conclusion
A Call to Harmony

As we reach the conclusion of this book, it's time to take the insights and tools we've gathered and put them into action. In this chapter, I will issue a call to harmony, urging you to integrate the practices of poetry, soundscaping, and mindful reflection into your daily life. You'll find encouragement to share the gift of serenity with others, whether through small acts of kindness or by inspiring those around you to embark on their own journeys. As you prepare to close this book, remember that the path to harmony is one we walk together, and that your commitment to serenity can be a light for others.

A Poetic and Visionary Reflection: The Ongoing Journey of Music, Poetry, and Wellness

Dear reader, imagine standing at the edge of a vast ocean, waves whispering secrets of the ages as they lap at your feet. Above, the wind carries a melody—a song woven from the threads of human voices lifted in poetry and music across centuries. This is where we've been together in these pages: exploring the timeless dance of words and waves, of poetry and soundscaping, as pathways to wellness.

Now, cast your gaze forward. We live in a world where artificial intelligence hums in the background, crafting symphonies and verses with mechanical precision. Yet, what sets us apart is not what machines can do, but what they cannot: feel the ache of a sunset, dream in metaphors, or find solace in a melody born of a broken heart. Music and poetry are not just art forms—they are the pulse of our humanity, beating strong against the tide of automation. Wellness, too, is more than a state; it's the harmony we cultivate within, a garden tended by human hands and hearts.

Picture a future where technology doesn't overshadow us but lifts us higher. Imagine Melodic Landscapes tailored to soothe your spirit, crafted with the aid of AI yet infused with the warmth of human intention. Envision poetry circles in virtual spaces, where voices from every corner of the earth weave a tapestry of shared stories—each word a testament to our lived experience. This is the ongoing journey: not a retreat from progress, but an embrace of it, with our humanity as the guiding star. In this vision, the crystals of our collections—symbols of strength, clarity, and peace—shine brighter, reminding us that serenity is ours to claim, no matter the age we live in.

An Invitation to Inspiration, Possibility, and Connection

So, where do we go from here? The beauty of this journey is that it doesn't end with the last page—it's yours to carry forward. Think of the busy parent who pauses each morning to read a poem, finding a moment of calm before the storm of the day. Or the friend who crafts a Melodic Landscape of rustling leaves and distant waves, sharing it to ease a loved one's restless mind. These are not grand gestures, but small ripples—ripples that spread serenity far beyond what we can see.

I'll let you in on a little piece of my own story: poetry and soundscaping have been my companions through life's highs and lows. When words felt too heavy to speak, a scribbled verse gave them wings. When the world grew loud, the hum of a Melodic Landscape brought me back to center. I share this not as an expert, but as someone who's walked this path alongside you, finding harmony in the chaos. And I believe you can too.

In a time when AI can mimic so much, it's our human spark—our ability to create, connect, and care—that lights the way. You don't need to be a poet or a musician to join this vision; you need only be you. Start small: jot down a line that moves you, hum a tune that lifts your spirit, or sit quietly with the sounds around you. Share what you discover—a poem with a friend, a moment of peace with your community—and watch how it grows.

CONCLUSION

This book may end, but your journey doesn't. You are part of something bigger now—a chorus of voices seeking harmony in life. In a world racing toward the synthetic, serenity is our rebellion, our gift, our superpower. Take it with you, nurture it, and pass it on. Let's build that future together—one word, one wave, one human heartbeat at a time.

In closing, here's a simple verse to carry with you:

> *"In every note, a story sings,*
> *In every word, the soul takes wing.*
> *Through waves and time, we find our place,*
> *A harmony of human grace."*

We've explored how poetry turns chaos into calm, how Melodic Landscapes soothe our nerves, and how mindfulness keeps us grounded. In this call to harmony, we must remember why being human matters today more than ever. In the next chapter, we will discuss the significance of our humanity in a rapidly changing world, highlighting the role of serenity in preserving our well-being and collective future.

You, with your unique voice, can ripple serenity outward.

Epilogue: Harmony in Life
A Vision for the Future

"Time could be made to serve the mind."
— **Frank Herbert, Dune**

As we come to the close of this book, let us take a moment to reflect on the journey we've undertaken together. In this epilogue, we will revisit the key insights and lessons learned, celebrating the progress made and envisioning a future filled with harmony and peace. Through the chapters that follow, we will explore the irreplaceable human spirit, imagine a world infused with serenity, and issue a call to action to integrate these practices into your daily life. As you turn the final pages, I hope you feel inspired to carry the gift of serenity with you, sharing it with others and contributing to a more harmonious world.

"A person's sense of balance is measured by how he handles the unexpected."

Brian Herbert and Kevin J. Anderson, Navigators of Dune

Your journey toward serenity doesn't end here; in fact, it's just beginning. To support you as you continue to explore and deepen your practice, I've compiled a list of additional resources. In this chapter, you'll find recommended poetry, soundscaping tools, guided exercises, and further reading to inspire and guide you. Whether you're looking for new poems to reflect on, apps to enhance your soundscaping, or books to expand your understanding, these resources will serve as companions on your path. As you explore them, remember that serenity is a lifelong practice, and there is always more to discover.

The following sections provide a curated selection of resources to support your journey toward serenity through poetry, sound, and creative wellness. Whether you're seeking inspiration, tools, or further exploration, these resources will help you deepen your practice. Both free and paid options are included to ensure accessibility for all readers.

Additional Resources
Major forms of poetry

1. Sonnet

A 14-line poem traditionally written in iambic pentameter (ten syllables per line with an unstressed-stressed rhythm). There are two main types:

Shakespearean (English) Sonnet: Three quatrains and a couplet with the rhyme scheme ABAB CDCD EFEF GG.

Petrarchan (Italian) Sonnet: An octave and a sestet with a rhyme scheme like ABBAABBA CDECDE.

Sonnets often explore themes of love, beauty, time, or mortality. The structured rhyme and meter provide a framework for deep emotional or philosophical expression. Famous examples include Shakespeare's "Sonnet 18" ("Shall I compare thee to a summer's day?").Sonnets often evoke **love, longing, introspection, and resolution**. The structured form creates a sense of order, which can feel stabilizing or constraining, while the "volta" (a shift in thought) often brings **clarity, revelation, or bittersweet acceptance**.

2. Haiku

A three-line poem with a syllable pattern of 5-7-5, originating from Japan. Traditionally, haikus focus on nature and include a seasonal reference.

Haikus aim to capture a fleeting moment with vivid imagery and simplicity. Their brevity encourages precision and evokes a sense of calm or wonder. Modern haikus may relax the syllable rule but retain the concise, reflective style. Haikus typically evoke **tranquility, wonder, melancholy, or fleeting beauty**. Their brevity invites a moment of **quiet insight or bittersweet awareness** of life's impermanence.

3. Limerick

A five-line poem with an AABBA rhyme scheme. Lines 1, 2, and 5 are longer and rhyme, while lines 3 and 4 are shorter and share a different rhyme.

Limericks are playful and humorous, often featuring absurd or witty content. Their bouncy rhythm makes them memorable and entertaining, as seen in Edward Lear's works.

Limericks evoke **humor, joy, surprise, or playful irreverence**. They often lead to **laughter or amusement**, though they can subtly convey **satire** or deeper commentary.

4. Ballad

A narrative poem typically written in quatrains (four-line stanzas) with a simple rhyme scheme like ABCB. Ballads tell stories of love, tragedy, or adventure.

Ballads often originate from oral traditions and are accessible due to their straightforward structure. They convey emotion and drama, as in "The Rime of the Ancient Mariner" by Samuel Taylor Coleridge.

Ballads stir **nostalgia, empathy, sorrow, or adventure**. Depending on the narrative, they can evoke **suspense, romance, or tragedy**, with a sense of **inevitability or fate**.

5. Ode

A lyric poem that praises or glorifies a person, place, thing, or idea. Odes vary in structure, from the formal Pindaric odes (with stanzas of strophe, antistrophe, and epode) to more flexible modern odes.

Odes elevate their subject with a celebratory tone, using rich imagery and emotion. Examples include John Keats' "Ode to a Nightingale."

Odes inspire **awe, admiration, reverence, or celebration**. Their tone can evoke **wonder, gratitude, or transcendence** as they honor their subject.

6. Elegy

A poem of mourning or reflection, often lamenting a death or loss. Elegies have no fixed structure but maintain a somber tone.

Elegies provide a space for grief and contemplation, blending personal emotion with universal themes. Thomas Gray's "Elegy Written in a Country Churchyard" is a classic example.

Elegies evoke **grief, sorrow, reflection, and sometimes acceptance**. They offer a space for **mourning and catharsis**, guiding readers toward **peace or remembrance**.

7. Epic

A long narrative poem recounting the heroic deeds of legendary figures, often with supernatural elements. Epics are written in a grand, elevated style.

Epics reflect cultural values and history, serving as both entertainment and moral instruction. Homer's *Iliad* and *Odyssey* are foundational examples.

Epics evoke **awe, excitement, admiration, and grandeur**. They can inspire **pride, courage, or cultural connection**, immersing readers in a sense of **wonder**.

8. Free Verse

Poetry without a fixed rhyme scheme or metrical pattern, allowing for natural rhythms and flexibility in line length and structure.

Free verse mimics speech and emphasizes imagery, tone, and line breaks to convey meaning. Walt Whitman's "Song of Myself" exemplifies its expressive freedom.

Free verse evokes a wide range of emotions, such as **intimacy, vulnerability, chaos, or freedom**. It often feels **authentic, immediate, or raw**.

9. Villanelle

A 19-line poem with five tercets (three-line stanzas) and a final quatrain. It features two refrains (repeated lines) and a rhyme scheme of ABA, with specific lines repeating in a set pattern.

The repetition creates a hypnotic, musical effect, often intensifying emotion. Dylan Thomas' "Do Not Go Gentle into That Good Night" showcases its power.

Villanelles evoke **obsession, longing, urgency, or inevitability**. Their repetition creates **insistence, desperation, or emotional intensity**.

10. Sestina

A 39-line poem with six stanzas of six lines each, followed by a three-line envoi. Instead of rhyme, it repeats six end-words in a complex, rotating pattern.

The sestina's intricate structure challenges poets to explore a theme deeply, often resulting in layered meanings. Elizabeth Bishop's "Sestina" is a notable example.

Sestinas evoke **complexity, depth, and layered emotion**. They create a sense of **interconnectedness or evolving meaning**.

11. Ghazal

A series of couplets (typically five or more) from Middle Eastern and South Asian traditions. Each couplet shares a refrain and rhyme, and stands somewhat independently.

Ghazals often address love, loss, or longing with emotional intensity. The form's repetition creates a meditative quality, as seen in the works of Rumi.

Ghazals evoke **yearning, passion, melancholy, or spiritual longing**. The refrain adds **insistence or unfulfilled desire**.

12. Pantoum

A poem of quatrains where lines 2 and 4 of each stanza repeat as lines 1 and 3 of the next, creating a circular pattern.

The repetition weaves themes together, giving a sense of continuity or obsession. It's effective for reflective or hypnotic poetry.

Pantoums evoke nostalgia, reflection, or cyclical time. Repeating lines can stir haunting, obsession, or inevitability.

13. Acrostic

A poem where the first letters of each line spell out a word or phrase when read vertically.

Acrostics combine wordplay with meaning, often serving as puzzles or tributes. They can be simple or complex depending on the hidden message.

Acrostics evoke playfulness, curiosity, or surprise. The hidden message adds intimacy or revelation.

14. Concrete Poetry

Poetry where the visual arrangement of words on the page forms a shape related to the poem's subject, enhancing its meaning.

The form merges visual art and language, making the poem's appearance as significant as its words. George Herbert's "The Altar" is an early example.

Concrete poetry evokes wonder, surprise, or harmony. The visual shape can amplify chaos, joy, or unity.

15. Spoken Word

Poetry designed for performance, emphasizing rhythm, delivery, and often social or political themes.

Spoken word engages audiences through theatricality and sound, thriving in live settings like poetry slams. It bridges poetry and performance art.

Spoken word evokes passion, urgency, anger, joy, or solidarity. It can inspire empowerment or communal connection.

Spoken word harnesses performance power, amplifying emotional release.

Additional Notable Forms

While the above list covers major forms, poetry's diversity includes many others. Here are a few more examples:

Tanka: A Japanese five-line poem with a 5-7-5-7-7 syllable pattern, often extending a haiku-like moment into a broader reflection.

Rondeau: A 15-line poem with a refrain and a rhyme scheme of AABBA AABR AABBAR (R = refrain), used for lyrical expression.

Terza Rima: Three-line stanzas with an interlocking rhyme scheme (ABA BCB CDC), famously used in Dante's *Divine Comedy*.

Blank Verse: Unrhymed iambic pentameter, common in English dramatic poetry like Shakespeare's plays.

Cinquain: A five-line poem with a syllable pattern of 2-4-6-8-2, creating a concise, evocative structure.

Poetry Referencing Serenity

Below is a brief list of poems related to "Serenity," each with a short excerpt and a source where you can read the complete work.

"Serenity" by Charles Bertram Johnson:

- Excerpt:

Cool, and composed, and calm as dawn,
He meets life's storms with tranquil breast;
No shadow mars his sky at morn,
No fears disturb his evening rest.

   - Source: Available on 'Poem-a-Day' by the Academy of American Poets. Read the full poem ("https://poets.org/poem/serenity-0").

"Serenity" by Edward Rowland Sill:

- Excerpt:

> Brook, be still,—be still, my soul;
> Peace, come in,—come in, my thought;
> Doubt, be gone,—be gone, my fear;
> Joy, awake,—awake, my hope.

- Found in 'The Hermitage and Other Poems' (1868), available via Project Gutenberg (https://www.gutenberg.org/ebooks/64467).

"Serenity" by Jean Malicsi

- Excerpt:

> Find that place within your heart,
> Where peace resides, a world apart.
> Let go of strife, embrace the calm,
> Serenity's touch, a healing balm.

- Published on PoemHunter.com. Access it [here](https://www.poemhunter.com/poem/serenity-22/).

"Serenity by the River" by Mahmudhasan6692

- Excerpt:

> Beside the river, still and deep,
> I find a peace that's mine to keep.
> The water's flow, a gentle song,
> In nature's arms, where I belong.

- Available on AllPoetry.com [here](https://allpoetry.com/poem/17742257-Serenity-by-the-River-by-Mahmudhasan6692).

Poems from 'Serenity: Poems by F.S. Yousaf '

- *Excerpt*

> *In the quiet of the night,*
> *I find my strength, my inner light.*
> *Serenity whispers, soft and clear,*
> *'You are enough, there's nothing to fear.*

- Published in 2022. Purchase the book on Amazon [here](https://www.amazon.com/Serenity-Poems-F-S-Yousaf/dp/1524872626).

Serenity by Robert Longley

- Excerpt:

> *Serenity is not a place,*
> *But a state of grace.*
> *It's found in the pause between breaths,*
> *In the space where the heart rests.*

- Featured on SacredPoems.com ("https://www.sacredpoems.com/serenity-robert-longley").

Acrostic Poem "Serenity" (Anonymous)

- Excerpt:

> *Silence wraps around me tight,*
> *Every worry takes to flight.*
> *Resting in this peaceful state,*
> *Embracing calm, I navigate.*

- Published on Medium.com in 2023 [here](https://medium.com/@example/serenity-acrostic-poem).

Various Poems Tagged 'Serenity on Hello Poetry'

- *Excerpt* (from a popular entry):

> *Serenity is the mountain's peak,*
> *Where the air is thin, and the soul can speak.*
> *It's the whisper of leaves in the autumn breeze,*
> *The quiet strength that sets us free.*

Poetry Without Borders – Multicultural and Secular Traditions

Poetic traditions that are multicultural or secular reflect the diversity of human experience, either by weaving together influences from multiple cultures or by exploring themes outside religious contexts. Below, I'll describe these traditions separately and highlight examples where they overlap, providing a clear picture of each.

Multicultural Poetic Traditions

Multicultural poetic traditions embrace the blending of diverse cultural elements, often emerging in societies where various ethnic, linguistic, or national identities intersect. These traditions reflect the poets' backgrounds or the globalized nature of contemporary literature, celebrating cultural diversity through language, form, and themes.

- **Harlem Renaissance**: This movement in the early 20th-century United States celebrated African American culture while engaging with broader American and global literary traditions. Poets like Langston Hughes incorporated jazz rhythms, blues influences, and African American folklore into their work, creating a vibrant, multicultural poetic voice that resonated beyond its cultural origins.

- **Postcolonial Poetry**: Emerging from regions shaped by colonialism, this tradition navigates the intersections of indigenous and colonial cultures. Poets like Derek Walcott from the Caribbean blend African, European, and indigenous influences, using multiple languages or hybrid forms to explore themes of history, identity, and belonging—often reflecting the complexity of multicultural societies.

- **Spoken Word and Slam Poetry**: A contemporary tradition, spoken word provides a platform for poets from diverse backgrounds to share their stories. Rooted in oral traditions like African American storytelling, it has evolved into a global phenomenon, with poets addressing identity, social justice, and cultural heritage in dynamic performances that transcend cultural boundaries.

Secular Poetic Traditions

Secular poetic traditions prioritize non-religious themes, focusing on personal, social, or political concerns rather than spiritual or doctrinal matters. These traditions span centuries and cultures, offering a space to explore the breadth of human experience without religious constraints.

- **Lyric Poetry**: Dating back to ancient Greece and continuing through the Renaissance and beyond, lyric poetry centers on personal emotions—love, desire, grief—rather than religious devotion. The sonnet, for instance, has been used by poets like Shakespeare to express secular passions, a practice that persists in modern free verse.

- **Nature Poetry**: This tradition, exemplified by Romantic poets like William Wordsworth, explores the natural world and humanity's relationship to it. While nature can carry spiritual undertones, poets in this vein often focus on sensory experience and emotional reflection, maintaining a secular perspective free of religious doctrine.

- **Political and Protest Poetry**: Addressing societal issues like inequality, war, or oppression, this tradition uses poetry as a tool for critique and change. Poets like Pablo Neruda, with his politically charged verses, focus on humanistic concerns—justice, freedom, solidarity—without relying on religious frameworks.

Traditions That Are Both Multicultural and Secular

Some poetic traditions embody both multicultural and secular qualities, creating inclusive spaces where diverse voices converge around universal human themes.

- **Beat Generation**: In mid-20th-century America, poets like Allen Ginsberg and Gary Snyder drew from Eastern philosophies, jazz culture, and global literary influences. Their work often carried a countercultural, secular ethos, challenging mainstream values—including religious norms—while embracing a multicultural tapestry of ideas.

- **Diaspora Poetry**: Written by poets navigating multiple cultural identities, this tradition often focuses on secular themes like migration, hybridity, and belonging. Poets like Li-Young Lee, a Chinese American, weave their cultural heritage into explorations of family and identity, typically without a religious lens, making their work both multicultural and secular.

- **International Poetry Festivals**: Events like the International Poetry Festival in Rotterdam bring together poets from around the world, celebrating linguistic and cultural diversity in a secular setting. These gatherings emphasize artistic expression over religious affiliation, fostering multicultural exchange on shared human ground.

Interplay and Significance

Multicultural poetic traditions celebrate cultural diversity, while secular traditions emphasize non-religious exploration. Where they overlap, they often provide a common space for poets from varied backgrounds to connect—whether through shared experiences of modernity, migration, or social struggle—without the divisions religious differences might impose. For instance, secularism in poetry can facilitate multicultural expression by offering a neutral platform, as seen in online poetry communities or university settings where diverse voices unite around art rather than faith.

In essence, multicultural and secular poetic traditions enrich literature by broadening its scope—drawing from the world's cultures and delving into the full spectrum of human concerns, free from religious boundaries. They are not mutually exclusive; many traditions and poets blend both qualities, reflecting the interconnectedness of our globalized world.

Resources for Ambient Sounds

Sources for Free Ambient Sounds

Ambient sounds encompass a broad range of audio environments, from natural settings to urban and fantastical atmospheres.

You can access free pre-made ambient sounds from several reputable websites, perfect for personal projects or relaxation. Here are some top choices:

- **Pixabay** (Pixabay) offers over 4,138 royalty-free ambient sound effects, no attribution required.

- **Zapsplat** (Zapsplat) provides more than 150,000 free professional ambient sounds.

- **Ambient-mixer.com** (Ambient-mixer.com) lets you listen and create custom mixes for free, ideal for relaxation.

- **PremiumBeat** (PremiumBeat) includes 15 free ambient background tracks for use in projects.

- **FreeSoundLibrary.com** (FreeSoundLibrary.com) offers free sounds for focus and sleep.

- **Mixkit** (Mixkit) has 36 free ambient sound effects ready for use.

- **A Soft Murmur** (A Soft Murmur) allows mixing ambient sounds for free to aid focus or relaxation.

- **Free Music Archive** (Free Music Archive) features free ambient music tracks.

- **Freesound.org** (Freesound.org) is a community platform with many free ambient sounds.

- **Uppbeat.io** (Uppbeat.io) offers over 1,470 free ambient sound effects for various media.

Sources for Paid Ambient Sounds

For higher-quality or commercial use, consider these paid options, which often offer subscriptions or one-time purchases:

- **BOOM Library** (BOOM Library) provides professional ambient sounds, including nature ambiences, with buyout or subscription options.
- **Pro Sound Effects** (Pro Sound Effects) has a wide range of ambient effects for purchase, ideal for professional projects.
- **SONNISS** (SONNISS) offers ambient sound libraries for creators, with various payment options.
- **Epidemic Sound** (Epidemic Sound) is a subscription service with royalty-free ambient music.
- **PremiumBeat** (PremiumBeat) offers paid ambient music tracks for licensing.
- **Soundstripe** (Soundstripe) provides subscription-based ambient music tracks.
- **Bensound** (Bensound) has paid ambient music tracks alongside some free options.
- **AudioJungle** (AudioJungle) is a marketplace for buying individual ambient sound effects and music tracks.

Soundscaping Tools and Apps

These tools and apps will help you create or access calming Melodic Landscapes, from nature sounds to binaural beats. Both free and paid options are included.

Apps for Custom Melodic Landscapes:

- **Calm** (free version available; paid subscription for full access): Offers ambient sounds and guided meditations.

- **MyNoise** (free with optional donations): Allows you to create personalized Melodic Landscapes.

Pre-Made Ambient Sounds:

- **Noisli** (free version; paid for additional features): Provides high-quality background noises like rain, forest, and café sounds.

- Binaural Beats and White Noise:

    - **Brain.fm** (paid, with free trial): Uses AI-generated music to enhance focus, relaxation, or sleep.

    - **White Noise** Lite (free): Offers a variety of white noise options for sleep or concentration.

Original Piano Compositions

Serenity Collection

Quest Collection

Enlightenment Collection

Endearment Collection

Nature Collection

Serenity Collection
Original Piano Compositions

- Mystic Journey
- Nostalgic Memories
- A Poetry of Solitude
- Organic Moment
- Extraordinary Life
- The Colors of Life
- Contemplations
- Life is a Journey
- Unto the Light
- Sweet Lamentations
- Harmonic Void
- A Warrior's Lullaby
- Rushing the Pulse

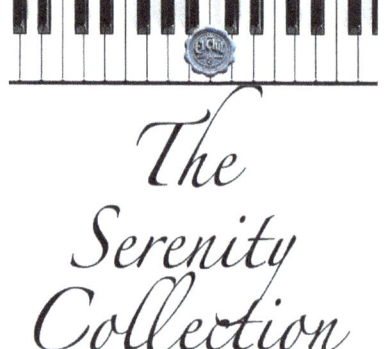

Quest Collection

Original Piano Composition

- The Wonder of Life
- Life Goes On
- New Beginnings
- The Arrival
- Into the Hope
- Fragile Delusion
- Strange Worlds
- Confetti Deceptions
- At the Vortex of a Purple Heart
- A Trapezist Walse
- Tearful Quest
- The Carousel of Inverted Dimensions
- The War Within
- Displace Me
- Impermanent Resilience
- Enduring Exiles

- Adiu Carina

Enlightenment Collection

Original Piano Compositions

- Enchanting Moment
- In Strength and in Weakness
- Sensing Joy
- The Soliloquy of the Wise
- The Call
- Mindful Intentions
- Authenticity
- Edging the Truth
- Dispirited Revelation
- Searching Into the Twilight
- A Perfect Tale of Imperfections
- Through the Storm of Tranquility
- Farming Consciousness
- Resilient Renewal
- Significant Dissonance

Endearment Collection

Original Piano Compositions

- Once and Again
- The Reencounte
- You are my Sanctuary
- Love Away
- Forbidden Serenade
- A Song for my Daughters
- Those Things we Feel
- The day you were born
- Tale of Illusions
- Ella
- This Is It
- A Brotherhood
- The Reunion

Nature Collection

Original Piano Compositions

- White Orchids in the Sunset
- Thirteen Brilliant Lights
- Nocturnal Light
- Spring Seven of Seven
- Distant Shores
- Season de Light
- A Dancing Breeze at the Sunrise
- Forestry Dreams
- Golden Rain
- Breath of a Feathe
- Navigating the Riverie
- A Tucan Awakening

Guided Exercises with Poetry and Sound

These exercises combine poetry and sound to create immersive experiences for reflection and relaxation. Start with simple practices and progress to deeper engagements.

Exercise 1: Mindful Poetry Reading:

Select a poem from the recommended list (e.g., "Wild Geese").
Pair it with a calming Melodic Landscape (e.g., ocean waves from Calm).
Read the poem aloud, focusing on your breath between lines.

Exercise 2: Sound-Enhanced Journaling:

Choose a reflective poem (e.g., "The Guest House").
Play a gentle Melodic Landscape (e.g., forest sounds from Noisli).
Write about the emotions the poem evokes while immersed in the sound.

Exercise 3: Immersive Sound and Spoken Word:

Record yourself reading a favorite poem.
Layer it over a custom Melodic Landscape using MyNoise.
Listen to the recording during meditation or relaxation.

Biblical Passages on Serenity

Old Testament Passages on Serenity

1. **"The Lord will fight for you; you need only to be still."** — *Exodus 14:14*

    - This verse, spoken by Moses to the Israelites as they faced the Egyptian army, encourages a calm trust in God's deliverance, promoting serenity by urging stillness in the face of danger.

2. **"The Lord bless you and keep you; the Lord make his face shine on you and be gracious to you; the Lord turn his face toward you and give you peace."** — *Numbers 6:24-26*

    - Known as the priestly blessing, this passage offers serenity through the gift of God's peace, tied to His favor and protective presence.

3. **"Submit to God and be at peace with him; in this way prosperity will come to you."** — *Job 22:21*

    - Eliphaz suggests to Job that surrendering to God brings peace, portraying serenity as a result of reconciliation and trust in Him.

4. **"In peace I will lie down and sleep, for you alone, Lord, make me dwell in safety."** — *Psalm 4:8*

    - David expresses serene confidence in God's protection, enabling restful sleep free from fear or anxiety.

5. **"He makes me lie down in green pastures, he leads me beside quiet waters."** — *Psalm 23:2*

    - This well-known verse uses imagery of quiet waters and restful pastures to depict the tranquility and serenity provided by God's care.

6. **"The Lord gives strength to his people; the Lord blesses his people with peace."** — *Psalm 29:11*

    - Serenity is presented as a divine blessing, where God grants peace alongside strength to His people.

7. **"Be still before the Lord and wait patiently for him; do not fret when people succeed in their ways, when they carry out their wicked schemes."** — *Psalm 37:7*

    - David calls for a serene patience and trust in God, resisting worry despite the apparent success of the wicked.

8. **"Be still, and know that I am God; I will be exalted among the nations, I will be exalted in the earth."** — *Psalm 46:10*

    - This verse promotes serenity through stillness and recognition of God's sovereign power, calming fears with His ultimate authority.

9. **"Better a dry crust with peace and quiet than a house full of feasting, with strife."** — *Proverbs 17:1*

    - This proverb highlights serenity's value, favoring peace and quiet over abundance marred by conflict.

10. **"You will keep in perfect peace those whose minds are steadfast, because they trust in you."** — *Isaiah 26:3*

    - Isaiah links serenity to unwavering trust in God, promising perfect peace to those who remain steadfast in faith.

11. **"The fruit of that righteousness will be peace; its effect will be quietness and confidence forever."** — *Isaiah 32:17*

    - This verse portrays serenity as a lasting outcome of righteousness, marked by peace, quietness, and confidence.

New Testament Passages on Serenity

1. **"So do not worry, saying, 'What shall we eat?' or 'What shall we drink?' or 'What shall we wear?' For the pagans run after all these things, and your heavenly Father knows that you need them. But seek first his kingdom and his righteousness, and all these things will be given to you as well. Therefore do not worry about tomorrow, for tomorrow will worry about itself. Each day has enough trouble of its own."** — *Matthew 6:31-34*

    - Jesus encourages serenity by urging trust in God's provision and focus on His kingdom, freeing believers from anxiety about material needs.

2. **"Come to me, all you who are weary and burdened, and I will give you rest. Take my yoke upon you and learn from me, for I am gentle and humble in heart, and you will find rest for your souls. For my yoke is easy and my burden is light."** — *Matthew 11:28-30*

    - Jesus offers serenity through rest for the weary, providing a gentle and light burden that calms the soul.

3. **"He got up, rebuked the wind and said to the waves, 'Quiet! Be still!' Then the wind died down and it was completely calm. He said to his disciples, 'Why are you so afraid? Do you still have no faith?'"** — *Mark 4:39-40*

    - Jesus brings literal and symbolic serenity by calming the storm, encouraging faith as the path to peace in chaos.

4. **"'Martha, Martha,' the Lord answered, 'you are worried and upset about many things, but few things are needed—or indeed only one. Mary has chosen what is better, and it will not be taken away from her.'"** — *Luke 10:41-42*

    - Jesus contrasts Martha's anxiety with Mary's serene focus on Him, teaching that devotion to Him brings lasting peace.

5. **"Peace I leave with you; my peace I give you. I do not give to you as the world gives. Do not let your hearts be troubled and do not be afraid."** — *John 14:27*

- Jesus promises a unique peace that fosters serenity, calming troubled hearts and dispelling fear.

6. **"I have told you these things, so that in me you may have peace. In this world you will have trouble. But take heart! I have overcome the world."** — *John 16:33*

    - Jesus assures serenity through His victory over the world's troubles, offering peace despite life's challenges.

7. **"Therefore, since we have been justified through faith, we have peace with God through our Lord Jesus Christ."** — *Romans 5:1*

    - Paul ties serenity to reconciliation with God through faith, establishing a peaceful relationship with Him.

8. **"May the God of hope fill you with all joy and peace as you trust in him, so that you may overflow with hope by the power of the Holy Spirit."** — *Romans 15:13*

    - Paul prays for serenity through joy and peace, rooted in trust and empowered by the Holy Spirit.

9. **"Do not be anxious about anything, but in every situation, by prayer and petition, with thanksgiving, present your requests to God. And the peace of God, which transcends all understanding, will guard your hearts and your minds in Christ Jesus."** — *Philippians 4:6-7*

    - Paul teaches that prayer replaces anxiety with God's transcendent peace, guarding hearts and minds for serenity.

10. **"Let the peace of Christ rule in your hearts, since as members of one body you were called to peace. And be thankful."** — *Colossians 3:15*

    - Paul urges believers to let Christ's peace govern their hearts, fostering serenity through gratitude and unity.

11. **"Now may the Lord of peace himself give you peace at all times and in every way. The Lord be with all of you."** — *2 Thessalonians 3:16*

    - Paul blesses believers with continuous peace from God, emphasizing serenity as a constant gift.

12. **"Now may the God of peace, who through the blood of the eternal covenant brought back from the dead our Lord Jesus, that great Shepherd of the sheep, equip you with everything good for doing his will, and may he work in us what is pleasing to him, through Jesus Christ, to whom be glory for ever and ever. Amen." —** *Hebrews 13:20-21*

    - This benediction invokes God's peace as a source of serenity, tied to Christ's resurrection and guidance.

13. **"But the wisdom that comes from heaven is first of all pure; then peace-loving, considerate, submissive, full of mercy and good fruit, impartial and sincere. Peacemakers who sow in peace reap a harvest of righteousness." —** *James 3:17-18*

    - James describes heavenly wisdom as peace-loving, linking serenity to a righteous and harmonious life.

14. **"Cast all your anxiety on him because he cares for you." —** *1 Peter 5:7*

    - Peter promotes serenity by encouraging believers to release worries to God, trusting in His care.

15. **"He will wipe every tear from their eyes. There will be no more death or mourning or crying or pain, for the old order of things has passed away." —** *Revelation 21:4*

    - This vision of eternity promises ultimate serenity, where God's presence removes all sorrow and establishes lasting peace.

Your Serenity Compass: The Twelve Pillars

Focus and Mental Clarity

- Attune Serenity
- Aquamarine
- Sit in silence for 5 minutes, focusing on a single soul
- Journal what clarity emerged from the silence.

Calmness and Serenity

- Sustain Serenity
- Jade
- Use a 4-4-4 breath when stressed today.
- Journal how calm flowed after breathing.

Healing and Balance

- Radiate Serenity
- Topaz
- Try 10 minutes of deep breathing for balance.
- Note how balance shifted with serenity's glow.

Confidence and Inner Resilience

- Ignite Serenity
- Peridot
- Set and achieve a small goal today.
- Reflect on how serenity fueled confidence.

Strength and Courage

- Fortify Serenity
- Diamond
- Face a small fear—write it down, take one step.
- Note how serenity felt facing your fear.

Wisdom and Increased Awareness

- Incarnate Serenity
- Emerald

- Pause before a decision, letting serenity guide clarity.
- Write the insight serenity shaped in your choice.

Tranquility and Inner Peace

- Root Serenity
- Amethyst
- Visualize a peaceful place for 5 minutes.
- Note a tranquil detail that rooted you.

Love and Affection

- Embrace Serenity
- Ruby
- Reach out with a kind word, embracing serenity.
- Journal how serenity felt connecting with another.

Abundance and Blessings

- Manifest Serenity
- Sapphire
- List three things you're grateful for today.
- Reflect on one blessing serenity brightened.

Prosperity and Compassion

- Invoke Serenity
- Gold
- Offer a small act of kindness today.
- Reflect on serenity's role in your kindness

Positivism and Optimism

- Infuse Serenity
- Citrine
- Reframe a challenge with a positive spin.
- Journal how serenity sparked a hopeful view.

Transformation and Self-Realization

- Transcend into Serenity
- Turquoise
- Reflect on an area to change—take a step.
- Journal what shifted with serenity's lift.

Key Studies on Internet Disruptions

Summary of Key Studies and Findings

- Casey, J. A., Fukurai, M., Hernandez, D., Lee, E. K., Morello-Frosch, R., & DeLone, C. (2020). Power outages and community health: A narrative review. Current Environmental Health Reports, 7(4), 371–383. https://doi.org/10.1007/s40572-020-00285-5

- Chen, J., Wu, X., & Zhu, W. (2016). What happened to our environment and mental health as a result of Hurricane Sandy? Disaster Medicine and Public Health Preparedness, 10(3), 314–319. https://doi.org/10.1017/dmp.2016.38

- International Rescue Committee. (2022). Social media, connectivity, and mental health in humanitarian settings. https://www.rescue.org/report

- Kim, H., & Cherry, K. E. (2021). Mental health effects of Hurricane Sandy on older adults. Clinical Gerontologist, 44(1), 47–59. https://doi.org/10.1080/07317115.2020.1837584

- King, G., Pan, J., & Roberts, M. E. (2017). How the Chinese government fabricates social media posts for strategic distraction, not engaged argument. American Political Science Review, 111(3), 484–501. https://doi.org/10.1017/S0003055417000144

- Loader, B. D., Vromen, A., & Xenos, M. (2019). Digital exclusion and its impact on mental health. Information, Communication & Society, 22(5), 689–703. https://doi.org/10.1080/1369118X.2019.1642937

- Lu, Y., & Casey, J. (2017). The mental and physical toll of living without power after a disaster. Environmental Justice, 10(3), 93–97. https://doi.org/10.1089/env.2017.0002

- Magrey, A. A., Wani, Z. A., & Dar, M. M. (2020). Psychological impact of the internet shutdown in Kashmir. The Lancet Psychiatry, 7(4), 301. https://doi.org/10.1016/S2215-0366(20)30045-2

- Savoia, E., Lin, L., & Testa, M. A. (2021). The impact of internet outages on mental health during the COVID-19 pandemic. Journal of Medical Internet Research, 23(7), e26285. https://doi.org/10.2196/26285

- Starbird, K., Dailey, D., & Palen, L. (2020). The emotional toll of online disconnection during disasters. In Proceedings of the 2020 CHI Conference on Human Factors in Computing Systems (pp. 1–12). Association for Computing Machinery. https://doi.org/10.1145/3313831.3376601

- UNICEF Office of Research – Innocenti. (2021). Digital connectivity during OVID-19: Global insights into adolescent well-being. https://www.unicef-irc.org/publications/

- Unknown author. (2016). Interconnected or disconnected? Promotion of mental health in the digital age. World Psychiatry, 15(2), 200–201. https://doi.org/10.1002/wps.20330

- Rydzak, J. (2020). Internet shutdowns and political violence: Evidence from India. American Political Science Review, 114(4), 1325–1341. https://doi.org/10.1017/S0003055420000300

Glossary

Abundance

A mindset of prosperity and gratitude, symbolizing the recognition of life's blessings. In the *Twelve Pillars of Wellness,* it is paired with the sapphire crystal, encouraging emotional and spiritual richness. Abundance fosters serenity by shifting focus to gratitude and plenitude.

Acoustic Ecology

The study of the relationship between living beings and their sound environments. Relevant to soundscaping, it emphasizes how sound influences well-being. Acoustic ecology informs the creation of harmonious personal sound sanctuaries.

AI Ethics

Principles governing the moral use of artificial intelligence. Explored in the book as part of the human-technology dynamic, questioning how AI impacts serenity. Ethical considerations highlight the balance between technological advancement and human values.

Alliteration

The repetition of initial consonant sounds in nearby words, a poetic device that enhances rhythm and mood. Used in poetry to create a soothing or emphatic effect, supporting emotional expression and serenity.

Alpha Waves

Brain waves (8-12 Hz) associated with a relaxed, calm state, often present during light meditation or creative flow. Enhanced by soothing Melodic Landscapes, alpha waves are key to achieving the book's vision of serenity.

Ambient Sounds

Background noises, such as wind or distant traffic, that set an atmosphere without demanding focus. Integral to soundscaping, they promote relaxation by blending into the environment or masking disruptive sounds.

Amplitude

The strength or intensity of a sound wave, determining its loudness. In soundscaping, softer amplitudes soothe, while louder ones may stimulate, affecting emotional states and serenity levels.

Artificial Intelligence (AI)

The simulation of human intelligence by machines. The book contrasts AI's capabilities with human creativity, noting its inability to replicate the soulful depth of poetry or intuition, emphasizing humanity's unique path to serenity.

Assonance

The repetition of vowel sounds in nearby words, a poetic technique that adds musicality. Enhances the calming flow of verse, aligning with the book's use of poetry for emotional alchemy.

Auditory Cortex

The brain region processing sound. Engaged during soundscaping and listening to poetry, it connects auditory stimuli to emotional and cognitive responses, supporting wellness practices.

Binaural Beats

An auditory illusion created when two slightly different frequencies are played in each ear, perceived as a pulsing tone. Used in soundscaping to influence brainwaves (e.g., alpha or theta), promoting relaxation and focus.

Biblical Serenity

Serenity as depicted in biblical contexts, such as the Serenity Prayer's call for peace and acceptance. Highlights a spiritual dimension of calm, encouraging surrender and trust as pathways to inner peace.

Cadence

The rhythmic flow of sound or poetry, created by patterns of stress and pause. In soundscaping and verse, cadence fosters a meditative state, guiding readers toward serenity.

Calmness

A state of tranquility, free from agitation. Linked to the jade crystal in the *Twelve Pillars of Wellness*, it represents a quiet mind and body, cultivated through mindful practices like soundscaping and poetry.

Catharsis

The release of pent-up emotions through creative expression, such as writing poetry or engaging with sound. A key mechanism in the book for transforming stress into serenity.

Consonance

The repetition of consonant sounds, often at word endings, in poetry. Adds harmony and texture, enhancing the soothing quality of verse as a tool for emotional grounding.

Cortisol

A stress hormone released by the HPA axis. Serenity practices like soundscaping and poetry reduce cortisol levels, offering physiological evidence of their calming effects.

Creative Expression

The act of conveying emotions or ideas through art, such as poetry or music. Central to the book as a pathway to serenity, it enables emotional release and personal insight.

Decibel (dB)

A unit measuring sound intensity. Understanding decibels helps in crafting Melodic Landscapes, where lower levels (e.g., 30-40 dB) promote calm, while higher levels may disrupt peace.

Digital Dependence

Excessive reliance on technology for daily life, often leading to technostress. The book suggests countering it with soundscaping, poetry, and digital detox to restore balance and serenity.

Digital Detox

A deliberate break from electronic devices to reduce mental clutter and stress. Promotes serenity by reconnecting individuals with the present moment and natural rhythms.

Digital Minimalism

A lifestyle reducing digital engagement to essentials, enhancing focus and peace. Aligns with the book's advocacy for mindful technology use to support wellness.

Elegy

A mournful poem lamenting loss, often used to process grief. One of the major poetry forms in the book, elegies offer a structured path to emotional healing and serenity.

Emotional Alchemy

The transformation of negative emotions into positive ones through creative outlets like poetry. A core concept, it turns pain into beauty, fostering resilience and inner peace.

Emotional Grounding

Techniques to stabilize emotions, such as engaging with sound or words. Essential for maintaining serenity amidst modern challenges like information overload.

Empathy

The capacity to understand and share others' feelings. Nurtured through poetry and human connection, empathy enhances wellness and contrasts with the limitations of synthetic beings.

Enjambment

A poetic technique where a thought runs from one line to the next without a pause. Creates a fluid, continuous flow, mirroring the ebb of emotions and sound waves.

Free Verse

Poetry without fixed rhyme or meter, allowing unstructured expression. Used in the book for personal reflection, its flexibility aids emotional release and mindfulness.

Frequency

The rate of sound wave vibrations, measured in hertz (Hz). Lower frequencies (e.g., 20-200 Hz) soothe, while higher ones (e.g., 2000 Hz) stimulate, shaping Melodic Landscapes for serenity.

Haiku

A Japanese poem with a 5-7-5 syllable structure, often evoking nature. Promotes mindfulness and brevity, distilling emotions into serene, poignant moments.

Harmony

The pleasing combination of sounds or ideas. In soundscaping, it balances frequencies; in poetry, it aligns rhythm and meaning, both fostering peace.

HPA Axis

The hypothalamic-pituitary-adrenal axis, regulating stress responses. Serenity practices deactivate it, lowering cortisol and enhancing well-being.

Imagery

Vivid, sensory language in poetry that evokes mental pictures. Strengthens emotional resonance and mindfulness, deepening the reader's connection to serenity.

Information Overload

The overwhelm caused by excessive data, a modern barrier to peace. The book offers poetry and soundscaping as antidotes, simplifying and refocusing the mind.

Internet Outage

A disruption in internet access, explored as a challenge to modern serenity. Encourages reliance on inner resources like sound and words for calm.

Intuition

Instinctive understanding without conscious reasoning. Guides creativity in poetry and soundscaping, distinguishing human expression from AI's logic-driven output.

Journaling

Writing thoughts or experiences for reflection. A companion practice to poetry, it fosters emotional clarity and serenity through private exploration.

Limerick

A playful five-line poem with an AABBA rhyme scheme. Offers light-hearted relief, balancing deeper emotional work with joy and ease.

Meditation

A practice of focusing the mind to achieve calm and awareness. Paired with Melodic Landscapes and poetry, it deepens serenity and mindfulness.

Melody

A sequence of notes forming a cohesive tune, often the emotional heart of a Melodic Landscape. Reflects human creativity and can soothe or uplift.

Metaphor

A figure of speech comparing unlike things without "like" or "as." Enriches poetry, deepening emotional insight and fostering serenity through symbolic connections.

Meter

The rhythmic pattern of stressed and unstressed syllables in poetry. Creates a musical cadence, enhancing the calming effect of verse.

Mindful Silence

The intentional practice of stillness and quiet awareness. Complements soundscaping, offering a counterpoint to sound for achieving inner peace.

Mindfulness

The act of being fully present, reducing stress and enhancing well-being. Woven into the book's practices, it's foundational to serenity.

Multicultural Poetry

Poetry from diverse traditions exploring peace and harmony. Broadens perspectives, showcasing serenity as a universal human pursuit.

Nature Sounds

Organic noises like birdsong or waves, used in soundscaping for their innate calm. Connect listeners to nature's rhythms, promoting relaxation.

Ode

A lyric poem expressing admiration or emotion, often to a subject. Inspires awe and peace, aligning with the book's themes of beauty and serenity.

Optimism

A hopeful outlook, tied to the citrine crystal in the Twelve Pillars. Builds resilience and serenity by focusing on possibility and light.

Oxytocin

A hormone linked to bonding and relaxation. Serenity practices like sound and poetry may increase its release, fostering connection and calm.

Personal Sound Sanctuary

A tailored sound environment for relaxation or focus. A practical exercise in the book, it empowers readers to curate their own serene spaces.

Poetry

A literary form using rhythm and imagery to evoke emotion. Central to the book, it serves as a tool for reflection, healing, and serenity.

Resilience

The ability to recover from adversity, linked to the peridot crystal in the Twelve Pillars. Built through creative practices, it supports lasting peace.

Resonance

The amplification of sound or emotion through vibration or connection. Links soundscaping and poetry to deep human experience.

Rhyme

The repetition of similar sounds in poetry, creating harmony. Enhances memorability and calm, aligning words with sound's soothing power.

Rhythm

The pattern of beats in sound or poetry. Drives flow and energy, guiding listeners or readers into a serene state.

Serenity

A state of calm and peace, untroubled by external chaos. The book's guiding theme, achieved through sound, poetry, and mindful living.

Simile

A comparison using "like" or "as" in poetry. Adds vividness, enhancing emotional connection and serenity through relatable imagery.

Sonnet

A 14-line poem with a fixed rhyme scheme, often exploring love or nature. Provides structure for reflection, leading to peace.

Sound Map

A record of environmental sounds and their effects. An exercise to heighten auditory awareness, aiding in crafting calming Melodic Landscapes.

Sound Wave

A vibration traveling through a medium, perceived as sound. Understanding its properties (e.g., frequency, amplitude) is key to effective soundscaping.

Soundscaping

The art of designing sound environments for well-being. A primary method in the book, it uses ambient sounds, frequencies, and rhythms to foster serenity.

Stanza

A grouped set of lines in a poem. Organizes thoughts and emotions, providing a framework for reflection and calm.

Synthetic Beings

Artificial entities mimicking human traits, like AI constructs. Contrasted with human creativity, they underscore the soulful depth of poetry and sound.

Technostress

Stress from constant technology use. Addressed as a modern challenge, countered by the book's practices to restore peace.

Theta Waves

Brain waves (4-8 Hz) linked to deep relaxation and creativity. Enhanced by Melodic Landscapes, they support meditation and serenity.

Timbre

The unique quality of a sound, distinguishing its source. Shapes emotional responses in soundscaping, from soothing to jarring.

Transformation

Personal growth and change, tied to the turquoise crystal in the Twelve Pillars. A key outcome of the book's practices, leading to serenity.

Twelve Pillars of Wellness

A framework of twelve principles for holistic well-being, each paired with a crystal (e.g., Strength and Courage with Diamond, Calmness and Serenity with Jade). Guides readers toward balance through sound, poetry, and mindfulness.

Visualization

Creating mental images to enhance relaxation or goals. Combined with poetry and sound, it amplifies their calming effects.

Wellness Pillars

See *Twelve Pillars of Wellness*. These principles underpin the book's approach to achieving lasting serenity.

White Noise

A consistent blend of all frequencies, masking other sounds. Used in soundscaping to promote focus or sleep, creating a neutral auditory backdrop.

Wisdom

Insight gained through experience, linked to the emerald crystal in the Twelve Pillars. Guides mindful living and creative expression for serenity.

References

- Adorno, T. W. (1973). *Negative dialectics* (E. B. Ashton, Trans.). Routledge. (Original work published 1966)

- Adorno, T. W. (1973). *The jargon of authenticity* (K. Tarnowski & F. Will, Trans.). Northwestern University Press. (Original workpublished 1964)

- Adorno, T. W. (1976). *Introduction to the sociology of music* (E. B. Ashton, Trans.). Seabury Press. (Original work published 1962)

- Adorno, T. W. (1997). *Aesthetic theory* (R. Hullot-Kentor, Trans.). University of Minnesota Press. (Original work published1970)

- Adorno, T. W. (1999). *Sound figures* (R. Livingstone, Trans.). Stanford University Press. (Original work published 1959

- Adorno, T. W. (2002). *Essays on music* (R. D. Leppert, Ed.). University of California Press.

- Adorno, T. W. (2006). *Philosophy of new music* (R. Hullot-Kentor, Trans.). University of Minnesota Press. (Original work published1949)

- Bohm, D. (1998). *On Creativity*. New York: Routledge.

- Church, D., & Dispenza, J. (2018). *Mind to matter:*

REFERENCES

The astonishing science of how your brain creates material reality. Hay House.

- Dispenza, J. (2012). *Breaking the habit of being yourself: How to lose your mind and create a new one.* Hay House.

- Dispenza, J. (2007). *Evolve your brain: The science of changing your mind.* Health Communications.

- Fromm, E. (1997). On being human (R. Funk, Ed.). Continuum.

- Fromm, E. (1989). *The art of being* (R. Funk, Ed.).Continuum.

- Fromm, E. (1976). *To have or to be?* Harper &Row.

- Fromm, E. (1968). *The revolution of hope: Toward a humanized technology.* Harper & Row.

- Fromm, E. (1947). *Man for himself: An inquiry into the. psychology of ethics.* Rinehart.

- Hayes JF, Maughan DL, Grant-Peterkin H. Interconnected or disconnected? Promotion of mental health and prevention of mental disorder in the digital age. Br J Psychiatry. 2016 Mar;208(3):205-7. doi:10.1192/bjp.bp.114.161067. PMID: 26932479; PMCID: PMC4939856.

- Herbert, F. (1965). *Dune.* Chilton Books.

- Herbert, F. (1966). *Destination: Void.* Berkeley Medallion.

- Herbert, F. (1968). *The Heaven Makers.* Avon Books.

- Herbert, F. (1969). *Dune Messiah.* G.P. Putnam'sSons.

- Herbert, F. (1970). *The Worlds of Frank Herbert*. AceBooks.

- Herbert, F. (1972). *Soul Catcher*. G.P. Putnam'sSons.

- Herbert, F. (1972). *The Godmakers*. G.P. Putnam'sSons.

- Herbert, F. (1973). *The Book of Frank Herbert*. DAWBooks.

- Herbert, F. (1976). *Children of Dune*. G.P. Putnam'sSons.

- Herbert, F., & Ransom, B. (1979). *The Jesus Incident*. G.P. Putnam's Sons.

- Herbert, F., & Barnard, M. (1980). *Without Me, You're Nothing: The Essential Guide to Home Computers*. Simon & Schuster.

- Herbert, F. (1981). *God Emperor of Dune*. G.P.Putnam's Sons.

- Herbert, F. (1984). *Heretics of Dune*. G.P. Putnam'sSons.

- Herbert, F. (1985). *Chapterhouse: Dune*. G.P.Putnam's Sons.

- Horkheimer, M., & Adorno, T. W. (2002). *Dialectic of enlightenment* (E.Jephcott, Trans.). Stanford University Press. (Original work published 1947)

- Matousek, R. H., Dobkin, P. L., & Pruessner, J. (2013).Cortisol as a marker for improvement in mindfulness-based stress reduction. *Journal of Clinical Endocrinology & Metabolism*, 98(2), E374-E382. https://doi.org/10.1210/jc.2012-3124

- Nifco, N.(2007). *Sense-making and communities of tolerance: Emerging outcomes in the modelling of a conceptual framework applying multi-agent systems* (Doctoral dissertation). Fielding Graduate Institute.

- Nifco, N.(2005). A conceptualization of knowledge management practices through knowledge, awareness, and meaning. *Electronic Journal of Knowledge Management, 3*(1), 45-52.

- Nifco, N.(2004). *Effective knowledge management practices under the constructs of knowledge, awareness, and meaning: An organic approach* (Master's thesis). Royal Roads University.

- Nifco, N. (2004). *Systems thinking and the notion to understand an organic self by modelling the principles of organic thinking in a complex adaptive system: Reflections from the Bethel, Main KA3 workshop experience* (HOD 703). Bethel, MA: Fielding Graduate University.

- Nilsson, U. (2007). The effect of music intervention instress response to cardiac surgery patients: A randomized clinical trial. *British Journal of Psychiatry*, 191(3), 234-240. https://doi.org/10.1192/bjp.bp.106.034884

- Oliver, M. (1986). *Dream Work*. Atlantic Monthly-Press.

- Peale, N. V. (1982). *Positive imaging: The powerful way to change your life*. Fawcett Crest.

- Singer, M. A. (2022). *Living untethered: Beyond the human predicament*. New Harbinger Publications.

- Singer, M. A. (2015). *The surrender experiment:

My journey into life's perfection. Harmony Books.

- Singer, M. A. (2007). *The untethered soul: The journey beyond yourself*. New Harbinger Publications.

- Stavish, M. (2006). *Kabbalah for Health & Wellness*. Llewellyn Publications.

- Whyte, D. (1989). *Songs for Coming Home*. Many Rivers Press.

- Whyte, D. (1994). *The Heart Aroused: Poetry and the Preservation of the Soul in Corporate America*. Currency.

- Whyte, D. (1997). *The House of Belonging*. Many Rivers Press.

- Whyte, D. (2002). *Crossing the Unknown Sea: Work as a Pilgrimage of Identity*. Riverhead Books.

- Whyte, D. (2003). *Everything Is Waiting For You*. Many Rivers Press.

- Whyte, D. (2010). *The Three Marriages: Reimagining Work, Self and Relationship*. Riverhead Books.

- Whyte, D. (2012). *Pilgrim*. Many Rivers Press.

- Whyte, D. (2014). *Consolations: The Solace, Nourishment and Underlying Meaning of Everyday Words*. Many Rivers Press.

- Whyte, D. (2018a). *The Bell and the Blackbird*. Many Rivers Press.

- Whyte, D. (2018b). *David Whyte Essentials*. Many Rivers Press.

- Whyte, D. (2021). *Consolations: The Solace, Nourishment and Underlying Meaning of Everyday Words*

(Revised edition). Many Rivers Press.

- Whyte, D. (2022). *The Sea in You*. Many Rivers Press

www.ingramcontent.com/pod-product-compliance
Lightning Source LLC
Chambersburg PA
CBHW040245010526
44119CB00057B/816